How to Survive Your Doctorate

How to Survive Your Doctorate

What others don't tell you

Jane Matthiesen and Mario Binder

Open University Press

Open University Press
McGraw-Hill Education
McGraw-Hill House
Shoppenhangers Road
Maidenhead
Berkshire
England
SL6 2QL

email: enquiries@openup.co.uk
world wide web: www.openup.co.uk

and Two Penn Plaza, New York, NY 10121-2289, USA

First published 2009

A catalogue record of this book is available from the British Library

ISBN-13: 978-0-33-523444-8 (pb) 978-0-33-523443-1 (hb)
ISBN-10: 0335234445 (pb) 0335234437 (hb)

Library of Congress Cataloging-in-Publication Data
CIP data applied for

100617048X

Typeset by RefineCatch Limited, Bungay, Suffolk
Printed in the UK by Bell and Bain Ltd, Glasgow

Fictitious names of companies, products, people, characters and/or
data that may be used herein (in case studies or in examples) are not
intended to represent any real individual, company, product or event.

Mixed Sources
Product group from well-managed
forests and other controlled sources
www.fsc.org   Cert no. TT-COC-002769
© 1996 Forest Stewardship Council
FSC

The *McGraw·Hill* Companies

This book is dedicated to all the brave graduate research students, who work hard to advance knowledge every single day and sacrifice many of the luxuries of life to do so, and to their respective families and supervisors, who work equally as hard in order to support their daughters, sons and graduate students.

Contents

List of figures

List of tables

Acknowledgements

First of all, we would like to express special thanks to our families for the support and understanding they showed us while we wrote this book. Without you it would have been much harder – even impossible – to complete this work.

Extensive thanks also go to our anonymous interviewees and storywriters (you know who you are). You have greatly contributed to this book. Your experiences and insights are what make this book special.

We would also like to acknowledge our friends Bhavesh Dayal, Maren Knappe and Paul Spee for their comments on earlier versions of the manuscript. You enabled us to improve the book with your insightful feedback.

We would also like to take the opportunity to thank Frances Meegan, Careers Adviser at Cambridge University, who kindly supported us with information on funding a doctorate through scholarships and bursaries (based on a paper she wrote while working as Career Adviser at the London School of Economics). You helped us shine light onto the difficult topic of funding.

Special thanks also to our friend and illustrator Ariane Hofmann, who drew the comics at the beginning of each chapter, for all your hard work. The illustrations are great.

Last but not least, we would like to express our deepest thanks to our editor Melanie Havelock and her editorial assistant Katy Hamilton for their constant support on all sorts of matters, as well as the anonymous reviewers for their encouraging and constructive comments.

1

Introduction

Who is this book for? • Why choose this book? • How to read and use the book • Who we are: the authors

Thank you for picking up this book. The fact that your interest was provoked by the title suggests that you are either doing or thinking about doing a doctorate, or know someone who is. This book is designed to serve as a survival kit for doctoral students and people doing similar research degrees. In other words, people who are planning to travel the academic road or have already begun their journey. Read on to find out how this book can help make the journey easier.

Who is this book for?

We think everyone who wants to understand more about the nature of post-graduate research degree programmes, including prospective and current doctoral and Master's researchers, supervisors, spouses, family and friends, should read this book. Although the book is largely targeted at the individuals actually completing or thinking about completing a doctorate in the United Kingdom (UK), we think others will also benefit from reading this book by gaining insight and understanding into life as a doctoral student.

For instance, we believe it will help supervisors to improve their supervision quality by enabling them to relate to the student experience, consequently strengthening the supervisor–student relationship. It will also help spouses, family and friends to understand the nature of doing a doctorate by showing them why doing it is not easy and why it can't just be done, and how much social support really matters for successful completion of this daunting task.

Why choose this book?

If you are looking for a book that will give you the truth about doing a doctorate, then this book is for you. We give you the R-rated version of events, without sparing any of the gory details. The premise behind this book is easy: we tell you what we wish someone had told us. Although the path towards a doctorate or similar research degree is winding and challenging, we believe that *everyone* can do a doctorate, as long as they have the right support and work hard. Thus our core message is – you can do it, you just have to know how to go about it!

Part of the journey is obviously finding and making an 'intellectual contribution' but that is only the tip of the iceberg and not the part of the journey we want to focus on in this book. Our key concern is about those issues that people do not talk about, the things that lurk in the shadows and are largely hidden from outside observers – the things that people do not become aware of until they have signed on the dotted line and are being confronted with them personally. We want to change that, demystify the process and tell you what it's really like: a doctorate, warts and all.

We know you have many other books to choose from, so let us tell you why we think you should choose ours. Although there are some excellent books currently on the market, most of them take a 'traditional' approach to writing about research degrees. Consequently, much of the literature guiding doctoral students either focuses on academic models of learning or offers clinical advice on how to achieve the content of a doctorate. This is generally done by offering students a systematic framework or set approach to use when physically conducting the research or writing the dissertation.

Furthermore, these publications are mainly concerned with technical issues of a doctorate, such as choosing a topic, selecting suitable data collection techniques and writing chapters. As such, these books are really fixated on technical competences and, although this is clearly important, it actually leads to most of the books overlooking many of the ancillary and soft skills necessary to complete a doctorate.

In our book, we are aiming to complement and go beyond what current texts offer by focusing (almost) exclusively on the ancillary issues in doctoral degrees and offering insights that go beyond pure description. We 'pull no punches' by offering an exposé-style review of the doctoral process. We do not hide the messiness, the politics, the tears. In other words, we give students a realistic preview of life as a doctoral student – something we believe none of the other books are able to offer.

We believe our book is unique and offers something that has been missing from the market so far. However, we also believe that many good books about doing a Ph.D. have already been written from an academic perspective. These books offer good complementary guidance on the content rather than the process of a Ph.D., both of which are key elements of successful completion. Some especially noteworthy titles include:

- Phillips, E.M. and Pugh, D.S. (2005) *How to Get a PhD*, 4th edn. Maidenhead: Open University Press.
- Rugg, G. (2004) *The Unwritten Rules of PhD Research*. Maidenhead: Open University Press.
- Davis, G.B. and Parker, C.A. (1997) *Writing the Doctoral Dissertation: A Systematic Approach*, 2nd edn. New York: Barron's Educational Series.

Interesting from the supervisory point of view is also:

- Delamont, S., Atkinson, P. and Parry, O. (2004) *Supervising the PhD: A Guide to Success*, 2nd edn. Maidenhead: Open University Press.
- Taylor, S. and Beasley, N. (2005) *A Handbook for Doctoral Supervisors*. London: Routledge.

We strongly believe that any book dealing with this type of topic has to be written specifically for doctoral students and also needs to be informed by student experience. The only way to offer legitimate and credible insight into life as a doctoral researcher is by telling it from the student point of view. We thus use many examples and case studies to illustrate the points we make throughout the book; these are populated by means of in-depth conversations with current doctoral students and recent graduates across a number of disciplines and universities and in most cases were written by the informants themselves.

Overall this is a light-hearted look at life as a doctorate student from the viewpoint of actual students, which incorporates some critical lessons along the way. Irrespective of which field you are researching in, we provide you with intriguing insights based on the experience of people who have gone through the process before you. Doctorate degrees are difficult, both academically and emotionally, which means that some of the things we say will be controversial, politically sensitive and can be construed to be very negative.

Thus, in order to avoid having any of the comments we make reflect badly on individuals and/or institutions, we provide jumbled examples that are concocted from the experiences of several students. Where names are used, these are fictional to preserve anonymity of the people and institutions representing our cases. However, everything we tell you in this book is rooted in the experience of real doctoral students – either current students or recent graduates. In other words, the experience is based on people who have gone through the doctoral process within the last five years.

How to read and use the book

We explore these ancillary issues and touch on all aspects of the doctoral experience by reviewing the doctoral process from application through to graduation. Each chapter covers what we consider a key issue for successfully completing a doctoral degree.

In Chapter 2 we describe the nature of a research degree and the graduate school environment, specifically focusing on the big change a doctorate often is for people coming from undergraduate degrees, postgraduate taught degrees or industry, and explain how to initiate the process.

In Chapter 3 we provide our top tips on how to overcome the serious and frequent lulls of motivation and persist in the face of adversity by managing the self. In particular we pay attention to common demotivators and potential solutions.

Your supervisor is undoubtedly one of the most important people in your life – or at least it feels that way while you are doing your doctorate. In Chapter 4 we discuss how to build a constructive relationship with your supervisor based on the multitude of different supervisory styles that exist (including supervision-by-committee).

Doing a doctorate generally does not only involve reading literature, collecting and analysing data and writing it up into a logical, concise and flowing piece of work. Doing a doctorate can also involve many additional tasks and activities. In Chapter 5 we discuss some of the key elements that accompany the doctoral process and focus on core decisions students face in relation to the 'sidelines' of a research degree such as publishing, going to conferences, professional development, networking and so on.

Finance is a serious consideration for most postgraduate research students as a doctorate can be a lengthy process. In Chapter 6 we discuss the various ways students can fund their studies, including scholarships and bursaries, funding and research grants, research work, teaching and other part-time work.

Politics are part of life, whether you are studying or working, so it should come as no surprise that universities are often a minefield when it comes to politics. In Chapter 7 we introduce and work through some of the more sensitive issues students may encounter during their time by talking about departmental and university hierarchies, structures, groups and relationships and ways to avoid getting caught up in 'messy' situations.

There are various different ways of doing a doctorate. Chapter 8 covers some of the main challenges faced by individuals choosing alternative paths to doing a doctorate and is thus dedicated to people that fall into the 'different from everyone else' category, such as 'new route' doctoral candidates, doctorate-by-publication students, part-time research degree candidates, overseas and international students, distance-learning postgraduates, and mature executive or professional doctoral students.

Doing a doctorate not only qualifies you for an academic career but also for a career in industry. No matter which route you choose after your doctorate, you should try to decide as early as possible. In Chapter 9 we give some examples of alternative career options and discuss the related doctoral strategies you should adopt to match them.

In the final Chapter of our book, Chapter 10, we talk about your exit point, the viva voce. We draw on reasons for early withdrawal from graduate school and how things shape up after you survived your viva and left university, for example interaction with former colleagues, friends, and so on.

We do not see this as an exhaustive list of issues but a sound overview of the most important topics that we and many other doctoral students were/are confronted with while doing a doctorate. Within each chapter we draw on various aspects that reflect not only our experience, but also the experience of many present and former students we talked to. Hence, we would like you to understand and use this book as a roadmap that guides you through the winding path of a doctorate.

You can use this book in various ways. If you are very motivated, curious or interested, you can read it front-to-back, cover-to-cover. If you are like most students we know, we suggest you skim through the table of contents and focus on the issues that are most relevant to you. Once you know what is in the book, you can always return to it at a later stage, as you move through the doctoral process. We also suggest for you to recommend this book to your supervisor(s). It will help you survive your doctorate together and help create a fruitful working relationship from the beginning until the end.

Who we are: the authors

Jane Matthiesen is a Lecturer in Strategic Management at Aston Business School in Birmingham, UK. She graduated from Brandon University with a Bachelor of Science in Psychology in 2001 and from the University of Nottingham with a M.Sc. in Occupational (I/O) Psychology in 2002. She received her Ph.D. from Aston University in October 2005. Her thesis entitled 'The effects of relocation on Royal Air Force families' won a series of awards from reputable organizations including the British Psychological Society, the American Psychological Association and the European Congress of Psychology. Jane also obtained a Professional Postgraduate Certificate of Learning and Teaching in 2004 and is now a Fellow of the Higher Education Academy. She is also a Chartered Occupational Psychologist with the British Psychological Society and an Associate of the Advanced Institute of Management Research (AIM).

 Mario Binder is a Project Manager at an international management consultancy based in Berlin, Germany. He also holds a Visiting Research Fellowship in the Operations and Information Management Group of Aston Business School in Birmingham, UK, where he received his Ph.D. in March 2007. He has published papers in various international journals. His co-authored paper 'Achieving internal process benchmarking: guidance from BASF' in *Benchmarking: An International Journal* was chosen as a Highly Commended Paper at the Emerald Literati Network Awards for Excellence in 2007. Mario also obtained a Certificate of Learning and Teaching in 2005 and is now a Fellow of the Higher Education Academy.

 We hope you enjoy reading the book and are always open to suggestions from readers. If you would like to make any comments about our book or share your experiences for future editions, please feel free to contact us using the address below:

survive.your.doctorate@gmail.com

2

Getting started

The nature of a doctoral degree: mind the gap! • The application process • Entering the academic community

Once you have decided to continue your education with a research degree, you will face many difficult questions and decisions from the very start, for example what university to apply to, how to apply, what field and topic to research, what the registration process looks like, what to expect in the first days and weeks and so on. This book is not about the research process; in other words, it is not about the technical aspects of how to conduct research or structure a doctoral thesis.

However, there are technical elements so crucial to the doctoral process that we want to touch on them briefly. Consequently, in this chapter we cover aspects such as the application process, that is selecting a university, writing research proposals, and getting together your application documents, as well as how you will find your way into the academic community as a researcher. Before elaborating on these issues, we would first like to focus on the nature of a doctorate in general and what it involves; what it is and what it isn't.

The nature of a doctoral degree: mind the gap!

What does it and what doesn't it mean to be a doctoral researcher? What does it and what doesn't it involve? Unless you experience the process yourself, you can only vaguely imagine what it is like to do a doctorate. So, how can you know whether a doctorate degree is for you or not? Admittedly, this is a dilemma most people experience in the early stages of the process. But, be assured, you are not alone. In order to assist you in your decision making, we want to clear up some of the myths surrounding doctoral degrees by giving you more insight into the nature of doing such a degree. More specific information is also available from agencies like UKGRAD and The National Postgraduate Committee; both provide national perspectives in graduate education for students.

Before we explain more about the Ph.D., we would like to offer a cautionary note: do not do a doctorate just for the title! Think about your motives for doing a doctorate and decide whether they are good reasons. If you are driven by superficial reasons like collecting titles or satisfying your ego, we fear that you will face many difficulties. A doctorate is difficult when you lack key motivational drivers like thirst for knowledge, challenging assumptions, curiosity, a desire to add to knowledge, and a willingness to conduct sound research.

As blunt as it might sound, unless you have a very strong desire to complete a research degree and are very ambitious, we suggest you do not even consider it. There are many valid reasons for going down the doctorate route but 'getting the title' is definitely not one of them. Be honest with yourself and think about whether you really want to do a doctorate, why you want to do it and what this will mean for you in the short- and long-term: remember, a full-time doctoral degree takes between three and five years.

Make a contribution, do not reinvent the wheel

A doctorate is basically about making an original contribution to knowledge. You achieve this with the empirical evidence and the theoretical argument in your thesis. In other words, a doctoral degree is awarded on the basis of original and valuable work. Looking back over our own time as research students, we are well aware that almost all doctoral candidates start their research with the aim of 'changing the world'. Most people want to do something very important, something that really matters and something that transforms the field they are working in.

Without implying that you do not have the potential to make such an outstanding contribution (if nobody ever had then there would not be any paradigm shifts or Nobel Prize winners), we want to highlight the importance of knowing your own limits. We know how easy it is to get caught up in the bureaucracy, the routine and the detail of doing research; and how this can all too often lead to a loss of enthusiasm, confidence and motivation (see Chapter 3 for more information). Do not throw your idealism and enthusiasm out of the window just yet – just be aware that you do not need to reinvent the wheel in order to make a sufficient original contribution to knowledge.

We will show you which ancillary and soft skills you need to achieve this successfully and how you can build confidence in yourself and what you are doing. This is the hidden agenda of doing a doctoral degree that will be covered in this book. You will realize that great researchers in your field are the same as everyone else and not inaccessible genii that are so clever that they operate in a different league to you. There is no reason for you to assume that people holding doctorate degrees are exceptionally intelligent and that you do not measure up to them and hence will never be able to get your degree. Well, if you really think that way, why are you even considering doing a doctorate? Why are you holding this book in your hand looking for advice and guidance, if you are so sure that you cannot survive the process? The feeling is just as superficial as we say it is, so do not take the easy way out. Bear up and face the challenge.

Nobody ever said it was going to be easy – and, well, we definitely will not. We have been there and know how difficult it can be. But despite all of this, we are nonetheless convinced that anybody can do a doctorate. So what is it going to be? Take a break and think about this for a few minutes before you continue reading the book. Sometimes a little time to reflect can work wonders.

Doing research is like doing a puzzle

Doing research is like putting together the pieces of a puzzle: you generally start off with a rough idea or expectation of your research outcome, which you normally describe in your initial research proposal (see p. 24). This is like looking at the front cover of your puzzle and knowing what it has to look like. Although people will tell you that you should ideally enter your research field free of any subjective bias, reality is different. Research is based on our own and other people's experience, therefore no research project can be 100 per cent bias-free. The key is to be self-reflective and aware of your existing knowledge, experience, education and expectations, as well as how these factors interact and impact on your research. Developing this consciousness and reflexivity is one of the main elements of research.

How you approach research depends very much on your underlying beliefs. Research is a passion and like most passions can be approached in different ways. Students typically enter the empirical field by collecting and analysing data utilizing an a priori developed research question or objective. This is equivalent to organizing and arranging individual puzzle pieces according to the guide or picture before you.

The final stage in the process is writing up your thesis, by tying together all the parts of your research from the past three or so years; this is like putting together your puzzle piece by piece. And every time a piece fits into another, you will experience excitement and a feeling of reward, until you ultimately see the light at the end of the tunnel and know that you can make it.

The very last step is the viva voce, the oral examination, in which you have to defend your thesis in front of a group of examiners. If you pass, which almost everyone who gets to this stage does, this means your research fulfils the high standard that comes with the degree and will be recognized throughout the academic world (more information on the viva is provided in Chapter 10). This is equivalent to your puzzle being sealed so that it cannot be torn apart anymore.

Determination beats brilliance

When beginning a doctoral degree, you are entering the postgraduate world and, more specifically, the academic research world. In contrast to the undergraduate world, which you should know pretty well and be familiar with by now, where pretty much everything is set and organized for you by the university and its staff, at doctoral level you are responsible for your progress and success yourself. Although you will generally have access to colleagues and supervisors for consultation and to help you work through problems, there may be times when nobody is there to help or push you. This is because most people will neither understand nor care about what you do – it sounds harsh but is true – it is a bit like talking to an outsider about your undergraduate degree or current job; there are not a lot of people you can keep interested for long.

Therefore, you need to bring along a good portion of motivation and curiosity, as well as the discipline and initiative to carry out what it requires for you to achieve your goal and finish your research successfully. Over time you will realize that it takes more determination than brilliance to complete your doctorate successfully and on time. In addition, you need to be flexible and constantly develop further, growing with your field as well as the research. It is not only you who changes; as you learn, your goals tend to change, too. The quicker you adjust to your new situation and environment, the sooner you can start being productive. With this book we want to help you to develop the necessary skills to do just that by offering you valuable insights into your future as a doctoral student.

Use our advice as a guide but also make use of your own experience and develop your own way and style of surviving your doctorate. The book will help you relate your own situation and experience to the experiences of others who came before you – but it is no panacea to your problems. Whether you get your doctorate or not depends on you!

Academia is not (always) an ivory tower

Research is not always a solitary task. Of course, there will be periods during your doctorate when you will have little interaction with others, for example when reviewing literature, analysing data or writing up results. But in general researchers are not sitting in their academic 'ivory towers', completely removed from reality and pragmatism, as the frequently used metaphor suggests.

Research is very much about interaction, communication, teamwork (especially in natural science projects) and establishing relationships within the academic community you are part of and working in, as well as with practitioners who often serve as key informants or gatekeepers. You will regularly interact with your supervisor and other faculty members, for example at research away days, will discuss your work with other experts at conferences or seminars (this is discussed in greater detail in Chapter 5 on 'Sidelines of a doctorate') and may also get involved in administrative activities related to research, for example as a doctoral representative. There are many opportunities to interact and communicate with others, and we strongly recommend that you seize them all. Research is not only about becoming an expert in a field of knowledge but also about developing interpersonal and other soft skills.

A doctorate is different to a Master's degree

Finally, it is important to distinguish between a doctoral degree and other research degrees, most notably the Master's by research. There are many similarities between the two degrees, which is perhaps unsurprising, since most universities start doctoral students by enrolling them in a M.Phil. programme – it is generally only after students pass the first major hurdle, the first year report, that they get registered as doctoral students (see p. 28).

It is thus possible to look at M.Phil. and Master by research degrees as a preliminary step towards a doctorate. Students have to demonstrate a sufficient understanding of appropriate research techniques and relevant literature to pass into a doctoral degree. However, depending on the discipline, the university and the research training programme, students also have to show that they are able to do independent research and are capable of analysing data. Familiarize yourself with these requirements to ensure that you can make this transition smoothly. It is hence common practice for students to start with a M.Phil. or Master by research and then expand their initial work into a doctorate thesis to gain a Ph.D. or similar degree.

A basic comparison of doctorate and Master's degree levels is provided in the following Table 2.1.

Table 2.1 Comparing doctorate and Master's degrees in business

Requirement	M.Phil./M.Sc.	Doctorate
Duration	1–2 years	3+ years
Application cost	£0	£0
Average tuition fees per annum for home students (varies widely; international fees are often double or triple that as they are not subsidized by the British government)	£6,000	£4,000
Nature of data	Secondary data or limited primary data	Primary data
Role in research	Secondary observer	Independent observer
Key aim	Replicate studies, test theory or parts of theories	Development of new theory
Length of dissertation	20,000 words	80,000 words
Internship	Not common	Not common
Common source	Self-funding	Research councils

Advantages and disadvantages of doing a doctorate

A doctorate is a very individual experience, so we do not advocate viewing it in monochrome. It is not black and white, good and bad. There is lots of grey (which is exactly what we are focusing on in this book) and it is important to keep that in mind. Nonetheless, we think it is useful to provide a synopsis of the advantages and disadvantages of doing a doctorate. This is not an exclusive list but rather a summation of the common themes students and recent graduates reported throughout our conversations with them (see Table 2.2).

Table 2.2 Advantages and disadvantages of doing a doctorate

Advantages	Disadvantages

• Opportunity to pursue an academic career
• Opportunity to work independently
• Pursuing your own research interests and do work that you enjoy
• Working with internationally recognized experts in the field
• Becoming an expert on a certain topic and field
• (Somewhat) flexible working hours
• Engaging with people on a highly intellectual level; sharing values and ideas
• Career catalyst: high entry position in industry after graduation
• Establishing an international network (personally and professionally)
• Compatible with having children
• Status: earning the highest academic degree possible; 'Doctor' title
• Scholarships are tax free
• Personal gratification; confidence through competence
• Improving knowledge, skills and abilities
   • Writing and presentation skills
   • Analytical and problem solving skills
   • Discipline & persistence
	• No guaranteed salary gain (your degree is unlikely to boost your earning power in industry)
	• In some cases overqualified for the job market (a doctorate is no job guarantee)
	• Sometimes too old when entering the job world (especially industry)
	• Expensive (if self-funded or prolonged)
	• Deadline pressure (especially at the end)
	• Performance pressure to create meaningful and publishable results
	• Time-consuming: lots of time spent reading/writing/analysing
	• Having to make sacrifices (restricting social life, forgoing other opportunities)
	• Risk of having a difficult or negative experience (e.g. difficult supervisor)
	• Emotionally exhausting; rollercoaster
	• Long-term commitment but research interests might change over time (may mean losing interest in chosen topic)
	• Research attracts limited interest outside of specialized segment of academic community

Concluding note

We hope that by now you are aware of the 'step up' you are planning to take or have taken already, and that you are sure that this is the experience for you. Certainly, it is a once-in-a-lifetime experience and, despite its ups and downs, people do gain a lot of enjoyment and satisfaction out of the challenge.

For illustrative purposes, we would like to conclude this section with a few quotes about the nature of a doctorate degree. We gained these insights by asking former and current doctoral students to describe what doing a doctorate is like. What follows are their original, unedited and unabridged answers:

> One of the most amazing things about doing a doctorate is knowing that I will make a completely unique contribution to the existing body of knowledge. Because as we all know, it is a prerequisite that there must not be ANY

theses on your topic, and after you have (finally) finished NO-ONE will be allowed to do a doctorate on your topic . . . Another thing is how rapidly your own knowledge grows. Now you just KNOW things which were difficult to grasp or remember a couple of years ago. I don't know how to describe it differently but to say that it feels as if you 'evolve' as a human being.

Jaidyn (final year student in biology)

I think undergraduates considering a PhD should understand that it takes a much higher degree of focus and commitment. Undergrad is work too, but it's more about going to classes, taking tests, and turning in papers. In a PhD program, you're pursuing a longer-term project, sometimes over several years, and often mostly on your own. There are fewer deadlines and guidelines, so it's up to you to stay disciplined and organised. Also, graduate students work much more closely with professors – almost as apprentices – so it's imperative that they find someone with similar interests with whom they can have a productive professional relationship. Most importantly, I think people should only do a PhD if they have a burning interest in their subject and are passionate about it.

George (first year student in sociology)

I think the most important thing to remember for prospective PhD students is that grad students like to complain . . . a lot. It's basically a right that we inherit when we enter our programs, but it's important to remember that we are often exaggerating and if it were really that bad, no one would be here. Pursuing your ultimate intellectual interests, working on your own time, getting paid to go to school, and graduating with the highest degree possible are all worth the stress (at least that's how it's been so far for me).

Azambe (second year student in business)

The application process

Now that you have a rough idea of what a doctorate is, the next decision you have to make is whether a doctorate is 'for you'. Specifically, you need to ask yourself whether this is something you want to do and also whether this is something you can do. If the answer to both questions is yes, it is time to start thinking about the application process.

This is the first obstacle you have to overcome on the way to your doctoral degree because without having been accepted into a programme, you cannot graduate from one. And without knowing where you will go, you won't know what the requirements will be and it does not make sense to start working on your research project. Although there are many similarities across universities, it is important to know that each university has its own collection of formal rules and regulations that you will have to adhere to. In addition, there are various ways of doing a doctorate (e.g. part time, distance-learning etc.). More information on this topic can be found in Chapter 8.

Remember, obeying these procedures is your responsibility not the university's and since your application may be rejected on the basis of not being in line with regulations, you need to make sure you adhere to them carefully – you do not want to get hung up on a formality.

In this section we introduce you to some of the formal elements of the system by providing you with information on:

- how to find a suitable university/department;
- how to prepare research summary documents;
- how to get references;
- how to find your way through the application process.

In order to achieve the desired result, in this case having your application accepted and being admitted into the doctoral programme, you need to start your planning well in advance of the deadlines. It is useful to know that doctoral programme deadlines differ from university to university, so you need to be clear about where you would like to apply. Some universities accept applications throughout the year on an ongoing basis but generally, Ph.D. programmes have one regular starting date time around the start of the academic year. As such, the most popular take-in period is late September/early October.

It is beneficial for doctoral candidates to register at this time of year, since it aligns with the regular academic year and the taught courses; consequently, most doctoral students will enrol at this time. However, it is common for most universities to offer a delayed registration in January, when graduate students from diverse backgrounds, including those coming into doctoral programmes from employment, who were unable to accommodate an autumn start, join the programme.

Since most doctoral courses accept applications on an ongoing basis throughout the year, there are no application deadlines as such. However, where enrolment is timed with scholarship or funding applications, or where the Ph.D. is offered as part of a research council researchship, deadlines may well exist. As a rule of thumb, funding deadlines are a few months before regular term, so regardless of when you plan to begin your degree, you need to apply well in advance and will thus benefit from taking an organized and structured approach to the application process. In the subsequent section we give you some advice on how this can be achieved.

Selecting a university and department

One of the earliest and most fundamental decisions you have to make in your doctoral career is to decide which university, department and research group you would like to join. This will be informed by your knowledge, skills and abilities, as well as your interest. So, before identifying suitable institutes, you will need to decide in which discipline and field you want to research. This will then help inform the decision about which university you would like to join.

In essence, the decision-making process should move outward from you – based on your interests. You decide which type of research group you would like to join; this in turn determines which department would be suitable, and of course this links to the type of university you will apply to. The most common mistakes doctoral students make is to follow this process exactly backwards and pick which university they want to go to first. This is a high-risk strategy because you may well end up in an area which you do not enjoy. For instance, if you want to study occupational psychology, it does not make sense to apply to Oxford or Cambridge – their specialities relate to experimental and neuroscience, both of which are very interesting but very different from occupational (applied) psychology. So, choose a topic you are interested in, you want to contribute to and which you expect to have some merit and relevance (more on this in the next section on 'writing a research proposal'). Remember, you will need to work in this area for three to five years, so it must be interesting enough for you to persist with the same topic for that long.

Many doctoral students continue with their degree at the same university they did their Master's or undergraduate degree or at least spent some time, for example during an exchange year just like James in the story below. This can carry many advantages:

- You are already familiar with the institution and its procedures.
- You do not need to invest time and finance into relocation and acclimatizing to a new environment.
- It is likely that you are already in contact with a few members of academic staff, including your dissertation supervisor – take the opportunity to talk to them about your interest in continuing your education with a doctorate and get information about the programme at the university.
- Working with someone you already know and are comfortable with has the advantage that you can work together well and do not need to invest much time into building a relationship or setting ground rules, as these already exist.
- You could also expand your dissertation and use your early work as point of departure for your doctorate, which would save you having to find your way around a new body of literature.

- The selection committee will look favourably on someone who has strong internal support.
- You probably already know about research groups and departments, scholarships and work opportunities at the university.

Sneaking in through the backdoor?

After my Erasmus exchange year at a UK university I decided to stay in touch with two of my lecturers for no specific reason. I went back to my home institution to finish off my university degree in business administration and spent two years there, not even knowing if I wanted to do a Ph.D. However, when I decided to continue my education with a doctorate degree at the end of my studies, my contacts proved very useful. I contacted both of my ex-lecturers with an initial idea in mind.

It quickly became clear that one of them was very interested in my idea and encouraged me to develop it further into a proper research proposal (the other one offered to be a potential associate supervisor). My contact also highlighted the importance of the proposal being of high standard, as the research group had a full-time scholarship on offer. He then said I should send my full application documents, including my research proposal, to him directly and that he would pass it on internally. I couldn't believe my luck!

From the extensive research I did about the university while preparing my application, I knew that I was applying to one of the leading business schools in the UK, a fact that I didn't realise during my exchange year. So, getting into their doctoral programme would be ideal for me. Furthermore, I knew my future supervisor already and knew that I would get on well with him because he was a great person who always put his students' concerns at the top of his agenda, even before his own. I know this was hard to find and made me even keener.

So, I sent my documents to him as he requested and waited. A few weeks later, I received a formal letter from the university, informing me that not only had I been accepted onto the doctoral programme but I had also been awarded a full-time scholarship. I couldn't believe it, I was ecstatic. Only applying to one university, getting a place on the programme and also a scholarship . . . That was amazing! I know it would have been far more difficult if I hadn't had kept the contacts up.

James (final year student in business)

Another way to choose a university is to rely on personal recommendations from people you know, which were or still are studying at that university (preferably as doctoral students). This option allows you to get valuable inside information about the university and its doctoral programme from people you trust; this information complements more objective information about the university, which is easily obtainable through websites, brochures, open days and so on.

If you do not know anyone at the university you would like to study at, you can always make contact. Take the opportunity to speak to doctoral students at the university's open day or get in touch with the university, specifically the doctoral, postgraduate or research degrees programme, and ask to be put in touch with current doctoral students. Of course you have to take everything that you are told with a pinch of salt, since the insights you will be gaining are subjective and biased by your contact's individual experience. So, make sure you interpret their comments with care and filter the information you consider necessary and, if possible, speak to several people to get a range of views.

A third way of identifying a potential university and department is to look through university rankings (e.g. *The Good University Guide* published by independent bodies like *The Higher Education Times, Financial Times, The Guardian*) or scan advertisements for doctoral positions. You can find the latter either on individual university websites or through popular search engines and job websites like www.jobs.ac.uk or www.monster.com. The advantage of electronic searching is that it will also allow you to get a feel for jobs in academia. This will help you understand the job market in your field and give you some ideas of the types of job you may like to aim for in the future.

The mere fact that doctoral posts are announced on job websites should send a clear message – a doctoral degree is like a job in many ways; you work full time, often in exchange for nominal payment. The posts that are advertised this way often link to specific research projects and questions, and they are commonly connected to time-bound research grants and student-ships. Applying for a post this way is a good opportunity for you to hit two birds with one stone: you get your place on the doctoral programme and sort out your finances at the same time. Of course, competition for this kind of post is strong. Finally, do not forget to contact the university and ask them directly about possibilities for scholarships if nothing is mentioned in your application pack (see also Chapter 6 on 'Finances').

Whichever option you choose, you will need to do some background research about the university and department you are targeting. A good approach is to consult the independent university rankings mentioned earlier, which are published every year. In addition, since you are going to undertake a research degree, it also makes sense for you to look closely at the outcomes of the Research Assessment Exercise (RAE), which assesses the research quality of UK universities and ranks them in accordance to the impact their research has (5 star being the top ranking). Visit www.rae.ac.uk for more information – the website not only allows you to search the results by university but also by discipline.

It is a useful way to compare and contrast universities and allows you to evaluate how well the university of your choosing performed in your particular field of interest. The exercise is conducted every six years and the most recent results were published in 2008; looking at the results gives you a pretty accurate image of the university and department you are looking at. *Note*: At time of writing the RAE was due to be replaced by the Research Excellence Framework (REF). Although in terms of Ph.D. programme selection the RAE is still likely to offer a valid reference point for some time, it will become increasingly meaningful to also look at the REF criteria. By using both sets of measurement exercise, you can ensure that there are no unpleasant surprises while you do your degree.

In case you are opting for an industrial career after your doctorate, you also might want to consider the ranking of employment rates, which serves as an indicator of the quality and intensity of the university's industrial network (see Chapter 9, pp. 165–71, for more information on pursuing an industrial career). Regardless of which field you are studying in and what career path you want to pursue, programme rankings will give you an idea of the quality of the programme you are applying for, including the quality of teaching and research at the university.

Traditionally there are some differences between 'old' and 'new' universities. In the UK, for example, a three-tier system operates: red brick universities, new universities and ex-polytechnics. You are also likely to come across the term 'The Russell Group', which is an association of 20 UK research-led universities, which together account for 66 per cent of UK research income. If you are interested in these distinctions, we recommend you consult one of the many websites dedicated to this division.

When researching the institute you are thinking about applying to, remember also to evaluate the work environment and work conditions. These differ widely from university to university. Check the work space that would be allocated to a student in your department and which resources they have access to. For instance, the university we graduated from had a separate doctoral suite for students across disciplines in the business school. This suite consisted of a computer lab, a small kitchen area, an area for socializing and relaxing and four-people-offices where each student was provided with their own desk, as well as some drawers and shelf space to store books and folders. Such a set-up can have advantages and disadvantages.

On the one hand, you have the chance to talk to and socialize with students from other research fields and disciplines, which can lead to very stimulating discussion and the development of innovative ideas that you otherwise might not have had. You might have very nice office mates that help you to get into the system much quicker (a medium that also facilitates this kind of interaction is some kind of introductory course or tutorial, for example in the form of a research training programme at the beginning of your first year; see also pp. 28–29 in this Chapter). If you favour a clear boundary between work and private life then having an office space will be important to you.

On the other hand, you could end up with office mates that use your stuff, are messy, and are very talkative, not only being on the phone half of the time but also asking all sorts of questions that distract you from your work.

A different and rare arrangement is for doctoral researchers to share their office with their supervisor. While this will undoubtedly intimidate some students because of the high visibility it creates, it also has advantages. For one, you are not isolated from your department or your supervisor and have the opportunity for extensive interaction with your colleagues.

Arrangements can be diverse, even within the same university, and what you evaluate as positive depends entirely on your personality type and working style. Inform yourself and you will know what to expect and can prepare for it. In terms of resources, policy also differs widely. For instance, we received a budget of £275pa to spend on research-associated costs (research equipment, books, conference costs etc.), free printing, free photocopying and free coffee. Some research students get none of this support, others get far more. Again, it pays to be informed. In addition to work space and resources, there are many other factors you should consider; we briefly summarize important selection criteria for you:

- reputation and image of university/department/staff;
- administrative support (e.g. induction procedure, programme handbook etc.);
- quality of courses (e.g. research training programme);
- facilities and equipment (e.g. laboratories, PC suites including software packages, office space, library including electronic sources, accommodation, sports facilities etc.);
- language support;
- professional development possibilities (see also Chapter 5);
- academic and industrial network of the university (this is especially important for doctoral students in the natural sciences as their projects are often funded by industry);
- attractiveness of city (e.g. cost of living, safety, infrastructure, opportunities etc.).

Before moving on to the next topic, we would like to make a final point with regard to department and university selection. If you are an international or distance-learning student and are considering a part-time option for your doctoral research, it might not even be necessary for you to move. Many well-known international universities have worldwide collaborations and hence also offer programmes at their overseas locations, or have a well-organized and supported distance-learning programme. Consider this when making your choice.

Selecting a supervisor

This section closely relates to the selection of a university and department. The selection of an appropriate supervisor is crucial, since you will be spending much of your time as doctoral student 'in their care'; much time will be spent under their instruction and many discussions will take place. It is important to remember that the reputation of the department and the university is generally built on the reputation of its members.

Usually, you do not tend to have much input into the allocation of your supervisor or supervisors (the issue of being supervised by a committee of supervisors is discussed in Chapter 4), since this is an internal process of the respective department or research group. However, you can (and we suggest you do) contact individual members of staff with a good reputation whom you think would be appropriate supervisors before you apply in order to arouse their interest, just as Peter did in his story below. This way they will already know about you when your application officially arrives in the department and can request to work with you.

You can research the profiles of prospective candidates for supervision on the university/faculty/department website. Normally, short biographical notes together with research and teaching interests, as well as selected publications will be provided. Usually people also provide some information on the kind of projects they have been or are currently working on and funds and grants they have been awarded either by government or industrial institutions. It is also becoming increasingly popular to include personal information on these websites; this will help you understand what type of person your potential supervisor is, which will also form an important part of the decision process. You are going to spend a lot of time with your supervisor, it is important you get along (see Chapter 4 for more information on this subject).

Most likely, scholars who publish regularly in highly ranked journals in your future field and also attract research grants and funds will be at the top of your list. However, these factors often have no bearing on whether an individual is good at supervising.

How I got to do a doctorate: Initiative pays off!

When I thought about doing a doctorate in early September 2005, I had just finished a Master's degree in Management at a UK university. Intrigued by the topic of my Master dissertation, I thought about delving into it more deeply.

I started by looking for a supervisor that may be interested in supervising me to do research in that area. Based on the literature in my Master dissertation I identified two potential supervisors, as they published extensively in the area that I wanted to focus on. Thinking about criteria that a supervisor might base a decision on, I wrote a short summary of my dissertation, a research proposal, and updated my CV. Then, I took the initiative and contacted the two prospective supervisors via e-mail and attached the prepared documents.

I was anxious and started obsessively checking my e-mail. One of the two answered on the very same day I sent the e-mails. Michael politely explained that he was not able to supervise any more students at that moment because he had reached the maximum of students he was able to supervise. However, he encouraged me to get in touch with Sophia, who funnily was the second person I had contacted. After two weeks, however, Sophia still hadn't gotten back to me, since she was about to change university.

Having job applications running at the same time, I felt pressure and needed to have an answer rather quickly. After obsessively checking my e-mails everyday, all of a sudden, I received a reply to my informal application. Sophia asked whether I would be available for a telephone interview on the same day. Without hesitation, I got back to her to fix a time for an interview.

During the interview, while my adrenalin steadily increased, I was asked about my proposal in more depth, in particular about the research questions, research methods in relation to them as well as the feasibility of the project. We also discussed funding which I would have to apply for once I arrived at the university. [You should be aware that universities often have internal studentships available, which may include a contractual relationship to teach or do other research related activities.] The conversation finished with Sophia saying 'Okay, I will take you. I just have to check whether there are some deadlines you have to consider'.

And so I went back to waiting, expecting another e-mail to be sent some time later in the week. I was just discussing the result of the call with my parents, when my phone rang again. Not expecting anything, I picked up. It was Sophia again and she informed me that I had the permission of the research degrees programme director to join the degree programme. After hanging up the phone, I honestly couldn't believe what had happened.

Within three weeks of contacting two potential supervisors I was offered a place on the doctoral programme at one of the best universities in UK under the supervision of an established expert in my future field of research. Although I didn't know much about what doing a doctorate meant, I felt it was a unique challenge. After filling out the administrative forms and sending them to the university, I was back to packing my suitcase again for another journey. I am sure it would have been more difficult, lengthy and probably not even successful without contacting my current supervisor . . . I suggest you try it yourself.

Peter (final year student in marketing)

Peter's case should be followed up with a word of caution: there is a thin line between persevering and pestering. So, although perseverance and initiative often do pay off, pestering and hassling do not. It is important to ensure you achieve the right balance and make the right kind of contact at the right time. Remember, the application process can be long and very involved for any number of reasons, so it may take a few weeks to make a decision. Respect this part of the process and give your potential supervisor the necessary space – being too persistent at this stage could actually end up being a disadvantage in the decision-making process.

Although many students are tempted to seek out professors to be their doctoral supervisors, we have to say that each faculty tier has its own strengths and weaknesses. Although professors, as established experts with wide-reaching academic networks, tend to be more experienced, many other faculty members compensate for their lack of seniority with motivation and enthusiasm. In addition, they tend to have more time to dedicate to supervision. We know students who, despite being their supervisor's first doctoral student, produced high-quality theses with very minor corrections after their viva – so being associated with a senior member of academic staff is by no means a must. Who is the best supervisor for you ultimately depends on the individual person and the relationship you have with that person (more on dealing with your supervisor in Chapter 4).

To inform your decision, we provide a brief overview of different career levels in the UK and US higher education system for you to gain a better understanding (see Table 2.3).

Table 2.3 Comparison of career levels in UK and US higher education systems

Level of seniority	UK system	US system
Early career (junior)	Lecturer	Assistant professor
Mid-career (mid)	Senior lecturer	Associate professor
Established career (senior)	Reader	No equivalent
	Professor	Full professor

It is also a good idea to set up a brief meeting with your potential supervisor to explore the possibility of working together in the future; this could include discussions about research topics and will be very useful in informing your decision making. Most academics will be happy to meet with you to discuss expectations and future directions if mutual research interests exist. This meeting will also allow you to explore more implicit factors like whether your personalities match and whether you could work together well.

We strongly suggest that you seize this opportunity if possible but are of course aware that it is not always feasible to meet your supervisor (especially for overseas students). If you are unable to arrange a personal meeting, we thus suggest you engage in email and/or telephone correspondence. Apart from anything else, it demonstrates your initiative and interest in joining the university's doctoral programme.

Finally, when approaching a potential supervisor, it pays to be prepared. The person you approach may well ask you for a short proposal or curriculum vitae (CV) in response to your queries, so make sure you have these documents to hand – it is too late to start thinking about preparing these documents when someone is asking for them. However, at the same time it is important to tailor your documents to the person/department/university you are approaching. So make sure you identify your potential supervisor first, draw up the draft documents and then make contact. In case you are interested in further reading, a more scientific approach to selecting a supervisor was developed by Ray (2007).

Writing a research proposal

Arguably the most important element of your application documents is your research proposal because it will be circulated around the department you are applying to and serves as the basis for your selection. Based on the quality of your proposal, staff members will decide whether they have an interest in supervising you or not. Depending on interest and university policy, they may offer you a place immediately or invite you for further discussion. Importantly, your proposal may also be used to decide whether you will be offered a scholarship or not. So, producing a high-quality research proposal is of utmost importance if wanting to get a (funded) place in a doctoral programme.

To aid your thinking on the topic, we present an extended structure for a proposal below, which aims to offer some generic advice for you to work with. Please remember that, as with many issues in this book, this is not the one and only way of doing it and much of how you build the proposal really depends on the university and departmental guidelines. Make sure you are familiar with these. We further suggest that you consult additional sources of information for advice on this topic (e.g. Punch, 2000). Nonetheless, some general guidance is helpful at this point. Based on our experience, a good research proposal contains the following:

- *Proposed topic*: The title you choose is not the final title; it is a tentative working title that summarizes the research you want to conduct in an informative and concise way.
- *Description of problem*: You need to provide the reader (your potential supervisor) with some background information on the topic. You also need to show that you are familiar with the relevant literature by relating your proposed topic to existing work.
- *Aims and objectives of the research*: Your aims and objectives can partly be derived from existing literature, for example improving/extending a concept or theory, creating a new framework, and so on. However, it can also be based on more practical issue, such as helping managers to improve their decision making. You do not need to outline your basic objectives in great detail – extended bullet points should be sufficient.
- *Central research questions*: Based on the aims and objectives you identified, you work out one or two key questions the research is going to address. These do not need to be your final research questions (in fact, most students spend their first year of research narrowing down their topic and refining their research question).
- *Relevance of the research to the field/discipline*: In this section you build on your knowledge of the literature by outlining the original value of your

work and explaining the implications your research will have on the field (known as 'the contribution').

• *How the research will be conducted*: This includes a rough description of the methodological approach you are planning to take and a time scale as the main elements. Do not worry – you do not need to be an expert on methodology yet. At this stage you just need to demonstrate that you actually thought about how you are going to address your research topic.

• *References*: At the end of your proposal you should include a list of all references, that is the bibliographic information for the books, journal articles, websites and so on you used when creating your proposal.

The key to remember is that it is quality not quantity that counts. Sometimes less is more. Hence, try to be as specific and concise as possible without losing any part of your argument. However, also do not worry too much if you slightly exceed the word limit that is set by the university; the word limit is often only a guide meant to save staff from reading hundreds of pages of research proposal and there is generally some flexibility. Check with a member of the administrative team to see what the guidelines are. There are often also example proposals available, either from the university directly or from various guidance websites. The good news is that once you have written your research proposal, you have actually overcome the most difficult part of the application process.

Preparing and submitting your documents

Before you start preparing your application, read the application documents carefully and make sure you do not overlook anything. Universities are bureaucratic beasts and we do not want you to get caught up in a technicality. Usually doctoral programmes offer comprehensive application packs; make sure you follow the guidance provided in them carefully. It is often part of the formal requirement to include the names of one or two referees (or even letters of recommendation) alongside your application documents. It is important that the references you provide are fairly recent, for example from your current academic or work supervisors, and that they come from competent and respected referees.

If you are an international student coming to study in the UK and your native language is not English, it may well be necessary for you to take a language test. The two most popular tests are the TOEFL (Test of English as a Foreign Language) and the IELTS (International English Language Testing System). Make sure you prepare for and take these tests well in advance, as there may be fixed testing dates during which you will have to take the test. In addition, you may well have to wait several months before receiving your results. The entry requirements related to these tests differ from university to university, so make sure you inform yourself about the threshold score required and whether you can realistically achieve that standard of English.

This type of information is available from the university, normally included in the application pack and generally also accessible via websites.

Some universities, largely US-based institutions but also some European universities, will additionally require you to take the GMAT (General Management Admission Test) or the GRE (Graduate Recruitment Examination) and this also requires preparation well in advance. Most universities require a certain score on one or several of the tests in order to make a student eligible for application. However, there may be some room for exceptions. For instance, if you have already completed your undergraduate degree in an English-speaking country or went to an English school abroad, you may be exempt from the English language test requirements.

Whether you find yourself in special circumstances or not, we suggest you inform yourself about the application requirements in good time to ensure you have sufficient time to prepare your application. It is also worth knowing that most universities also provide crash courses in English for overseas students when arriving on site; although it should be noted that the quality and cost of these courses vary from institution to institution.

Also be aware that your highest degree needs to be sufficient for acceptance to a higher degree programme at the chosen institution. In most cases this is a Master's or an equivalent degree. Sometimes universities also accept high-performing undergraduate graduates, for example based on the quality of their final dissertation or their achievement of a good degree result overall. A minimum requirement tends to be a good 2:1 degree; however, because of the strong competition in the UK higher education market, a first class honours degree is generally preferable.

In educational systems that do not use Bachelor and Master degrees (e.g. Germany's 'Diplom' degrees) you will have to provide evidence, often translated and certified, that your degree qualifies you for a doctoral research degree in the UK. Do not be discouraged if at a first glance you do not have the necessary qualification; take advantage of the programme administrators and get advice from academic staff to verify whether your understanding is correct – a lot can get lost in translation and conversion, so make sure you do not sell yourself short!

Do not become discouraged if you are rejected by the university of your choice, especially if you are aiming high. Being rejected by one institution does not mean you will be rejected by all. Take it as a learning experience and enhance your application portfolio based on the feedback you got from the institution. Do not put all your eggs into one basket by applying to only one university. Instead, create a short list of interesting institutions and apply to more than one. Remember, you have got nothing to lose by trying. Indeed, it is still free to apply for higher degrees in the UK (unlike the US, where you often pay significant application fees). Of course that does not mean you should fire blindly – every application you make needs to be grounded in research about the institution you are applying to, otherwise you waste your time and theirs.

If your application is successful, you will be formally notified by the university (depending on the university procedures and the nature of your relationship with your prospective supervisor, you may also receive informal notification in advance). Formal notification generally comes in the form of a letter outlining an offer of a place on the university's doctoral programme and requesting a response by a specific date. Depending on the department or university you applied to, your supervisor(s) may or may not be outlined in the letter. Often, but not always, they will simultaneously inform you about whether you qualified for a scholarship and, if so, outline the terms of your contract.

The 'offer letter' is generally accompanied by some induction material, which introduces the university, the department and the doctoral programme, as well as outlining the length of study, payable fees, resources and so on. You now have the option of becoming a doctoral candidate and moving one step closer to your goal. This is a very exciting prospect and a minor success in itself. The fact that you made it this far means that you submitted a strong application and that your research proposal made for interesting reading. Congratulations!

Entering the academic community

If you decide to accept the terms of the offer, then you are about to embark on the journey of a lifetime by entering the academic community as a professional researcher. As mentioned earlier, the (unstructured) postgraduate world of research is different to the (taught) undergraduate and postgraduate world you are already familiar with. Regardless of which educational system you come from, you will now be required to work much more independently. This starts on day one when you register for the doctoral programme.

Registration

Although you have probably already submitted your application documents, most registration processes additionally require personal enrolment on site. This is often done during official induction or welcome days, and combined with campus tours and information sessions. You will often have a pre-registration pack to guide you but, if not, you will find out about the process as soon as you arrive. Most universities have support on site to help you familiarize yourself with the procedures and guide you through the process. Activities typically associated with registration include:

• formal course enrolment (often initially as a M.Phil. student);
• payment of tuition fees;
• creation of university student card;

- departmental induction;
- induction to departmental tasks and projects (crucial if teaching or research is part of your student contract or if you opted to increase your experience and income);
- introduction to doctoral programme structure;
- doctoral meet and greet;
- allocation of office space (if available);
- collection of accommodation keys (only applies if you opted for student accommodation).

At enrolment, you may choose between different modes of study, including full and part time, on-site or distance-learning student and so on (see Chapter 8 on 'Alternative routes to a doctorate'). Make sure that you discuss these options with your department ahead of time and know which option is most suitable for you. Registering correctly the first time helps you avoid lengthy administrative problems and inconveniences like restricted access to resources. If you do not already have a M.Phil. or Master by research, you will normally be registered as either a M.Phil. or general research student. Later you will be formally registered as doctoral student (see upgrading to doctoral research status later in this section).

The doctorate

A doctorate degree is usually completed in three stages:

1 *Year 1*: You will have to complete a research programme, which involves some assessed modules. In addition, the formative stage of the doctoral process is generally used to begin your literature review, develop or refine your research question and prepare the qualifying report – see below (depending on the discipline some data collection, for example lab work, may also be required in your first year).
2 *Year 2*: The second year is normally dedicated to conducting field or laboratory research, including data collection and analysis. In addition, research students often write industry reports and academic papers.
3 *Year 3+*: The last part of your doctorate is used to consolidate your research work, write your thesis, defend your work and look for postdoctoral employment.

The above is the most commonly used model of doctoral degrees; however, there are of course many variations on the above. For instance, qualitative researchers may do only very limited reading until they have completed their research and then do their literature review in the final stages of their degree. Other students already come to the programme with a dataset and thus can circumvent the data collection in year 2. Whatever the case may be, it is important that you familiarize yourself with the requirements of the programme. You need to know what the standard of research and writing is that you have to produce and what the requirements of you as a student are.

Wherever you decide to do your degree, it is very likely that you will have to attend a structured induction course as part of your doctoral programme. Generally, this is a basic methodology course comprising different modules covering different parts of research (e.g. introduction, philosophy, methods, writing, presentations etc.). There may well be some specific subject-knowledge courses, workshops or conferences your supervisor would like you to participate in as part of your learning process (see also Chapter 5 on 'Sidelines of a doctorate').

Since doctoral programmes are generally made up of people from a variety of educational and ethnic backgrounds, researching a plethora of different areas, these courses tend to be very general. Even if you feel that you are already familiar with the topic presented in the lectures, make sure that you attend and put sufficient effort into your assignments. You will need to pass the modules to be able to prepare your qualifying report and move into your second year (as a full doctoral researcher).

Upgrading to doctoral status is an important milestone in a doctoral degree and often associated with a formalized process, not dissimilar to the final oral examination or viva voce. Most universities employ a mini-dissertation or report structure, the qualifying report, which is an extended version of your initial research proposal, informed by a year of study at the institution. Often the information presented in the report is then reviewed in either an oral examination or informal chats with faculty members; generally, at least one of these is from your department. Although many students find this process very daunting, it is helpful to remember that it prepares you for your final defence.

While some universities treat this part of the doctoral process as a formality, others take it very seriously – there are reports of students finding this initial step more difficult than the final viva. Of course a lot of that has to do with the amount of learning a student does between the qualifying report viva and the final thesis viva, but some of it also has to do with your faculty trying to test and push you. They want to make sure that you have thought through your work and that it is defensible, when you reach your final viva. You will need to demonstrate familiarity with your field including literature and methodological knowledge and show the competence to complete your doctoral research successfully.

It thus pays to take this process seriously and prepare for it like you would for a final exam. There are four outcomes that the examiners, who are normally members of your university, may recommend based on reading your report and listening to your explanations in the oral defence:

1 Pass to Ph.D. (with guidance, advice and revisions).
2 Recommend for resubmission (major revisions).
3 Recommend for M.Phil. (with guidance, advice and revisions).
4 Recommend for withdrawal from programme.

First of all, you will be pleased to know that option (1) is the most common outcome. If the university did not think you were capable of doing a doctoral degree, they would not have admitted you to the programme in the first place. Secondly, the fact that you have submitted your qualifying report and had your oral viva means that your supervisor has signed off your work and believes you to be competent enough to pass this stage of the process – otherwise they would not have advanced your work. Options (3) and (4) are rare and tend to be a mutual decision. Do not dismay if you are not happy with the results of your qualifying viva – you often have the opportunity to submit your report again six months later as per option (2). Think carefully about whether this is an investment you want to make given the examiners' recommendation, make sure you incorporate the examiners' feedback into your new proposal and, as always, consult your supervisor and members of your department before making the final decision.

Once you have passed this stage of the doctoral process, the rest is achieved on the basis of hard work and persistence. Welcome to the wonderful world of doing a doctoral degree! Welcome to the academic community!

3

Managing the self

Make sure your basic needs are met first • Figure out how you learn best and what motivates you • Common demotivators and potential solutions • Keeping sight of the end goal

Some people describe the doctorate as a constant battle. They are not wrong but what they often fail to mention is that the doctorate is a battle you fight largely with yourself. Academic staff, departments and politics may make your life as a student more difficult but ultimately you are the person who controls whether you succeed or not. In this chapter we show you how you can successfully 'control' the emotional rather than the intellectual aspects of your personality by discussing the all important topics of self-motivation and persistence.

Thinking about a doctorate brings to mind an image of a student (well, let us be honest, we are talking about ourselves) sitting in front of a computer staring blankly at the screen, wishing that words would appear on it, flicking between email and solitaire, and wondering whether to clean the oven. Whatever your preferred distractions may be, it is likely that you will feel like this at some (possibly many) points as you move along in the process. Doing a doctorate can feel like climbing a mountain – standing at the bottom and looking up at that mountain can be overwhelming and demotivating.

Similarly, starting out with an idealistic and ambitious research project (in academic circles often referred to as 'setting out to save the world'), and later having to concede that doing what you set out to do is impossible because research is all about endless dedication and nitty-gritty detail, can be a very disappointing experience. When you reach that point, any given day can feel like a drop in the ocean, which makes it easy to become distracted and deeply unhappy about the task that lies ahead. Matters are compounded by the fact that, for better or worse, a doctorate is mostly a solitary task.

As most students face these issues at one point or another, we use this chapter to discuss some of the common demotivators doctoral students encounter and provide some tips about how to overcome them successfully. We start off by discussing how important it is to make sure your basic needs are met to avoid unnecessary distraction or complication, and allow you to fully focus on the task at hand. We then move our discussion on to how you can find out what actually motivates you and work through different ways of using that knowledge to keep your motivation levels high. We conclude by reminding the reader what doing a doctorate is all about.

Make sure your basic needs are met first

In line with Maslow's (1943) theory of human motivation, we suggest you start battling yourself by satisfying your basic needs first. These include your physical and financial needs, social needs and also psychological needs. By keeping these needs satisfied and in balance, you will be able to create a solid foundation for your motivation that is necessary for you to survive your doctorate and succeed in the process.

Physical/financial

Are you thinking about how you are going to put the next meal on your table? Or where you are going to sleep tonight? Let us hope not! Although this might sound like an awkward thing for an intelligent educated person to worry about and thus seem silly to you right now, it is an immanent and omnipresent threat that lies at the very core of your successful doctorate. If you face financial difficulties, not only will it occupy your mind and distract you from you work but in the worst case scenario may even force you to quit your doctorate altogether. We sincerely hope you never have to face a situation like this.

No matter whether you are supported by your family, self-funded or on scholarship, you should not have to worry about your finances. See Chapter 6 on more information about sources of funding and income. Remember, if you are struggling, do not be afraid to seek help and advice. Universities offer various support services, which students can take advantage of confidentially and free of charge. Do not be too proud to use them if necessary. This includes postgraduate, pastoral and welfare tutors, as well as various advisery teams (e.g. international student office, specific student advice functions, chaplains etc.). There is no shame in asking for advice and, in fact, it often takes a lot more strength to ask for help than to ignore the problem.

Regardless of what happens, remember to keep physically active. We know how tough it can be to fit sports into your busy time schedule but, as we all know, it is a critical part of anyone's routine. Physical activity helps stimulate mental activity and, believe it or not, actually increases your energy levels and has a positive effect on motivation; not to mention the negative effects if you do not keep fit as Andrew will tell you below. Already the Romans knew that a healthy mind resides in a healthy body (*Mens sana in corpore sano*). It does not mean that you have to work out like crazy. Thirty minutes of daily activity in the fresh air is sufficient. Besides, it can actually be fun. If you do not believe us, try it – who knows, you might even enjoy it. And often it also helps you to get in touch with other people as well. What follows is an outline of the benefits of using the university recreational facilities sent to all students by a head of sports and recreation.

Regular physical activity for adults is important to help prevent premature death from heart disease, some cancers and the health risks caused by obesity. A half-hour swim gives the body a thorough work-out using almost all the muscles and increasing the heart rate. It is a low impact exercise with so-called aerobic benefits. Aerobic exercise raises the heart rate, causing blood to circulate more quickly around the body and deliver more oxygen to the muscles. In addition to reducing your chances of developing high blood pressure, diabetes and obesity in later life, other potential benefits of regular exercise include improved circulation and the reduction of stress, depression and anxiety.

Andrew (Head of Sports and Recreation)

Avoiding permanent health damage (PHD)

One day I woke up with terrible pain in my lower leg. It was a few days before Christmas and at the very end of my doctorate. I was in the last stages of writing up and was under considerable pressure to finish in order to be able to submit my thesis to the examiners on time. At that stage of the process, I was working nights mostly, sometimes up to 14 hours straight. Just sitting at my desk in front of the laptop. And of course no exercise whatsoever, unless you count the walking distance between my room and the kitchen.

All of a sudden, this pain was there and wouldn't go away. The way over to the university health centre was torturous already, just to be told that I would need to see a doctor at the hospital ... an even further distance to struggle with for a limping man. After endless hours in the waiting room of the hospital on a Saturday and seeing an assistant doctor the tentative diagnosis was: Deep Vein Thrombosis (DVT). I was shocked! To make things worse, I was told I wouldn't be able to fly home to see my parents over Christmas. Too risky they said. I had to come back on Monday to take some tests with another doctor to be sure. Then I was dismissed limping my way back home again. All weekend I was sitting in my room, watching the lines on the screen in front of me unable to focus.

What was I going to do? Is my Ph.D. really worth that much? I could think of nothing apart from the tests on Monday morning. At that time I didn't even realise that I lost 1.5 full days of work – at a stage where every minute was precious and every lost minute was a disaster. Fortunately, when the long-awaited Monday finally came, I was told the test results were negative. However, the pain was still there. The good news was that I was at least allowed to fly home over Christmas. The doctor advised me to undertake extended walks to loosen the cramped muscles until I would be able to do proper exercise again. 'What exercise?' I was thinking ironically.

But this unfortunate incident enlightened me. I realised that if I had done some exercise (maybe only 30 min a day) I probably could have avoided that unpleasant situation and ultimately saved myself a lot of lost days of work. From then on I exercised regularly again or at least went for extended walks in case I wasn't motivated enough to go to the gym. I hope you guys don't make the same mistake. Nothing is worth risking your health!

Mark (final year student in physics)

Social/relational

As already touched upon, doing a doctorate can be a lonely journey. Unlike taught postgraduate degrees, research degrees do not tend to follow a structured programme. While you take modules with other students, generally in small classes, most of your time is actually spent in the lab, in your office or in the field doing research by yourself. Being alone so much can sometimes lead to people feeling sad, isolated, neglected or alienated – this is especially true for outgoing and extroverted personalities, who thrive on social contact. Of course feeling unhappy does not facilitate productive work; in fact, quite the opposite is true. Demotivation can lead to sad emotion, which in turn can compound the motivational problems.

It is really important while doing a Ph.D. that you avoid social isolation. Ali and Kohun (2007) developed a framework for dealing with social isolation in various stages of doctoral studies. Although based on the US model, it offers some helpful guidance. Remember that when adapting this model to the UK context, there is some overlap between stages II and III.

- Stage I: Pre-admission/enrolment
  - Causes: ambiguous description, lack of integration, insufficient admin support
  - Solutions: orientations, formal and informal events, admin liaison
- Stage II: First year
  - Causes: discrepancy from other academic degrees, adjustment, avoidance
  - Solutions: integration, cohort structure, ice-breakers
- Stage III: Second and third year
  - Causes: unpreparedness (for assignments and exams), lack of guidance on research topic, lack of guidance on choosing an adviser
  - Solutions: collaborative supervisory relationship, presentations and feedback, adviser selection guidance
- Stage IV: Writing stage
  - Causes: lack of structure, distrust, lone working
  - Solution: increased structure, collaborative supervisory relationship, face-to-face meetings

It is all too easy to let work take over your life (see Samantha's story below), especially if you are doing something you like and are enthused by. But this is not healthy in the long term and you need to make sure you are also meeting your social needs. If you are not readily provided with opportunities to meet others through your degree programme, then seek them out!

Social support is beneficial in many ways. For one, it provides a good way to balance your working life by giving you a break, that is some time away from work. It is a way to release your frustration, vent, enjoy. It is also a good way to share your experience with peers in similar situations and to find out that you are not alone. Talk to people who are in a similar position as you, such as other graduate students or early career academics. They will be able to understand your perspective, help you see things from another angle and possibly even give you some solid advice for getting past any tricky issues you are dealing with.

So, bottom line, interpersonal relationships are often critical to academic success. In our interviews, we found that the lack of social interaction leads to self-doubts that often result in the loss of interest in the doctorate and ultimately a poor, inefficient and unproductive research performance that will delay your progress.

Why don't you want to be our friend anymore?

When I was doing my Ph.D., I had a very good friend, flatmate even. She was a very social and gregarious person, who loved meeting people, loved going out, loved having fun. Her life was so wonderfully clichéd, that she was often called the 'life of the party'. Whatever happened, if Lisa was there, we knew we'd have a good time.

But one day, that all changed. Lisa fell behind in her work – there were some problems with data collection – a very common phenomena in medicine (I mean, seriously, our participants tend to be people that make appointments they don't keep, not little cells in Petri dishes!). Anyhow, the point is, Lisa changed. She started to feel the pressure and became very stressed out. The change in her demeanour was evident to everyone but no matter what we said to try to cheer her up or help her academically, nothing worked. She withdrew more and more; she stopped taking up our invitations; started socialising with other people; and working (long) nights instead of days. Things got worse and worse and worse. Eventually, she cut us off completely.

In retrospect, I think she couldn't handle the pressure we were inadvertently putting on her and she thought it was easier to avoid the situation all together by avoiding us. We tried really hard to help her turn her project and her moods around but with no avail. Eventually, it all culminated in a serious nervous breakdown and an extensive period of hospitalisation. We could all see it coming a long way off but felt completely helpless.

Lisa is recovered now and going strong. She's very near completion and you can't see a trace of emotional instability. I think in her case, a new supervisor was associated with new confidence and hope. All it took was a bit of rest and change, and then things jumped right back on track. Anyhow, I learnt an important lesson through this experience, even if it wasn't my lesson to learn. First of all, we all need a little extra help sometimes – and that's totally okay. I'd rather shout for help from the top of my lungs than fall and have no one hear me. Plus, doesn't everything seem a lot easier when you've got a shoulder to cry on . . .? Secondly, whatever happens, I need to keep a balance in my life. All work and no play makes for a very unhappy person . . .

Samantha (final year student in medicine)

Some of the things you can do to keep socially active include joining study groups, clubs or societies (there are a lot of virtual communities if you prefer more anonymous interactions); or find a strong mentor (some departments or universities have very successful student-to-student mentoring and tutoring programmes). Many graduate schools have programmes specifically designed for postgraduates, research students or doctoral researchers – or all of the above. There is probably a postgraduate representative or society. If your school does not have this type of scheme already or you like to take on a more active role, there are opportunities for this too. Where there are no schemes, propose them and help to organize postgraduate events. Where the schemes are ineffective or unsuitable, get involved and help transform them. Sometimes you have to help build a community.

Do not forget your family. Although they do not face the same situation as you do or have similar experiences as your peers, they will always be there for you. Involve them in your doctorate. They are your family and will always be there to support you no matter what. Besides, it is often relieving to talk to 'outsiders' who are not involved in the process but will offer emotional support. This also gives you the advantage of an objective and uncoloured view on your problem that often helps to put things into perspective again. Do not forgo this opportunity.

Emotional/psychological

Doctoral degrees are full of ups and downs and over time this emotional rollercoaster ride can take its toll. Do not think of this as a reflection of your character but rather think of it as a reflection on the difficulty of the journey. It is important that you remember to take care of your psychological welfare as well – ensure you are happy and healthy.

Throughout your degree, you may sometimes feel so down that you find it difficult to pull yourself back up. And this is not helped by one of the common myths of graduate school: 'Everyone else is doing great'. Well, simply put, this just is not true. Everyone struggles at one point or another; it is just a natural part of the growth process. Many people do not talk about their plights but do not let that fool you into thinking you are the only one that is having problems. Instead, talk to those around you openly and share your experiences with others; you will soon see that you are not alone. This links back to the earlier section on relationships and the importance of social support. Remember: the work you do in your doctorate is mainly independent and solitary work; however, this does not mean your whole doctorate life has to be solitary and lonely.

Friends and family, colleagues and supervisors are great sources of social support. Talk through the issues you have and do not let them rest with you. And, remember, if things ever get too much for you, you can always seek confidential advice from advisers, counsellors or psychologists. There is no shame in asking for help when you need it, or even just stopping by for a friendly chat 'just because' you feel like it.

Another way to keep 'sane' while doing a research degree is to make sure that you get the work–life balance right. Make sure you take sufficient breaks and 'mental health' (work-free) days. It can be tempting to let yourself get caught up in work; but work hard to avoid that trap. If you work too much, you will not be efficient and you certainly will not be happy. Do not let your Ph.D. lead to PHD (permanent health damage, see p. 34).

Also make sure to enjoy and celebrate small successes, for example when you achieve a set goal, no matter how minor it is. Do not exaggerate but consume these moments consciously and reward yourself with little 'goodies'. This will help you to stay on track, push your confidence and actually enjoy what you are doing. Always remember: humour and happiness are the strongest weapons against demotivation and depression because a positive mood will increase your productivity and stress resistance and hence enable you to adopt and achieve challenging goals (Fishbach and Labroo, 2007). Make sure you use this to your advantage. You can do it!

Figure out how you learn best and what motivates you

People learn in different ways and have different needs; it is important that you know what works best for you if you want to take advantage of your personal strengths by tailoring your actions accordingly. If you do not know what works best for you, find out! The best way to do that is by trying out various ways of learning and personal motivation, and seeing what pays off. While doing that, it is important to understand and remember that different ways of working may be better at various times or for diverse tasks, so do not be too quick to dismiss any one way of working. What does not work in one situation may work in another.

When figuring out what works best for you, under which conditions and when, it is important to consider the following factors:

- *Work environment*: What setting you are working in (e.g. office, library, study room, bedroom, kitchen etc.).
- *Working conditions*: What conditions you are working under (e.g. noise level, lighting, location in the room, people around you, background distractions like music or TV, etc.).
- *Task*: What you are working on or trying to achieve (e.g. literature review, writing a chapter or paper, analysing data etc.).
- *Method*: How you are trying to reach your goal (e.g. structured, unstructured, individual or group work etc.).
- *Timing*: When you are trying to do the work (e.g. morning, afternoon, evening; well in advance or close to the deadline etc.).

When evaluating your way of working, remember to consider four outcome variables:

- speed of work;
- persistence, that is the ability to endure the work;
- quality of work;
- enjoyment of work.

It is not enough to be quick; you also have to be good. And, just the same, if you are quick and good but only manage to do about five minutes worth of work and spend every second despising it, there is probably a better approach for you. And overall do not forget to have some fun as well. If everything you do is like torture, then you will not succeed. We assume that nobody forced you to do your doctorate, so there must be some desire somewhere inside you. Locate it and draw on it from time to time, then you will find your work easier and success will follow naturally. Having said that, there are various key principles of learning and motivation that can help you direct your actions. Some of these are reviewed in the section below.

Common demotivators and potential solutions

This section looks at some of the common demotivators people encounter while doing a doctorate and offers potential ways forward. Not everything will work for everyone; so try several of these in combination to find out what works best for you.

So many things to do, so little time: the magnitude of the task

One of the common complaints of graduate students is that a doctorate degree is so much work, that they do not even know where to start. Students often report being overwhelmed, especially in the first year of their studies. This is perhaps unsurprising, seeing as students embark on a three to five year degree, often largely by research, with little instruction, limited guidance and little experience in the area (even if this is not the case, it certainly feels that way). Even when you are working hard, it can feel like you are treading water because so much lies ahead of you. That is the nature of the doctorate and part of the reason why it is such an incredible learning journey. However, it can also be very demotivating. Some of the things you can do to make the task less daunting include:

- breaking the task down;
- planning backwards;

- linking new information to previous knowledge (e.g. mnemonics, spider diagrams, rhymes, riddles etc.).

Our capacity for processing information is limited and it is often cited that people can process seven plus or minus two pieces of information in their mind simultaneously (Miller, 1957). Anything more than that will be difficult for us to remember and work with in our mental space. Hence, **breaking the task** into between five to nine segments should make it easier for us to cope with. Create goals, sub-goals and micro goals to achieve what you set out to achieve. Work hard to meet your goals but do not get too agitated if you do not succeed. Instead, work to a set timeplan, identify risks and dependencies, and adjust timeplan to counter the risks.

At the beginning of your degree you will only have a vague plan on how to accomplish the long-term goal of handing in your thesis after about three years, for example literature review and developing research question in year one, data collection and analysis in year two and writing up in year three. At this stage three years seems an awful lot of time, so most students do not feel the urge to get started right away. However, be assured that this deadline will approach very fast, especially towards the later stages of your doctorate and you will wish that you had done more work at the beginning or at least kept track of your aims and deadlines.

Planning backwards can be an effective means to help you focus on what you need to achieve because it gives you a fixed end goal to work towards. If you want to defend your thesis, you will first have to submit your final copy, your draft copy, all your chapters, do your research, design your methodology, build your theoretical framework, read the literature and come up with a research question. One builds upon the other and they are all necessary steps towards the achievement of the end goal, the defended doctoral thesis and the prestigious title associated with it.

If you want to finish in a set period of time, set a deadline. Say, if you want to defend your thesis on day x, you know you will need to submit your final copy by day x − y, where y is the amount of time it takes at your university to arrange a viva voce. Keep in mind the time the examiners require for reading your work, which is generally between one and three months. In other words, you will have to submit the complete thesis three months before you defend it. Using this method, you can work your way back through the timeline, working out exactly what needs to be completed when.

Deadlines are important for monitoring your progress as it enables you to discuss your developments with your supervisor. Whatever happens, remember to build slack into the plan for unavoidable mishaps, delays, breaks from work and so on. Remind yourself that research is creative work that cannot always be forced into a routine timetable. Having contingency in your plan will help you stay as much on track as possible. This is what most people will consider as effective and successful time management.

An example of how a rough timetable for your doctorate can look like is outlined in Figure 3.1. Be aware that although the diagram shown outlines a chronological sequence of steps to work on, in reality you will find yourself going through many iterative steps of revising and replacing work from earlier stages. Furthermore, the outlined timetable is just an example of what it could look like. You will have to develop your own timetable that fits your own work pace and research purpose.

The final method we discuss is **linking the new information** you are confronted with during your Ph.D. to existing knowledge. It is easier to remember things you are already familiar with, so linking new information to existing knowledge will help to solidify the learning and help you remember better. This links with Miller's (1957) principle of simplifying and reducing the amount of information processing your mind actually has to do. An example would be a foreign language student, studying Indian language who is trying to remember the Gujarati letter (Kh = ખ) by remembering that the symbol looks like a (kh)amel. It will help you remember because you are associating new knowledge with already existing schemata, therefore making the thought process less strenuous.

No matter what you study, it is likely that you have come across certain abbreviations. For instance, as a psychology student, you might have used the acronym OCEAN (openness, conscientiousness, extraversion, agreeableness and neuroticism) to remember the commonly cited big five personality factors (cf. Goldberg, 1981; McCrae and Costa, 1990). Or, as commonly used to remember the order of the planets, you can use a sentence 'My Very Excellent Mother Just Sold Us Nine Pizzas' or the acronym MVEMJSUNP (Mercury, Venus, Earth, Mars, Jupiter, Saturn, Uranus, Neptune, Pluto). Now that Pluto is no longer a planet, it may need some rejigging but it helps to illustrate the point. If you have a difficult time remembering, there are legitimate ways of tricking your mind into remembering. There is nothing wrong with being efficient, right?

I don't know what to do: lack of direction

Another common issue for graduate research students is that they often lack direction. A doctorate is like nothing you have ever done before and like nothing you will do again. This means that students often do not know what to do and how to do it. Combined with the fact that they are one of the few people researching in their chosen area with limited supervisory support (after all, a doctorate is about self-directed learning), students can sometimes feel like they are floating around aimlessly. One graduate student always talked of her colleagues 'running around like chickens with their heads cut off'. When we asked her what she meant by that, she explained: 'Everyone's working very hard but nobody around here really ever seems to be sure that what they're doing is actually right'.

The fact that most people come into a doctoral degree from a more structured educational or professional environment only compounds the problem – the

Figure 3.1 Outline of timetable

Task	Year 1	Year 2	Year 3	Year 4	Progress
Research Methods Course					
Qualifying Report					
Literature Review					
Empirical Work					
Select cases					
Design + test interviews					
Conduct interviews					
Analytical Work					
Within-case analysis					
Cross-case analysis					
Enfolding literature					
Writing up					
Draft Methodology					
Draft Literature					
Draft Results					
Draft thesis					
Finalise Thesis					

(Year columns subdivided by month: O N D J F M A M J J A S)

strong contrast helps to highlight and make salient how different the new environment is from the old one. And, regardless of people's natural tendencies, change is difficult for almost everyone because with change comes uncertainty. Uncertainty creates unease and fear because it forces us out of our comfort zones. The good news is that positive adaptation often leads to profound personal growth; the bad news is that the adjustment period can be very difficult.

So, what can you do? Some of the things you can do to give yourself more direction include:

- set your own goals;
- ask for advice (e.g. supervisor, peers, colleagues, friends etc.);
- be adaptive (e.g. have a Plan B);
- spread the workload.

To ease the transition into the new and fast-paced doctoral environment, an important lesson to learn early on is that you have to **set your own goals**; nobody is going to set them for you. They are *your* goals and only you know what you are setting out to achieve. Although many of you will have good guidance from your supervisors or colleagues, you will have to make many of the critical important decisions that you are confronted with throughout your degree alone.

The nice thing about doctoral degrees is that you have a lot of freedom; you have the opportunity to really shape your research over time and set out the scope of what you are going to do. Some people find this overwhelming and describe it as 'being thrown into the deep end', 'chucked overboard', 'plunged into cold water' and so on. The point is, more often than not, it is a shock for most people that they are now expected to learn rather than just be taught. The more active role you take in a doctoral degree demands a lot of self-discipline and hard work. For instance, if you want to work in a structured environment and have tangible objectives (and, of course, not everyone works best that way), you need to create this for yourself.

One of the simplest ways to give yourself a direction is to set your own goals as goals constitute the focal points around which human behaviour is organized (Fishbach and Ferguson, 2007). We know from the literature that goals should be challenging and specific, and that knowledge of results and performance against the target is important (Locke, 1968). Applying these principles to your doctorate will help to give you aims. We have included some core considerations and principles of goal-setting in Table 3.1.

If you are also having difficulty setting your own goals, there is no shame in seeking direction and **asking for advice** from others. Ask your supervisor, other academics or industry members, colleagues and recent graduates for their input. Feedback is one of the best developmental mechanisms. Do not forgo the opportunity to ask others who have 'been there' for their views. You might be surprised about just how helpful this can be. It also might speed

Table 3.1 Do's and don'ts of doctoral goal-setting

Principle	Don't	Do
Personal involvement in goal-setting	Let your supervisor set all your goals ('s/he runs the show')	Get involved; outline what you want to achieve in the long term; identify and set clear and achievable milestones (short-term goals) along the process
Challenging goals	Make the goals too easy ('anyone could have done that'); make the goals too difficult ('set out to conquer the world')	Set goals that take you outside of your comfort zone and stretch you but lay within your competence ('work hard and challenge yourself')
Specific goals	Make goals so vast and vague that you cannot measure achievement against them ('I will write the best Ph.D. in neural networks'); these types of goal are ambiguous, and unachievable, and thus do not drive you forward	Break down the task into manageable chunks and make sure you can measure achievement; have overarching and subordinate goals ('After my first year I will have chosen a preliminary research question, have a solid basis for my literature review and have designed my methodology; By day X I will have written one chapter')
Knowledge of results/ performance	Just look at the overall feedback, ranking or grade (where applicable) on your assignment	Ask for feedback: How did you do, what went well, what could have been better, in which area and how can you improve your work. How did you do compared to expectation for someone at your stage/level? How did other people do?

things up. Instead of wasting days and weeks by going around in circles, you can benefit from the advice others can provide you with.

But be careful and do not make it a habit to ask for help and guidance unless you have tried to solve your problem on your own. Only use it as a last resort. Developing a sufficient solution on your own will even be more rewarding. It will increase your confidence in your skills and competence, thereby also making you more independent of your supervisor and other sources of help. Eventually you will be more motivated and become increasingly interested in and absorbed by your work, sometimes even to the extent that the thesis becomes one of the most important things in your life.

Another helpful mechanism is to **be prepared to change and adapt** your goals and milestones several times as you progress in your research. Doctoral degrees are dynamic and flexible degrees that take on new shape and grow as you grow. Do not limit yourself by trying to force all of that into a neat little conceptual black box you drew up three, four or five years earlier. We suggest setting yourself reasonable goals and trying to improve on them as you learn and grow.

For example, you could write two doctoral proposals: one setting out the ideal research project, and another considering the minimal threshold at which a project would pass for a Ph.D. The first proposal sets the standard against which you are able to evaluate and judge your research; the second highlights which cutbacks or compromises can be made without challenging the main aims of the research. This is important because you will come across issues that will make you change your outlook on the research and will have to overcome barriers, which again will reflect on how you eventually conduct and present your work. It is thus important you are clear what the minimum is you need to achieve. However, that is not to say that you should aim for the bottom but always set yourself demanding goals in order to exceed the minimum.

Especially towards the end of your doctorate when you find yourself writing up your thesis, the pressure to finish will be very high. You will face the task of merging three or four years worth of work into a concise thesis that has to meet certain standards; not even to mention the intellectual contribution you have to make in order to receive your degree. This is a daunting task and many doctoral students feel overwhelmed by it. Whereas a little pressure might be healthy because some students find it difficult to work without it, too much pressure is counterproductive.

One way of avoiding or at least reducing that pressure is to **spread the workload**, for example by engaging in regular writing, as you move along in your process. This can involve conceptual ideas, extended chapter outlines, analytic results, literature reviews and so on, just as Andrew describes in his story below. Writing journal publications, conference and working papers can also contribute to this. It will not only improve your writing skills but also relieve you of some pressure and provide you with more structure and direction because it can be seen as a small thesis in itself that you can build on. You can use the given structure of the publication and expand on it when writing up your thesis by including more details of your research work (the issue of publishing will be discussed in more detail in Chapter 5).

Fortnightly literature review

I remember the first meeting with my supervisor as if it were yesterday. He welcomed me at the university and as a part of the research group. He asked how I felt and what my expectations were. But he didn't beat around the bushes for long before he hit me straight with his expectations and demands.

One, passing all the assignments of the research methods course. *Two*, teaching tutorials on one of his modules two hours a week. *Three*, handing in a literature report about all the papers I have been reading every two weeks.

What was that? Did I get this right? He wants me to write a report on all the articles? 'It doesn't need to be essay style, bullet points will do', he said. 'Now, that makes a big difference', I said sarcastically to myself. Since it was my very first week as a doctoral student I wasn't tough enough to veto this.

So I ended up doing as he required. For each paper I dedicated one page of review stating the full paper reference, summarising the main points and concluding how it might contribute to my research topic. In case of really bad papers that I thought I would never use anyway, I omitted writing up a review. For the rest I handed in my report every two weeks for almost as long as my first year producing dozens of pages of literature review.

In retrospect I have to say that it was challenging, a really great amount of work (no illusions there!) but also rewarding. Writing up these literature reviews helped to organise my thoughts. Not to speak of the advantage this posed when it came to actually writing up my literature chapter in my thesis. I could go back to my notes and copy and paste them into the chapter. All that was left to do was to connect the various ideas and form a structure.

Andrew (graduate in business)

The same thing all over again: the repetitiveness of the task

Although a doctorate is an intellectually challenging journey, you sometimes end up doing repetitious monkey work. Repetition is the key to success in many areas because you need to be able to reproduce your evidence; the fact that a lab or social experiment works once, does not make it fact. You need to make sure that your results are robust to demonstrate that you are adding value (in research this is referred to as reliability).

Remember also that practice makes perfect. Things may not always work out just the way you plan and this may mean having to repeat the odd task – the good news is that your doctoral degree will give you plenty of time to do just that. Unfortunately, unless you have the funds to pay someone to do the nonessential repetitive parts of the research (e.g. transcribing interviews), there is no way to avoid this kind of work.

Research revealed that the longer you work on a single problem or task, the more likely you are to lose enthusiasm about it (Phillips, 1980). Although the monotony of repetitive work often kills the initial enthusiasm of students, you can make it less painful. A few things you can do to improve this type of work and make it more enjoyable (and thus make it less likely for you to become demotivated and distracted) include:

- increase the variety;
- engage in forward thinking;

- improve the task;
- break it up;
- use it as a distraction task.

You are doing a doctoral degree, which means that you are most likely an inquisitive person. You are curious and want to know things, and enjoy the surprising aspects of change. However, there will be times when you feel stuck or just bored from concentrating on the same task over and over again thereby having to discipline yourself to continue. By **introducing variation** in your work, you will be able to focus for a longer time. Thus we recommend varying your work – switch back and forth between tasks when you notice that you are becoming fatigued with the monotony of the work.

Another thing you can do is to trick your mind into thinking this work is more interesting than it actually is. You can do this by adding additional stimulation, for example playing some music in the background, or engaging in some **forward thinking**, for example focus on all the wonderful things you will be able to do once you have completed the tasks. Always remind yourself of the superordinate (desirable) goals; this will help to keep you motivated.

You can also **improve the tasks** by adding another dimension to it, for example peaking your interest in the activity by adding an edge to it. For instance, when logging journal articles into a data file, you can make the task more interesting by counting the frequency of publication in an area over a given period or grouping the articles into topic subgroups. In physical terms, this may take a little longer but if it focuses your attention and increases your efficiency, the benefits of doing this will outweigh the costs.

What you can also do is to **break the tasks down**. Sometimes breaking down a task like this will make it more manageable and thus easier to complete. Take, for instance, the example of entering questionnaire or lab result data into a computer, you may find it easier to do five sets of results per day or half an hour each morning and afternoon. Try it and see what works for you. There is no sense in forcing yourself to do it all in one go, if you just end up sitting in front of the screen, staring at the keyboard and thinking about how nice the party on Saturday will be. Be efficient, it will help you work more quickly in the long term and also help you avoid oversights or making simple errors.

Last but not least, you can use these repetitive mind-numbing tasks to take a break from more challenging and exhausting creative work. Think of them as a **distraction task** in their own right. If you have read a journal article, you probably need some time to digest the information and do not want to dive straight into the next one. Use the 'break' your mind needs to refresh itself to do something that does not require a lot of thinking – your monotonous little break tasks.

Whether these techniques work for you really depends on your personality and learning style: some people take the plaster off slowly and others prefer to pull it off quickly. Try some of these methods, even in combination, to see what works for you. Maybe the story of Anne will help you to find your own mechanisms.

Transcribing: the evil of qualitative research

Transcribing interview data, that is turning the interviewee's words into a computer document by listening to the recording over and over again to capture each sound as text, was one of the most stupid, boring and frustrating tasks I have ever done in my life. Unfortunately, interviews being one of the most fruitful data collection techniques in qualitative research there was no way around it. On top of that I couldn't afford to outsource this obnoxious task and neither my supervisor nor my department would fund it. What a nightmare!

Looking back I have to admit that this period was one of the worst during my doctorate so far. I never suffered so many days of frustration and demotivation. In order to survive this seemingly never ending task I had to come up with some strategies to trick myself into actually enjoying it. Well, maybe not enjoying it but at least accepting it and getting it over with. So, what did I do?

Firstly, I frequently changed my work place. That way it somehow appeared to me as if I hadn't been transcribing forever. It almost seemed like a different kind of work every time I changed my routine. I switched back and forth between my office, my dorm room, and a friend's place where I could work.

Secondly, I set myself tough but achievable targets, e.g. 20 pages per day or 1 hour of interview per day. Every time I achieved my goal I rewarded myself, e.g. with half a day off, or going to the movies with friends. Believe it or not, this way I was actually motivated to outreach my set targets and achieve more. Of course not all the time but at least sometimes.

Thirdly, I talked to a lot of people that went through the same torture and sharing our experiences actually helped to lift off some of the weight off my shoulders. I always felt relieved and motivated afterwards and for a while was even more productive than before. Unfortunately this state or condition didn't last for too long. I guess you have to find your own way and figure what works for you. But I am almost sure that you won't be able to do it without one or two little psychological tricks.

Anne (final year student in language studies)

I'm bored: limited attention span

You will invest a lot in your doctoral degree, not only in terms of time and financial resources but also intellectually and emotionally. However, as we know, humans have a limited capacity to pay attention. Although this clearly depends on the person and the environment, studies suggest that the average attention span of adults is between 15 and 20 minutes (Johnstone and Percival, 1976). In addition, it appears that the attention span becomes shorter over time and can fall to three or four minutes after a period of intensive engagement.

So, if you feel your attention waning, take a short break. Get up and stretch – walk around the room, get a drink of water and allow your mind to refocus. Take decent lunch breaks and do not work ridiculous hours because you will end up being far less efficient and also far unhappier. Diet and exercise are also important. Research suggests that eating healthily and keeping fit is linked to improved attention and memory, two things crucial for a successful completion of a doctoral degree.

One thing you should definitely do every week is to take 'mental health days' – it is a day completely free from work, dedicated to doing something you love. Do not fall into the common trap of working continuously and taking few breaks. Remember that working more, does not mean working better or being more productive. Take breaks, spend time doing things you enjoy and visit friends, that is make sure that you satisfy your basic needs (see above). Relax and unwind; this will leave you refreshed for work and will stop your attention from constantly drifting.

At this stage we are pretty sure that you think of us as backseat drivers or smartypants. But trust us, we and hundreds of other students have been there. We worked endless hours, dozens of night shifts and so on ignoring signs of fatigue and exhaustion only to find ourselves mentally exhausted to such an extent that we were not able to work the next day or even for a couple of consecutive days. The price you pay is a disruption in your creative process and ultimately a delay to your research.

Of course we are aware that sometimes the pressure is very high, especially towards the end of your doctorate. The writing up stage is normally 'crunch time'. Although you can prevent situations like these, for example by writing up ideas, results and literature analyses regularly throughout your doctorate (see above), it is easy to get caught out. If you do end up in a high-pressure situation, then do not just try to take breaks, force yourself to. You need to give your mind some time to rest and recover or you will inevitably regret it at a later stage. Use the time sensibly and combine work with other activity, like exercise for instance, because this is all too often neglected and can cause severe problems (see Mark's story on pp. 33–34). That way you can do something that is good for you in more ways than one – a multi-purpose break.

Everything else is more fun: never-ending distractions

Distractions are everywhere. There is always something you would rather do than work. This is especially true if you have ended up with something that does not stimulate your interests and you find a real chore.

What can you do? Some techniques to help you circumvent distractions include:

- remove distractions;
- engage in behavioural self-management.

We suggest that you ensure you **remove yourself from all distractions**. When you are working on something that is 'dull by nature' and frustration is setting in, any distraction will do. Make sure you work in an environment that is free from diversions, interruption and unnecessary activity. For instance, do not work in the living room, while your partner or flatmate – who is not doing a doctoral degree – watches your favourite Chuck Norris film on DVD (this may be a silly example but there are still some die hard Chuck Norris fans out there; (see www.chucknorris.com/ for proof). Anyhow, the point is that when you are doing something you do not really want to do, it is easy to find other things to pursue. Make your life easier by removing the temptation. This will help you to focus on the task at hand and increase your ability to concentrate.

A formal method of avoiding distractions is called **behavioural self-management** and was introduced by Luthans and Davis in 1979. According to their theory, you need to identify and limit undesirable behaviour. They suggest learning which environmental prompts trigger the desired and undesired behaviour and managing them accordingly. Among the suggestions for improving behaviour are providing cognitive support for the new behaviours and self-reinforcement. There are various different forms cognitive support can take including:

- symbolic coding (imagery and verbal coding);
- mental practice (repeating the task often);
- self-talk (convincing yourself that you can do it).

Reinforce positive behaviours: make them more likely to occur again in the future by rewarding them. You can do this by simply rewarding yourself every time you achieve the task you set out to achieve (like Anne in her story on p. 48). For example, you can reward yourself with half an hour of TV once you have written 5,000 words or buy new shoes once you have finished data entry. People also use punishment and deprival to eliminate negative behaviours. However, you will be pleased to know that reward is actually a more powerful motivator than punishment – we thus recommend using reward over punishment every time. It does not have to be big things that break your bank; it could be a cup of tea, a five-minute stretch, a piece of fruit and so on. The choice is yours. The symbolic effect is what counts.

However, we would strongly recommend staying clear of negative stimulants like alcohol, cigarettes, chocolate and so on; these types of 'reward' can carry negative consequences with them and are thus best avoided. Further, as touched upon earlier, engaging in positive behaviours, like healthy eating and exercise, which are linked to positive consequences, are more beneficial in the short and long term. We realize not everyone is a master of self-control, so if you must indulge yourself, do so in moderation.

Of course, 'being in it alone' is not always easy. It can thus be very helpful to get feedback, recognition and rewards from others in your doctoral environment, for instance your supervisor or colleagues. However, not everyone recognizes the importance of this type of behaviour. Whatever the case may be, not everyone engages in reinforcement activity. Nonetheless, it is important for you not to think of an absence of external reinforcement as criticism. Instead, actively seek feedback from others when you think you have done something well to make sure that you are on the right track and also to get the praise you deserve.

I'm afraid to fail: big shadows

A sentence we often heard from fellow doctorates and even from ourselves is: 'I am not sure whether I can do it. I am not as intelligent as all those other people'. Especially at the beginning of your doctorate career, you will often have this feeling. It will be triggered by certain events, such as reading an excellent piece of research work, reading someone else's thesis and so on; it will hit you straight in the face and fill you with doubts: Am I clever enough, can I make an original contribution, will I finish in time? – to name only a few thoughts that might come into your head.

Let us just tell you this: successfully surviving your doctorate is not about brilliance but dedication and determination for what you are doing and how you are doing it, that is in a structured way with high-quality output. If you have to be brilliant at something, then you have got to be brilliant at mastering your fears, frustration, boredom and so on.

The good news is that by going to conferences, reading research work, discussing with colleagues and so on, you will eventually discover that supposed experts in your field of research are just like everyone else, not necessarily more or less intelligent than you (the issue of going to conferences is discussed later in Chapter 5, pp. 96–100). They go to where they are now through hard work and determination over the years; sometimes even a good portion of luck.

It will also help if you consider your doctorate a job and behave as though it is just like any other job in the world. You need to perform and to produce some kind of output over a certain period of time; not more, not less! If you manage to reach that stage of awareness, you are already on a solid path towards your goal. All that is left for you to do is to tie together all the parts of your research, capture it on paper and hand it in to the examiners for review. We can tell you, you will never forget the relief you feel when you type the last word of your thesis.

Another common concern among research students is making a sufficient and unique contribution. In other words, it is the ability to find a gap in existing knowledge that causes sleepless nights. Undoubtedly, the word 'unique' before the term 'contribution' is what really strikes fear into the hearts of all doctoral researchers. There is always anxiety that someone else is working on the same topic and will publish their results before you do, thereby eliminating your contribution and deeming your research pointless.

Remember: what the eye does not see, the heart does not grieve over. You can make yourself crazy by searching for every relevant journal in your field for days and weeks hoping not to find 'your' work. We suggest you do not. No person is alike and so no two research projects will be exactly alike. Even if someone does research in 'your' area or an area very close to 'yours', there will always be enough differentiation. Original value can come from the results, the methodological approach, the theoretical framework, the research question (or aims) or your data sample. You will be fine!

However, we do advise you to stay informed of the latest developments and findings in your field because, for one, this is part of your job as a doctorate and it also enables you to remain adaptive and flexible in your own research. A similar point is made by Phillips and Pugh (2000) when they state: 'The worst that can happen is not that someone else publishes on your topic, but that someone else publishes on your topic and you are not aware of it' (p. 84).

Keeping sight of the end goal

Anyone who has ever done a doctorate will agree that it is hard to do a doctorate. It is easy to become discouraged when confronted with difficulties and so it is important to keep all the positive things you gain from the journey in mind. We know from experience that it can be really challenging to keep the positive elements of a doctorate in mind when faced with adversity. Hence we have decided to write it down for you here, so you can have a reference section for those rainy days.

Despite all the niggles and issues, most doctoral students will tell you that doing a Ph.D. is really an amazing journey and that you gain a lot personally and professionally. Of course they will tend to do that only after they have finished because, let us face it, graduate students like to complain. Consequently you will hear a lot of negative things and even if you try to ignore this negativity, it is likely that cynicism will penetrate some parts of your life. Keeping in mind the greater goal will help you move past those issues and focus on the thing that you really came to graduate school for – completing and defending your thesis successfully thereby becoming a fully accepted member of the higher academic community.

One of the most obvious benefits of a research degree is that you make a significant academic contribution. You will have conducted some unique research, which will help advance knowledge and be meaningful in your field of study. By the end of your time as a graduate student, you will be an expert in your field, publish your ideas and results and people will start to come to you to ask for advice (see Chapter 5 for 'publishing', pp. 83–96). Take some time to bask in your own glory and reflect on what you are achieving and how your results can meaningfully be used – you are contributing to knowledge, society, organizations and possibly even individuals. This is not something everyone can say for themselves, so take pride in it.

On top of the more idealistic contribution, you will also be developing yourself professionally. Throughout your doctoral degree, you will acquire key skills that are important in your field and will make you more employable within your specific specialism. In addition to the very specific knowledge you gain, you will also take a number of generic and transferable skills away from your time as graduate student. These include analytic thinking, endurance, independence, initiative, presentation skills, writing skills, negotiation skills, teamworking skills, networking skills and leadership skills to name but a few. Much of this progress will be incremental and perhaps not always easy to observe. But just pick up a paper you wrote in your first year and compare that to something you wrote in your third year. The progress will be more impressive than you suspect.

The third and often most profound learning you undertake as a graduate student is learning about yourself. Recent graduates will tell you that doing a doctorate was a personal growth experience. Apart from stretching yourself academically, you will also gain personal insight, self-understanding and grow as a person. You will know a lot more about yourself than when you started. And that alone is often worth the journey.

Also do not forget all the contacts and friendships you develop during your doctorate time with peer students, research colleagues, university staff, flat-mates and many more. With some of your newly gained friends you will stay in touch forever and your paths might cross various times in life, for example working together on a joint project such as a book like ours. Consult Chapter 2 for some positive quotes graduant students and recent graduates gave about their time as a Ph.D. student.

4

Dealing with your supervisor

The nature of supervision • Coping with different supervisor styles • Changing supervisor(s) and/or university • Being supervised by a committee of supervisors

Your supervisor is undoubtedly one of the most important people in your life – well, it certainly feels that way while you are doing your doctorate. They help mould your work, sign off your assignments and ultimately have the power to pass or fail you or at least have some influence over the process and the decisions made. Your supervisor holds the power in the relationship, which puts you somewhat at their mercy and means that you need to be careful about how you manage the relationship.

Hence, getting the right supervisor and developing a fruitful relationship with them is one of the most important requirements for successful completion of your doctorate. Although doctoral students are generally not able to select their supervisors due to department and/or faculty allocation policies, there are some ways to increase the probability of finding your Dr Right. However, who your 'Dr Right' is depends entirely on your personal characteristics and preferences, which will also shape the interactions and the relationship you will have with your supervisor.

In this chapter we set out to explore issues related to supervision, that is the process of actually being overseen once a supervisor has been assigned. We begin by discussing the nature of supervision, where we address issues like reconciling discrepant aims, building a constructive relationship and establishing paths of communication between student and supervisor.

We then go on to outline different roles supervisors can occupy at different times in the supervisory process and explain how you can best cope with these. We also review some of the more difficult situations and decisions students may face during their doctoral process, including the emergence of 'irreconcilable differences' between you and your supervisor. We review some of the options and offer advice on the issue of changing supervisors and/or universities. In addition, we talk about some emerging models of supervision. For instance, we discuss the advantages and disadvantages of being supervised by a committee, a model increasingly gaining popularity in recent years in the UK.

The nature of supervision

What is supervision all about and who does it involve? In colloquial terms, supervision means one person guiding another person. Generally, the person offering the guidance is an expert in the area in which the person receiving the guidance would like to gain knowledge, skills and abilities. Since it is a process that involves considerable cognitive skills to facilitate learning as well as interpersonal skills to facilitate the relational aspects of the process, it is a complex progression. In any relationship of this sort, a host of factors come into play including:

- personality;
- preferences;
- habits;
- behaviours;
- goals;
- culture;
- expectations.

Each of these factors impacts on the way a person behaves and thus also shapes how any two people will interact. Given the importance of these issues, we thus outline some of the fundamental issues in supervision in the subsequent section to help raise awareness of these issues and make them more salient to you.

Differing aims and expectations of doctoral students and supervisors

There are many reasons why students set out to do a doctorate and many reasons why academics would take on a doctorate student to supervise. However, these reasons may be vastly different and when student and supervisor are matched, each of them will have certain expectations.

As in any relationship, it is important to understand each other's aims and objectives in order to develop and sustain a mutually beneficial student–supervisor relationship. The broad aims and expectations of students and supervisors are briefly outlined below. They are based on insights gained from interviews with both doctoral students and academics who supervise(d) doctorates. We pick up on these issues at various points throughout the chapter to discuss them in greater depth.

Some of the reasons why students become doctoral researchers and what they expect from their supervisors is summarized in the following Table 4.1:

Table 4.1 Aims and expectations of doctoral students

Aims	Expectations
• Pursuing an academic career (teaching and researching) and becoming an expert in the field • Learning the craft of academic research • Making a contribution to knowledge (ideally also in an area of personal interest) • Delaying employment and gaining time to decide on a future career • Using the doctorate as a career catalyst or stepping stone in industry • Gaining status and reputation by getting the highest academic title	• A supervisor who is an expert in the field (versed in the literature and the methods) • A supervisor who is not only interested in but also actively engages in the progress of the student • A supervisor who provides constructive (sometimes this means negative) feedback on a regular basis • A supervisor who gives the student room for trial and error and allows for development of own ideas • A supervisor who is approachable and available

• Building an international network (personally and professionally) • Fulfilling a personal dream • Need for a flexible schedule	• A supervisor who sees the doctorate as a collaborative partnership and treats the student like a colleague • A supervisor who cares about the student and is supportive (academically and emotionally) • A personable supervisor • A supervisor who checks the student's work and gives them confidence in their abilities

People often start their time as doctoral students with lots of ambition and idealism. Over the years they tend to become more realistic and eventually even enter the 'just wanting to finish' stage. This is mainly due to the intellectual, emotional and political complexity of doing a doctorate (see Chapter 3 for more information about motivational aspects of the process). You probably think this is silly but – trust us – almost every doctoral student goes through this metamorphosis.

There is one more point we would like to reiterate at this point. Although it feels good to be called 'Doctor' by others, no matter whether that is in an academic or an industrial context, the title alone is not worth the journey (see Chapter 2). Do not enrol in a doctoral programme just for the title; if you do, there is a high likelihood that you will regret it. Most people who have completed a doctorate degree will tell you that once you get to graduate school 'the journey is the goal'. It is about the process and what you learn along the way, not about the piece of paper you receive at the end. Certainly, there are still people who do it just for the certificate, but they tend to struggle. Make sure you are 'in it' for the right reasons.

The reasons supervisors take on doctoral students and what they expect from them often differ from the reasons why students enrol in a programme and what their expectations are. Supervisory views are outlined in the subsequent Table 4.2.

From reading through Tables 4.1 and 4.2 it should become clear that just like doctoral students, supervisors also have different motives for taking on doctoral students and supervising their theses. It is therefore really important that you talk to each other about your individual goals right at the beginning of the degree in order to work out what kind of relationship is best suited to achieve both your aims. This is important in order to set the basis for a mutually beneficial relationship.

Table 4.2 Aims and expectations of supervisors

Aims	Expectations
• Gaining insight and developing new ideas about a specific research topic together with the student • Gaining reputation and promotion by successfully supervising doctoral students (preferably with minimum effort) • Using students as a resource to promote own research • Educating and raising the future academic elite, that is independent, committed and knowledgeable scholars who are well known and respected in their field • Working with bright minds and developing relationships with potential future colleagues • Contributing to the advancement of the research group and university (intellectually and financially) • A chieving personal satisfaction through high-level intellectual discussions • Expanding personal and professional network • Satisfying the requirements of a research grant • Fulfilling teaching commitments	• Students who are independent, that is they are able to plan and deliver their research projects • Students who produce written work for the supervisor to help evaluate the student's progress • Students who are honest and hard-working • Students who are willing and able to establish an effective (working) relationship with the supervisor • Students who make an effort to deliver high-quality work and desire to excel in their chosen field • Students who strive to publish their work (or parts of it) together with the supervisor • Students who are open to criticism and use it to develop their ideas further • Students who (aim to) complete their thesis on time • Students who are excited, motivated, committed and take ownership • Students who come to meetings prepared • Students who accept direction but are not passive • Students who challenge their supervisors intellectually and come up with their own ideas

Developing a relationship with your supervisor

The relationship between you and your supervisor should not be left to chance. A good relationship is one that is developed actively, and this requires determination, commitment and patience (the related issue of networking is reviewed in Chapter 5). It takes time and effort to build strong relationships – take a minute to think about that because this is the key to successful engagement.

Also be aware that your relationship with your supervisor could take a number of forms ranging from a strong friendship to a formal working relationship. Neither of these is right or wrong. In fact, it does not matter what kind of relationship you foster, as long as it is a relationship that suits both you and your supervisor. Only if you and your supervisor do not get along at all, and the relationship ends up being hostile and counterproductive, do you have to seriously consider changing your supervisory team (see pp. 73–78).

Establishing a relationship with your supervisor often involves clarifying general terms and issues such as defining:

- how to address each other (first name or last name);
- the frequency of your meetings (e.g. weekly, monthly etc.);
- the location of meetings (e.g. supervisor's office);
- the meeting format (only prescheduled meetings or also drop-in sessions).

It is noteworthy that the Anglo-Saxon system – and this does not only apply to academia – is generally less formal than other systems, for example the German system. You should thus expect to deal with your supervisor on a first name basis. However, this gesture of informality does not mean abandoning professionalism. Do not be fooled into being any less professional, conscientious or respectful. Give your relationship some time to evolve. Over time it will naturally develop into either a friendship or a purely work-based relationship.

It is also useful to try to inject some routine into your relationship, for example regular meetings or written submissions like a literature review or a draft chapter. Having some structure will ensure you both get the most out of the meeting, since you will each have had time to prepare and thus can make productive and constructive use of your actual meeting time.

See whether your supervisor is happy for you to stop by without appointment from time to time to have an informal chat about your doctorate or request some additional advice. Some supervisors do not like making this option available to their students, due to their high workload and other commitments. If this is the case, always make sure you book appointments well in advance. This will require good planning and time management but will pay off in terms of your quality of relationship.

It is very important that you do not forget to show appreciation for the help and guidance you receive from your supervisor. This not only signals your awareness of the efforts they invest in you but this 'giving and taking' also allows you to enhance your relationship. The key to a healthy and positive relationship with your supervisor is finding the right balance between giving and taking based on both of your aims and expectations (see Tables 4.1 and 4.2). So, make sure you discuss these issues with your supervisor at the very beginning and come up with a verbal agreement or even an informal written contract.

Communication is the key

Verbal and written communication is our main means of interaction and hence also forms the basis of your relationship with your supervisor. That may seem pretty obvious but there are a few ground rules that will help you to positively shape the interaction with your supervisor.

- *Take responsibility*: It is your duty to keep your supervisor informed about your progress and to get feedback about the ideas you share with them. You need to accept responsibility for this by taking an active role in driving the process forward. In order to facilitate effective meetings with your supervisor, we recommend that you engage in preparation, for example by developing a tentative agenda or making a note of topics you want to discuss. This will ensure that you get all the information you need to continue progressing by asking all the right questions. Set yourself clear targets that are ambitious but also realistic, and monitor your progress against them.
- *Listen and be open-minded*: When you are speaking to someone else, listen carefully to what they have to say. It is important for you to understand your conversational partner's perspective and the argument they are trying to make. This will help avoid misunderstanding and ensure you are both discussing the same issue. This is especially important in supervisory meetings, which will often be highly intellectual and theoretical. Treat each meeting as a learning opportunity – an opportunity to learn more about the field and have a seasoned academic reflect on your work.
- *Do not make it personal*: Should your discussions ever get difficult, intense or controversial (and this is possible when debating various theoretical viewpoints), stay focused on the academic content. Even if you think your supervisor is wrong or unfair, either at an intellectual or interpersonal level, do not make it personal by slipping into an inappropriate way of engaging. Things said in the heat of the moment will often be regretted later and you would be better served to address the conflict at a different time. However, that is not to say that you should never argue with your supervisor; just ensure you remain focused on the academic and technical discussion.
- *Do not be shy*: It is also important that you are open and honest in your interactions with your supervisor and you do not leave too many things unsaid. If there is anything that prevents you from performing and progressing in your work, then you should talk to your supervisor about it. Whether you are facing professional or personal difficulties, honesty is always the best policy. Similarly, if you do not understand something your supervisor has said, then ask them to repeat and/or clarify it. Doctoral supervisors recognize that the doctorate is a learning process and want to help. Often the only way they know how to best support you is if you tell them. Indeed, most doctoral supervisors will expect their students to ask questions, since this is one way to demonstrate that you are engaging with the material. So do not be ashamed to ask. This is true for all forms of support, including intellectual, social and financial support (e.g. conference funding).
- *Keep a record*: It is good practice to keep a log or write up the notes from your meetings, so both of you have a record of what has been agreed and what needs to be achieved until the next meeting. This process of defining goals and allocating responsibilities is very important because it serves as a reminder for both of you and also ensures you have evidence of your developmental process.

These five strategies will help you to ensure good communication in practice, which is the foundation of a healthy relationship.

Coping with different supervisor styles

Everyone is different and that is also true when it comes to doctoral supervision. Every person has a different way of dealing with supervision; consequently, a multitude of supervisory styles exist. In this section we work through these styles and give examples of what you may encounter when you start your doctorate. Of course, just because your supervisor is supportive or makes mistakes at one stage of the process does not mean it will stay like this forever. We operate on the premise that it is possible for a supervisor to occupy different roles at different times in the process and we think this is a sensible view for doctoral students to adopt. In order to get the most out of your supervisor, it is imperative that there is a degree of fit. Where discrepancies exist, you have three basic options:

1 You try to influence your supervisor's behaviour.
2 You adapt to the situation by changing your own behaviour.
3 You try to find a new supervisor.

In this section we focus on options (1) and (2), although it should be noted that it is difficult to change other people's habits and behaviours. Thus, more often than not, you will need to adjust. We will reflect on different supervisor roles and provide you with insights about the competences, skills and attributes you need in order to best deal with them. This will help you make decisions about how to identify a suitable supervisor and how to engage with your supervisors effectively, but also highlight your role in making the relationship work by responding favourably to your supervisor's behaviour.

You should be aware that the aims and expectations of supervisors (mentioned above) are reflected in their supervision behaviour and hence the role or roles they adopt. Based on our own knowledge and experiences as well as insights we gained through a plethora of interviews with peers, we provide a basic overview of supervisory styles in Table 4.3. The description of each behavioural pattern should be used as an indication only rather than being seen as a taken-for-granted norm. Various shades of each supervisory style exist, and you will find plenty of overlap between them in real life. They have been made extreme and polarized in order to make them more tangible for you.

Academic research reveals similar results. In a recent study on doctoral supervision and the role of supervisors Wright et al. (2007) identify five generic role models – as perceived by supervisors – based on interviews with

Table 4.3 Description of supervisor roles

Supervisor role	Description of behaviour
The perfect supervisor	Everything you ever wanted in a supervisor; supportive in every imaginable way; no conflict or issues, the perfect fit
The supportive supervisor	Emotionally, intellectually and physically (resource) supportive; equal relationship between student and supervisor; helps student grow, and develop confidence and independence
The idealistic supervisor	Wants to train student in craft of research; wants to educate future academic elite. Is passionate about supervision and considers supervision a mission
The ignorant supervisor	Lacks expert knowledge in various aspects of the doctorate (e.g. methodology, literature etc.); generally nice and supportive. Often no interest in developing knowledge and capacity to better support the student
The inexperienced supervisor	Naïve and perhaps optimistic about how system works; little supervision experience; not sure how to direct the student, generally giving little input into the process; knowledgeable about research
The awkward supervisor	Lacks interpersonal skills; interactions are socially awkward; discussions are difficult; not unfriendly or uncaring but uses an unusual communication style
The demanding supervisor	Has high expectations of student; pushes hard (sometimes too hard); does not understand limits; wants to achieve excellency; often offers small specific topics for the thesis that contribute to a bigger project
The selfish supervisor	Uses student to fulfil own personal and professional goals; sees student as a kind of free labour; only gives support if beneficial to them; exploits student
The absent supervisor	Too busy or too far away to support you; lack of personal contact; hardly responds to emails, calls and so on
The arrogant supervisor	Think they are the best; do not accept different ideas; do not listen; may try to drive you out if you disagree; often gets too involved (total control); impedes the development of independence and growth
The friendly supervisor	Wants to build a social relationship with the student; wants to move away from formal arrangements and spend time together outside of work. Supervision is not always effective

academics. The roles identified include: quality assurer, supportive guide, researcher trainer, mentor and knowledge enthusiast. Further, Wright and colleagues found that often the role supervisors adopt and their conception of supervision is influenced by their own experience as doctoral researchers. So, do not blame everything on your supervisor *per se* but make an effort and try to cope with the behaviour you are confronted with. In the following we discuss how you as a student can deal with the different roles outlined in Table 4.3 by talking you through each in turn.

Note: Although many of the examples and the advice we offer on the following few pages will help you to better understand your supervisor, adapt to their behaviour, and ultimately improve your relationship, the guidance we offer is not to be seen as panacea. It is important that you use your own experiences and develop your own strategies and tactics to cope with your supervisor.

Dealing with the perfect supervisor

Congratulations – you have just won the supervisory lottery! The chance of this is about one in a million, so consider yourself lucky – you have got the kind of supervisor every doctorate student dreams of. Make sure you do not mess things up by giving your supervisor reasons to be unhappy with you, for example due to a lack of performance, initiative or commitment. Be enthused about what you do and show it to your supervisor. Engage in highly intellectual discussion, surprise your supervisor with new ideas, and demonstrate that you are capable of carrying out your research and finishing your doctorate on time. However, this does not mean that you have to give up your own ideals and agree with everything your supervisor says, wants or thinks. Discuss things constructively in an open dialogue and you will find that everything will work out just fine.

Dealing with the supportive supervisor

Unfortunately, in the real world, the perfect and flawless supervisor described above is rare indeed. From our experience, perfection is rare and only very few students are lucky enough to find everything they are looking for in a supervisor in a single person (another one of the benefits of being supervised in a committee; see p. 78 for more information). Indeed, having most of your criteria satisfied is about 'as-good-as-it-gets' in terms of a good student–supervisor relationship.

Although these supervisors might not be the ultimate experts in all matters of your research unlike the perfect supervisor (e.g. versed in the respective literature and research methods), they tend to be very supportive not only intellectually but also emotionally and physically. This means that you can turn to such a supervisor for support in almost all circumstances.

Another very important feature of a supportive supervisor is viewing the doctorate as a collaborative partnership in which the student is treated like a colleague. For you this means that you not only have the chance to interact with your supervisor on an equal level; you also have to live up to that expectation. So, make sure you act as a reliable and supportive colleague for your supervisor in the same way they are reliable and supportive to you.

Supportive supervisors are in general very accessible for their students to discuss important issues. Make sure you maintain a good balance of self-study and collegial work to avoid becoming too much of a resource drain on your supervisor. This will be counterproductive in several ways. First of all, if you always call on your supervisor, they may eventually not have the time to support you in more important situations. Secondly, you could strain your relationship and risk losing future postdoctoral collaboration opportunities.

Dealing with the idealistic supervisor

The idealist is enthusiastic, almost to the point of being an academic 'missionary'. In terms of behaviour, there is much overlap between this type of role and the supportive supervisory role. The major difference between these two styles is the extreme passion of the idealistic supervisor about research, teaching and learning. These individuals tend to consider doctoral supervision, the training of the future academic elite, as one of the most important duties of an academic, and as such gain much personal gratification from the process. Hence, you may receive an extraordinary amount of supervision and support throughout your degree.

The flipside of this is, of course, high expectations directed at the student. Enthusiastic supervisors will provide you with enough room for trial and error to learn from your own mistakes, to develop your own ideas, and most importantly learn to evaluate your own work. Enthusiastic supervisors will follow your progress with interest and actively engage in the process of making you an independent scholar.

One important way of doing this is by providing constructive feedback on a regular basis. This also means providing negative feedback from time to time – do not be upset about this; instead use it as a chance to develop your skills and abilities further. Your supervisor is on your side and would not confront you with criticism if they did not think it was necessary for your learning and development. So, listen and learn, and eventually you will succeed at your doctorate and also become an established academic, just like your supervisor.

Dealing with the inexperienced supervisor

Inexperience does not equate to ignorance or incompetence. Indeed, inexperienced supervisors may know a lot about the technical issues of doing research. However, they have little or no experience in actually supervising doctoral students. This often results in a quite naïve and overly optimistic view about how the supervisory and doctoral processes work. Thus, inexperienced supervisors – in most cases but not always junior members of staff such as lecturers – sometimes underestimate the workload that comes with supervision and as a result may feel overwhelmed with their duties. Culminated, this may create the impression with you that your supervisor is not helpful or supportive which, however, is not the case.

Having an inexperienced supervisor does not mean that you cannot get good supervision; it just means that you need to be more independent and find out about the formal issues of a doctorate (i.e. administrative paper work, scholarships etc.) for yourself. Once you have obtained the information, discuss it with your supervisor and involve them in the process, thereby simultaneously enabling them to gain experience about these issues.

Sometimes inexperienced supervisors may also have difficulty putting themselves in their students' shoes. For instance, it may also mean that they overestimate how much you are capable of in a certain amount of time, consequently setting you unrealistic targets for achievement. They may also be very self-focused, relating supervisor issues back to their own experiences of being a doctorate student (also see Wright et al., 2007), which may differ significantly from your own experience. The aim in this relationship is really to help educate your supervisor about the doctoral process while drawing on their experience of the research process.

Dealing with the ignorant supervisor

In contrast to the inexperienced supervisors, the ignorant supervisor actually does demonstrate a lack of competence in certain areas. For instance, despite much research or supervisory experience, they may lack subject knowledge in various aspects of your research (literature, methodology etc.), thereby being unable to provide sufficient guidance to you in these areas of study. Although at times frustrating, this is not necessarily a major problem, as it is expected that you will eventually surpass your supervisor in certain areas of subject knowledge, for example specific bodies of literature or certain data collection and analysis methods and techniques.

The ignorant supervisor is most obstructive during the first year of the doctoral programme, where students are most dependent on and benefit most from guidance. In order to ensure that you have a capable academic to engage with, you need to keep your supervisor informed about recent developments in the field (e.g. new papers) as you move along in your doctorate. This can be difficult and requires a lot of tact – you do not want to become arrogant yourself or demonstrate a belief that your supervisor is incompetent in certain areas.

After all, the basis of your relationship should be communication and you cannot expect your supervisor to be an omniscient superhuman, who excels in all areas – everyone has their weaknesses and flaws. The best way to approach this situation is to gain your supervisor's respect by demonstrating increasing confidence and strength in argumentation. After all, you are their guide to new developments and recent knowledge in the area/discipline. Share your insights with your supervisor and do not cut them off because you think they are not contributing sufficiently.

Remember, if you have reached a stage where you can recognize some weakness, it does not only highlight your own skills; it also demonstrates your supervisor's ability to lead you there. Ignorance only gets problematic if your supervisor does not show any interest in developing their knowledge and capacity further to better support you. The only thing you can do in this situation is either to rely on other academics or make it through on your own, as the subsequent story by Christie illustrates.

Bite the bullet – you can't wait for your supervisor forever!

When I first met my supervisor I thought 'cool, not one of these established Professors who think they know it all'. Unfortunately, despite being very ambitious, it turned out that my supervisor didn't know much at all in terms of my research. Her background was in quantitative techniques and I wanted to use qualitative methods in my work, which meant that I was faced with a significant skill gap. Of course I only discovered that towards the end of my first year when I started to plan my data collection and analysis. What made things worse was that she didn't even show any aspiration at all to develop her knowledge in that particular area.

So, what did I do? Well, not sit around and wait. I educated myself in the particular research technique, since no one else had experience or expertise in this area. I even started thinking about changing my research question because I knew I would never receive any genuine guidance but decided to persist in favour of my true interest. So, I spent endless hours looking for useful literature and then, to add insult to injury, additional time explaining the methodology to my supervisor.

I can't tell you how frustrating, time-consuming and exhausting that was. I mean, isn't the supervisor supposed to be the one who should educate the student and not vice versa? When I confronted her with this, she simply responded that there was no need for her to know all the details about my research. Ouch.

If I had to do it again (and I'm really glad I don't), I would seek out an experienced supervisor, someone who is competent in the methodology I was using. Of course having an experienced supervisor doesn't mean that you're going to have an easy ride – But it does mean that you will be given a good start by reading the relevant core literature first. If you are out on a limb and stuck with an ignorant supervisor, I suggest you try to battle through on your own (and this takes lots of effort and persistence) or collate a group of advisors who you can consult on a variety of issues. Whatever happens, you'll need to show some initiative.

Christie (graduate in public management)

Dealing with the absent supervisor

Just like any other relationship, your supervisory relationship is based on personal interaction. We would even go as far as saying regular personal contact between supervisor and student is crucial. Of course, there are many issues that can be solved with modern information and communication technology (ICT). This includes using email to facilitate the iterative process of writing joint papers by sending an electronic copy of the work back and forth. Other issues might also be solvable via video conference, teleconference or voice over IP (VoIP) meetings, thereby reducing the number of physical meetings and travel requirements, something especially important in long-distance supervisory relationships.

Nonetheless, some issues in doctorate supervision require (or at the very least are facilitated through) personal interaction. This includes discussing theoretical ideas, sounding out your supervisor or requesting emotional support – to name but a few. Because of this, an inaccessible supervisor may cause some difficulties.

Supervisors may be away from the university for a number of reasons, including very legitimate reasons such as:

- maternity leave;
- illness;
- sabbatical;
- research exchange;
- transfer.

In many cases this absence is managed and mitigated through the aforementioned ICT methods. However, there are also cases where supervisory absence and inaccessibility becomes a major concern, specifically because they are too busy or too far away to interact with you personally. There are also cases where this escalates, entering a phase marked by unresponsiveness to your emails and phone calls, and makes you feel like your supervisor is the world hide and seek champion.

What to do? Since most absences are planned or at least foreseeable, we suggest managing the issue before it comes a concern. Set rules for engagement and find ways to interact meaningful, given the limitations of the situation. Useful mechanisms include:

- having a second on-site supervisor (associate supervisor);
- making use of regular meetings;
- setting deadlines and timeplans.

Just because your supervisor is not there physically does not mean you have to accept them being absent in all senses of the word, that is completely unresponsive – your supervisor plays too central a role in your development and your doctoral progress.

Remember, busy and absent supervisors are not 'bad' supervisors. Indeed, they are often very competent supervisors. However, this competence is part of their downfall, as they are the ones with the toughest timetables due to the duties that come with excellence, for example acting as reviewers, guest speakers, visiting scholars and so on. However, just because your supervisor has many diverse and important tasks to complete does not mean that you do not deserve their attention. Politely remind them of that fact from time to time.

Dealing with the awkward supervisor

Academia plays host to some of the brightest people. However, brilliance does not necessitate social competence. And so it may be that you are paired up with a supervisor who lacks interpersonal skills. Yes, this is the eccentric and slightly weird academic – the stereotypical image of a geek. This means that interactions will be socially awkward, at times uncomfortable or painful. It also means that you may find it difficult to follow conversations or understand their line of argumentation (they forget to contextualize their thoughts, assuming you can follow, thus leaving you stranded intellectually). However, that does not necessarily make them less likable or insensitive (although it may). Awkward supervisors are generally competent in their field and supervision, and genuinely care about the progress of their students; the only problem is the social interaction and even that can become manageable over time. So what can you do?

- *Do not try to change who your supervisor is*: People skills are not something that someone can pick up overnight, and trying to reprogramme someone is likely to cause offence at some level. It is actually much easier to adapt your own cognitive processes and behavioural patterns to the situation. Remember who you are dealing with and call to mind the intention rather than the action when working with someone of limited social competence. Contextualize the actions and behaviours of your supervisor – recontextualize the limited tact and inability to read emotions.
- *Do not take 'harsh words' to heart too often*: Remember that what they are trying to do is drive you forward and, although it may sometimes feel hurtful, their heart is in the right place. They are doing it to help you. Develop a thick hide around this person and be more forgiving and generous in understanding than you would normally be, otherwise your relationship will falter early on. Being awkward, difficult, insulting or inappropriate will only escalate the situation – just because they cannot assess your feelings or do not know how to interact with you does not mean that you cannot hurt them.

In summary, engage with your supervisor in light of their limitations but seek social support elsewhere – a little bit of social awkwardness never killed anyone – it could be worse, much much worse!

Dealing with the demanding supervisor

Working with someone who excels in a given area often comes at a price and may translate into high (possibly unrealistic) expectations and demands. It could be that your supervisor tries to push you hard, sometimes too hard because they do not understand what your limits are. This arises out of a drive for excellence and a need for perfection. More often than not this will mean that you will be given a small specific topic that contributes to a larger research agenda the supervisor has. This in itself is not unusual; for many reasons it makes sense to research a similar (or the same) area as your supervisor.

However, this may also go too far when you are expected to not only satisfy your supervisor's research interests but also adhere to the same quality standards they are capable of, which is not necessarily easy for a doctoral student, who has considerably less experience, training and expertise in the area. This may consequently lead to a conflict between student and supervisor, where the student is constantly trying to achieve performance that is unrealistic given their knowledge, skills and abilities. This may lead to student burnout, in the case where students try too hard to meet these expectations and deliver high-quality outputs, or actually in supervisory tension, where the supervisor cannot understand why you are unable to deliver those outputs that are expected (possibly even agreed).

Of course, having a demanding supervisor also has benefits. Expect to receive excellent training and guidance throughout the process, expect to learn a lot, expect to challenge yourself and grow, and expect to operate in a whole new league of research (in terms of research quality and network). Working hard will open up a lot of opportunities for you.

But what can you do when the demands exceed your capability? The best thing, as with all issues, is to take the bull by its horns and address the issue before it becomes problematic. Outline a work schedule and adhere to it. If demands increase to an unrealistic level (some fluctuation is to be expected and even necessary in the natural evolution of a research proposal) and not in line with this plan, then rebuff your supervisor's requests for additional work. Explain to them why you reasonably cannot oblige with their demands, justifying your decision throughout, and referring to the agreed plan of work.

Rationality works with most people, so do not be afraid to use it as a tool in this circumstance. Avoiding the problem and not bringing it into discussion will not be beneficial – it entrenches behavioural patterns, making excessive demands more acceptable, and will only delay the inevitable. Because when the issue is finally raised, conflict is likely, as neither you nor your supervisor will be able to find an amiable solution quickly (due to work backlog) – you may even find yourself in a difficult position, for example where you cannot deliver a client report on time because you did not flag to your supervisor that you did not have the capacity (or capability) to complete it.

Dealing with the selfish supervisor

Selfishness is more difficult to deal with but unfortunately you will encounter it in any walk of life, which includes your doctoral period. A supervisor with selfish traits will try to use you as a tool to fulfil their own personal and professional goals. Doctoral students are seen as a type of free labour, being engaged and involved in a variety of projects, not all of which are relevant. Often the supervisors will only offer you support in areas where it is beneficial to them and advances you in a way that ultimately pays off for them. There is no problem with this if your goals are well aligned but in some circumstances they may even exploit the student for personal gain and this may have no advantage for the student or even detrimental to them (see Daniel's story below).

The best way to deal with a selfish supervisor is to ensure that your personal and professional objectives match those of your supervisor – this way advancing their goals will ultimately also advance yours. This is another reason why it is so important to know a lot about the person you will be working with, both professionally and personally. If, however, despite these efforts, you arrive at a situation where they are unreasonably taking advantage of you, there are only a few things you can do to restore the situation. First and foremost, it is important that you are assertive.

Be firm and explain your goals and objectives, if possible in ways that bring your objectives closer together, but do not let them push you over. Even when disagreements arise, you need to remain professional and stay calm, otherwise your difference of opinion may escalate into conflict and future collaboration will be difficult. We have seen cases where relationships were damaged beyond repair because of misunderstandings or unintentional selfishness.

Remember, conflict never resolves anything. Nonetheless, you also have to be fair. You need to understand that it is unreasonable to expect your supervisor to advance you in areas that do not benefit your progress as a doctoral student and/or are unrelated to their expertise. If you were unable to define the terms of your relationship and collaboration at the start of your relationship, we suggest trying to find a middle ground. Reassess and ask yourself: How can you achieve your goals together? Where are clear areas of synergy? Where do your goals overlap? Focus on those goals with your supervisor and they will be inspired to drive you forward.

Ménage à trois with a greedy supervisor

At the beginning of my Ph.D. everything was fine. My project got fully funded by a company that was interested in the practical outcomes of the research, which would eventually result in some patents for them. For me this meant that I was financially sorted for the duration of my Ph.D. I also knew my supervisor from my undergrad already and hadn't had any problems with him.

So, the triangular relationship company–supervisor–me seemed ideal to me. It looks good on a resumé, right?

So it seemed until I found out that my supervisor was playing a bit of a double game by distorting the information the company received. I didn't find out about that until I started to get in touch with our company contact myself. And let me tell you, both of us were surprised and certainly not happy about what we discovered. Our whole ménage à trois reached the tip of the iceberg when we found out that my supervisor applied for a patent based on my research results (that were funded by the company), thereby not only betraying me but also the sponsoring company. I never saw it coming and maybe that is why I was hurt really badly – Stabbed in the back by my own supervisor!

When the company manager found out he forced the university to remove my supervisor from the project; a condition which would avoid them pulling the funding altogether, which would have resulted in a loss of image for the department and university. The whole thing ended with me changing supervisor at the very end of my Ph.D.

I certainly didn't want to move down that path but I certainly also didn't want the name of a greedy supervisor on my thesis. I am glad I had the courage to distance myself from my former supervisor, although it was very difficult as I was almost finished with my project and could have used his support in the final stages of my work.

Daniel (graduate in environmental studies)

Dealing with the arrogant supervisor

The arrogant supervisor is not dissimilar from the selfish supervisor – they try to drive you forward in the way that suits them best. However, there is one important difference. Arrogant supervisors generally are not trying to advance their own goals. They are actually trying to advance yours; they just have very specific thoughts about what your goals are and how progress in those areas should be achieved. This type of supervisor tends to think that they are the best. They are set in their ways and will not accept different and new ideas, or innovative ways of doing things. This means that they may not listen to you and even try to suppress your suggestions. This is difficult, especially if you are an independent person and a creative type of student, who has their own ideas about how they want to do their Ph.D. and achieve the goals they set out to achieve.

An arrogant supervisor also has a tendency to get overly involved in the details of the doctorate, trying to control even the minutiae of the process. This need for total control means that they tend to dominate and may take actions that impede the development of independence and autonomy of their students. They do not leave enough room for trial and error because of their preconceived notions of doing things. They also do not tend to be interested in developing a personal relationship with the student, focusing only on the professional sphere. In extreme cases, this type of supervisor may even try to suppress or drive the student out if they persistently disagree.

How do you deal with arrogance?

- First of all, stop trying to tell them that they are wrong. That will get you nowhere fast. Concede that the way they do things may well serve a purpose but also go to lengths to explain that your way of doing things may also yield success. Use reasonable and sound arguments to introduce them to new ways of doing things. Just because they are set in their ways, does not mean that they cannot learn.
- A second useful mechanism is to get the support of another senior academic or member of your department. This legitimizes what you say and offers some strength through numbers. You may be wrong, but not everyone else can be too.
- Finally, it may also be helpful to try to find a middle ground, a way of doing things that makes both of you happy. Explain your need for intellectual independence and what you need to develop academically. Find ways of working towards these goals in a mutually satisfactory way; for instance, agreeing on milestones that you commit to meeting in exchange for additional freedom in the ways that you achieve them.

However, regardless of which approach you take (and a combination of techniques may be most suited, depending on you, your supervisor and your relationship), remember to stay professional and respectful. Your supervisor is where they are for a reason; respect their expertise and seniority, even if you do not always agree with them on an intellectual or academic level.

Dealing with the friendly supervisor

As opposed to arrogant and oppressive supervisors, friendly and open supervisors try to build a social relationship with their students, probably going as far as adopting a kind of nurturing parental role. They often move the relationship away from mere formal interaction and arrangements, and sometimes even spend time with their students outside of the work environment. From our point of view there is nothing wrong with this *per se*, for example there is no issue with you and your supervisor playing in the same basketball league or going for a pint after work from time to time. However, there are two possible problem areas: relationship boundaries and work focus.

Though rare, your relationship may move to a level with which you are not comfortable as a student – this is where it has the potential to get complicated. We thus recommend that you clearly set out the boundaries of your relationship, and this can be done informally rather than formally (e.g. by turning down invitations that you think would constitute inappropriate interaction and make you uncomfortable in your professional relationship with your supervisor). What makes people uncomfortable really differs from person to person, so we cannot give specific guidelines on where to draw the line. However, we recommend you adhere to your beliefs and, especially where these have a cultural or religious basis, explain them to your supervisor to avoid causing offence.

Friendly supervisors are essentially nice people and it is normally not their intention to come 'too close for comfort' or to cause any unintentional anxiety; it is simply in their nature to be sociable – they want to be liked. So if you do get into a situation where you feel uncomfortable, you have to let your supervisor know about it. This is very important. Do not feel obliged to go along with situations or behaviour that you cannot tolerate. It is always easier to define personal space and set relationship boundaries early on, otherwise your supervisor may not be aware of how you feel and your response to their behaviour may cause significant embarrassment on both parts.

Also note that informal supervisory relationships are not necessarily effective supervisory relationships. At times the social nature of the relationship may actually hamper your progress and quality of work. For instance, friendly informal meetings may not provide enough focus or drive for all students. In terms of your long-term development, you will actually need your supervisor to be critical and firm at times, even if that firmness is not always appreciated immediately. There is such a thing as 'being too nice' and by not critiquing your work as thoroughly as your examiners will do, your supervisor is not doing you any favours.

Remember, most people are reasonable and if your supervisor is as open and friendly as they seem, then they will understand and respect your need for distance. If you do this, there will generally be no need to take further action – just make the point that you feel uncomfortable and would prefer a more formal relationship. If things escalate and you really feel that you cannot cope with your supervisor, then consider involving a third-party arbitrator (e.g. another member of your department, a pastoral tutor, or the international student adviser). If all else fails, you may need to consider changing supervisor(s). The various options and what the process involves are discussed in the next section of this chapter.

Changing supervisor(s) and/or university

In some instances the afore-mentioned discrepancies between student and supervisor cannot be overcome and, for a variety of reasons, you feel that continuing the relationship with your supervisor is impossible. If this is the case, you need to consider changing your supervisor. In this section we provide you with some guidance when it comes to changing supervisor(s).

This is a very sensitive and political issue at every university (see also Chapter 7), so you should always proceed with caution. Thus, even if you are very unhappy with your current situation, find it emotionally difficult to cope with and want to get out of it as quickly as possible, it is important to approach the topic with a degree of rationality. Getting objective third-party advice often helps to contextualize these types of situation and find satisfactory solutions, even for the most difficult cases.

However, before making the definitive decision to change your supervisor(s), you should try various ways of resolving the situation and make use of existing escalation mechanisms, for example by consulting the student advice services, speaking to a (trustworthy) senior faculty member, the Head of Department or the Ph.D. Director. These people could serve as mediators in the relationship between you and your supervisor by helping to reduce communication barriers (remember: communication is the key!). We know students who only interacted with their supervisors through mediating mechanisms, for example only having meetings when an objective third party was present to ensure that discussions did not escalate and become personal. Although the relationship was bordering on contentious, as the necessity of these drastic means demonstrates, the students we talked to refrained from changing their supervisors, as the overall working relationship was productive on a professional level.

So, if you want to leave your supervisor, you really have to do a serious bit of soul searching to find out the real reasons why you want to leave your supervisor(s) and which part of the relationship you may wish to salvage. Is it because you do not like them personally? Are they not providing sufficient or satisfactory support? It is imperative that you ask yourself these kinds of question because this will be exactly the kind of questions you will be asked by the Head of your Department, the Director of the Doctorate Programme or the committee you could potentially face when you announce your desire to change supervisor(s).

Hence, preparation is crucial (it is advisable to keep records of the relationship with your supervisor). It will also help if you are able to clearly outline what you are trying to achieve with your doctorate and what you expect from a supervisor, that is how they can facilitate you in reaching these goals (see Table 4.1). Make sure that what you expect is realistic and in line with the support that doctoral supervisors should provide – unrealistic expectations cannot be satisfied for a variety of reasons and will end up having the case decided in a way that is not necessarily in your favour. For instance, you may be asked to readjust your expectations and, if this is not possible, even to move to another institution.

In addition, you need to be aware that changing your supervisor(s) is a lengthy process, which cannot be accomplished overnight (see Mark's story on p. 76). Agreeing to supervise a doctoral student is a major commitment and not every potential supervisor is willing to take on that responsibility, especially if you have a poor track record in this area. From a supervisory point of view, this may increase the risk of something going wrong in their relationship with you, and this is something anyone would prefer to avoid. As such, changing supervisors should really be considered a last resort – a mean only to be utilized if all else fails. This is especially true in the later stages of your research, as you will already have developed your work in a certain direction and your new supervisor will either have to fit this direction or you will need to consider reworking your project – again, something best avoided at that stage of the process.

Furthermore, it could be that you cannot find a suitable replacement, as research groups and departments tend to be built up of academics with heterogeneous research interests covering a range of issues. This might mean that you not only have to change supervisor(s) but in fact may also need to leave the university in order to facilitate this process. This could have a host of connotations, including implications for funding arrangements. As a rule of thumb, the later in the process you want to change supervisors, the more difficult it is to find a suitable replacement and the more likely it is that it will disrupt your progress.

The sensitivity surrounding the issue and the associated consequences mean that it is uncommon though not impossible for students to change supervisors. Especially in cases where this split is acrimonious, conflict is likely to arise. Since academics are partially rated on their doctoral success rates, your supervisor's reputation may suffer by losing you as a doctorate student. As such, you should expect some difficult times ahead if you do decide to change supervisors, especially if you remain within your department. It is a bit like a divorce – no one will know the whole story and there will be lots of gossip.

Having a mediator can be very useful and help calm troubled water. They can assist you in finding a new supervisor and officially support your action in front of your group/department in order to avoid unnecessary discomfort. It is also easier for your supervisor to accept your decision if a senior member of staff, who has a certain role within the group, takes charge of the situation and helps to ensure it is handled appropriately. Making a big deal out of the issue generally does not help anyone, least of all you. Even if you feel like it is all their fault, take the high road and be the bigger person.

There might also be situations where it is *necessary* rather than *desired* to change supervisor, for example your supervisor moves to a different institution (*Note*: you may also have the option to move with them – something to consider carefully), your supervisor passes away (let us hope not), your supervisor may go on maternity leave for a significant period of time, or for a variety of other reasons that cannot guarantee sufficient supervisory support. These cases are slightly different and although still constitute a significant change, which by its very nature is always associated with some degree of difficulty, may actually be easier because there are fewer sensitivities.

To stay or not to stay, that was the question

My Ph.D. was off to a great start. My supervisor offered me a Ph.D. post at the university he was moving to and asked me to join him there to help build up a new physics lab. Unfortunately, we never really hit it off on a personal level and so when plans for a physics lab failed and our personal relationship deteriorated, I ended up almost quitting my Ph.D.

The decision was then to either (A) stay at my part-time job, which I'd started after about one week into my Ph.D., thereby quitting my Ph.D. or (B) go into a full-time studentship and leave my job. The latter option, however, was only feasible if I moved to another supervisor (and, for that matter, another university). Difficult decision. I set myself a deadline to either find another supervisor I could work with or to leave academia for good and focus on my job in industry. I gave myself one week to find a new supervisor. (Which, in retrospect, was a very short period of time.) The worst thing during that week was the uncertainty I was facing.

After endless hours of internet search and phone calls I finally found a potential new supervisor. In order to make sure that I got on with him on a personal level and that the university had a good community – something I realised was very important to me – I set up a personal meeting with my potential future supervisor to talk about these issues. Both of us talked very openly and it became clear to me very quickly that this relationship would work for me. So, once I'd satisfied the basic conditions for continuing my Ph.D., I handed in my notice at work and became a full-time Ph.D. student.

Based on my experience I can only emphasise to everyone contemplating a Ph.D. how important it is to make sure you get along with the person or persons supervising you because you will have to rely on this person throughout the process.

Mark (final year student in physics)

No matter whether you want or need to change supervisor(s), there are a number of aspects you need to consider as you move along this sensitive process. Some of the core issues are outlined below:

- If you are unhappy with your supervisory situation, talk openly to your supervisor about it first. Do not be impolite but be unambiguous: outline what you expect from your supervisor and what support you need. Also offer some suggestions on how both of you can improve your relationship and communication.
- Talk to an objective third party in confidence and get advice about the situation. This could be any number of people; for example, someone in the student advice centre, a welfare tutor, your Head of Department, the Director of Postgraduate or Doctorate Programme, a senior faculty member

with some responsibility for doctoral supervision or a representative from an external agency. Whatever the responsibility of this person, you should trust them and feel comfortable talking about your supervision-related problems as it is a sensitive issue. If you do not feel comfortable talking to your supervisor about your problems one-on-one, then involve a mediator in the discussion. Explain the nature of the issue and how you would ideally like to resolve the situation.

- Meet your supervisor together with the mediator. Ask the mediator to explain the situation to your supervisor as they might be more open to 'criticism' if it comes from an objective third party or a well-respected colleague. However, do not expect the mediator to be your advocate and to fight your cause without regard for your supervisor's opinion – a mediator's function is to facilitate objective communication between you and your supervisor, ensuring that both of you have the opportunity to express yourself and be heard, and hopefully help you arrive at a reasonable solution. The core of your problem may arise out of a basic misunderstanding between you and your supervisor, with the actual relationship being productive. With the help of a mediator you should be able to work this out in a constructive discussion. Regardless of what the situation is, it is important to be prepared and offer clear reasoning. Hence, it is good to keep records of your relationship with your supervisor as soon as things start to become unpleasant. You do not want your supervisor to turn your arguments and use them against you, just because you are not assertive or clear enough. This is potentially dangerous as it could cause you to lose your credibility and could cost you the opportunity to change your supervisor.
- Identify potential new supervisors and talk to your mediator about it. Try to agree on a short list of three suitable candidates (never back only one horse). They do not necessarily need to be from your department but could be from other departments or even faculties as long as their research background and interest overlaps significantly with your topic. Hence, do not narrow your options down too quickly. Ideally, your mediator will support you in establishing contact with the candidates. It is a good idea to send them some information about your research before meeting personally. This should, for example, include your original research proposal (if you are still in your first year), a summary of your recent activities, insights, ideas and so on, and your current CV. This will help them to evaluate whether they are interested in and suitable for supervising you.
- Meet with interested supervisor candidates. If you feel uncomfortable ask your mediator to come along. In case you are staying in the same department, we advise you to take along your mediator to all events as close colleagues of your former supervisor might be a bit more distanced and reserved. In this meeting you should talk openly about the problems you had with your former supervisor. Do not make unsustainable accusations but stick to the facts. Also make sure that you understand what your

potential new supervisor expects from you and vice versa as this will be the basis for your future relationship.

• Finally, familiarize yourself with the appropriate regulations and protocols on changing supervisor(s) at your institution, as a failure in adhering to them could lead to disciplinary measures for you as a student.

In cases where no suitable alternative to your current supervisor exists within your university and you definitely cannot continue that relationship, then you should consider changing university. In general it is more important for you to get along with your supervisor than which university you are studying at. Especially when you are at the beginning of your degree, the disruption a move causes may be acceptable. However, the effort you have to put into finding a new supervisor is much higher as it is unlikely that you will be able to draw on the help of a mediator. Basically, you will have to go through the application process from the start (see Chapter 2).

In case you are further into your degree, you really need to think hard about this. Nobody can make this decision for you but make sure you get some good advice, as this may cause major disruption. Ultimately, you need to consider the pros and cons and make a well-balanced decision.

In some cases, going through the hassle of changing your supervisor and risking a disruption to your progress, which could impact on the quality of your doctorate, can be avoided by being supervised jointly by two or more supervisors. This will allow you to draw on the core strengths of each supervisor, thereby hopefully allowing you to circumvent many of the issues reviewed above. In the next section we discuss the multi-supervisor model in more detail.

Being supervised by a committee of supervisors

Apart from being an increasingly popular mode of supervision in the UK, being supervised by a committee or panel of supervisors can be beneficial for many reasons, including the polyvalent and interdisciplinary nature of modern research, the use of specialized research methodology, access to industry contacts and so on. In this section we outline the pros and cons of being supervised by a committee or panel of two or more supervisors.

Without the aspiration of exclusivity, Table 4.4 briefly outlines advantages and disadvantages associated with joint supervision of a panel of supervisors.

There is one very important point that you should keep in mind: having only one supervisor does not mean you cannot seek advice and help from other academics (e.g. in your department) for aspects of your research in which your supervisor does not excel or if your supervisor is absent at an important

Table 4.4 Advantages and disadvantages of being supervised by a committee

Advantages	Disadvantages
• Each supervisor is an expert on a certain topic or methodology; this is helpful for the research in terms of literature or methodology expertise and where a broad range of academic and industry contacts is advantageous • Ability to avoid or minimize interactions with supervisors where the relationship is not ideal • Not being completely dependent on one individual supervisor as the responsibility is distributed across the panel • Balance of gender (male and female supervisors) • Access to multiple research projects and/ or opportunities for additional funding or future employment	• Illusion of support: *de facto* ending up with one supervisor with the other ones just being free-riders without providing useful support • Being guided in different (sometimes conflicting) directions as each supervisor wants to put their stamp on your doctorate (be aware of politics!) • More time-consuming if each supervisor wants to meet with the student separately on a regular basis (and probably in addition also as a group) • Feeling overwhelmed and sometimes even backed into a corner if supervisors unite against you • Diffusion of responsibility: none of your supervisors may commit to your doctorate; only responsible for part(s) of your research

point in the process. Of course it is more convenient to formally have various persons to rely on in a regular fashion, but again this is no guarantee of commitment, since each of your supervisors only commits to you to a limited degree.

You might also think that having more supervisors gives you the chance to avoid the ones you do not get along with and focus on the other ones. This may or may not be possible, but what if you do not get along with any of them? Or, if they try to pull you into their political power games? Whether you benefit from interacting with different academics (or industrial experts, if you have an industry supervisor) really depends on you and your needs. There is no guarantee that this will all be sweetness and sunshine. Supervision by committee has its own disadvantages, as described in Charles's story below, and it pays to be aware of them.

Musical chairs – A continual coming and going of supervisors

I originally started my Ph.D. in the School of Health Science – Initially with a scholarship, and later with research council funding. Towards the end of my second year, my supervisor and several other members of staff moved into another faculty within the university. There was no question of me changing supervisor, but I was left the choice of whether or not I wanted to move to the new department and faculty. However, it quickly became clear that I would have to stay in the School of Health Science because of my funding and as a result also had to get a second supervisor from within this faculty.

A second supervisor was found and we started to build a working relationship. However, shortly afterwards she also left. It was obvious that nobody had thought out what would happen to me, effectively in limbo between two departments. Eventually another member of staff provisionally agreed to be a second supervisor but later decided she couldn't commit the time. After a couple of months, I finally wrote to the Head of Faculty to express my concern, and she said that she would take on the roll of second supervisor. We had an initial meeting, but it was clear that my main supervisor (belonging to a different faculty) was not going to have an easy working relationship with her. We thus suggested another person who was interested in my work and subsequently agreed to be my second supervisor.

There were times when I felt I needed a second opinion on aspects of my research but was not in a position to get that feedback. At these points I was really affected by the frequent changes and gaps in supervision. I feel that the periods of uncertainty were disruptive to the progress of my research and how concerned I was that a new supervisor might come with new ideas and try to alter the course of my research. It also became clear that my main supervisor didn't actually want another person involved. There were supervision meetings when he spent a lot of time defending my work instead of making real progress. In the end, my way of dealing with this was to simply focus on finishing and trying to ignore the problems with supervision.

Charles (graduate in optometry)

In order to facilitate your doctorate life and minimize supervision conflict, we provide you with a few basic guidelines on how to ensure a good and effective relationship with your supervisory panel:

- Agree on the terms of the relationship(s) up front. This is even more important in a multi-supervisor relationship than it is with a single supervisor, as there may be power struggles between supervisors. In fact, it is best to have one main supervisor who is generally responsible for your overall progress and performance, and one or more associate supervisors who will assist in certain areas of your research. This should guarantee that someone feels responsible for your whole doctorate (and eventually you passing) rather than only parts of it. Regardless of the constellation, it is important that you clearly define who is responsible for which aspects of your research and hence will provide guidance and advice in that particular area. Agree also on the formal format of supervision, for example meetings with the full panel every six months to discuss your future direction and set targets, as well as bilateral meetings with one supervisor at a time in order to discuss ideas and activities as you move along the process.

- Inform all supervisors of your activities with other supervisors, as well as any agreements made in bilateral meetings. In short, everyone needs to know what is going on. This way you can also avoid any envious feelings coming up between your supervisors. In addition, this means that you need to develop a very effective means of communicating within your little supervision team and managing the relationships, otherwise your work may escalate drastically. It may help to introduce a standardized format for minutes and memos that you can circulate around the supervisory panel.
- Try to follow their individual advice and meet their requirements as well as possible. This will keep them happy and minimize conflict. However, do learn to make your own decisions, especially when the advice you are given by your supervisors is contradictory. This also involves developing your self-evaluation skills and becoming increasingly independent.
- Do not get involved in any political power games. Also do not try to play them off against each other (see Chapter 7) – in most cases you will end up being the loser. Try to treat them alike in order to avoid any envious feelings that might be redirected at you. They are peers and will communicate, even if you are not around. So treat them all equally, with respect for their expertise and gratitude for their support.
- Remember that regardless of what your supervisors have achieved, they are not omniscient gods who know everything. They are humans, so give them a break if they happen to make a mistake. Always adopt a professional attitude, be committed and excited about your work, and over time your relationship will develop into one of mutual respect.

As with most things in life, when it comes to supervision there is not one best option. Whichever mode of supervision you choose, it needs to work for you and meet your aims and expectations (see above). Make an informed choice about what works best for you.

5

Sidelines of a doctorate

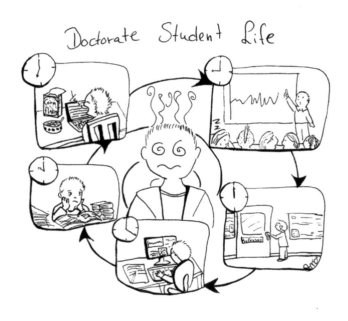

Publications • Conferences • Teaching • Networking • Professional development • Exchanges

Doing a doctorate is not only about reading literature, choosing or designing a methodological approach, collecting and analysing data, and finally describing the process in a clear, logical and concise way in your thesis. Doing a doctoral degree also involves many additional tasks and activities, some of which are not even related to research. This may come as a surprise to some, since research is often seen as being at the heart of a doctorate and consequently is the core focus for most doctoral students. This is true (and rightly so in order to complete your degree on time) but, for one, research does not exist in isolation and, for two, your doctorate is a learning process preparing you for a career in your chosen profession.

So, if you want to get the most out of your degree, your doctorate should be about more than just 'doing research'. To prepare you for these ancillary activities, we set out to introduce and discuss some of the key elements that accompany the doctoral process in this chapter; in other words, we talk about the sidelines of a doctorate. These include:

- publications;
- conferences;
- teaching;
- networking;
- professional development;
- research exchanges.

We discuss each of these in turn, focusing on decisions and problems students are confronted with when participating in these types of activity. Additionally, we would like to emphasize that the purpose of a Ph.D. is to complete a manuscript – your thesis – which satisfies an academic standard. Hence, the more activities you engage in, the less time you have at your disposal for working on your thesis.

Publications

One of the most important – maybe the most important – sideline of your doctorate is publishing your work in one way or another. In this section we introduce and explain 'publish or perish', a phrase so commonly used by academics that it has become stereotypical of academia. We then go on to outline and explain features of the Anglo-Saxon publication process, discuss various publication outlets and categories, focus on how publishing may affect your doctorate and outline the problems and decisions you are confronted with when embarking on publishing for the first time.

Remember, this chapter should and can only function as a starting point for your future publishing endeavours and hence only covers what we consider essential aspects. However, a magnitude of detailed guides offering specific advice on publishing and/or academic writing exist (e.g. Kitchin and Fuller, 2005; Swales and Feak, 2004).

'Publish or perish'

Regardless of your discipline, university or department, 'publish or perish' is an expression you will come across many times while doing your doctorate. You will hear your peers and colleagues talking about it repeatedly to the point that you will likely feel either a desire or a degree of pressure to publish. But what does the phrase 'publish or perish' actually mean? What is 'publishing', why would you 'perish' and what does all this have to do with your degree? In this section we try to clarify these elementary questions and their relevance to you as a doctoral researcher.

The phrase 'publish or perish' is very daunting and implies that something bad will happen (you will perish) if you do not publish. Remember where you are when you are doing your doctorate – you are in an academic context and the people who use the phrase will most likely be academics or young researchers striving to be professional academics. Publishing is very context-specific and is by no means as exciting or dramatic as it sounds. Originally the phrase 'publish or perish' was used to indicate that those who do not publish are forgotten (i.e. perish) because their work is not recorded for future generations to refer to (see also Hills, 1999). As such, it broadly implies that research is conducted in vain if the knowledge arising from it is not shared with others, since the main aim of research is to advance and extend knowledge. The phrase was thus used to encourage a wide variety of people to share knowledge by publishing their work, and this includes not just empirical research but also literary works.

Over the years the term 'publish or perish' has taken on a slightly different meaning. In academia, one of the most common ways of sharing knowledge is by publishing work in academic journals or books. In recent years, a strong focus on research combined with the quantification of research output, for example through mechanisms like the Research Assessment Exercise (RAE) (which was already explained in Chapter 2) has meant that academics are increasingly under pressure to publish; not only to advance knowledge but also to advance their own careers, since promotion in the Anglo-Saxon academic system is heavily based on the quality and quantity of the scholar's research output. As a result some cynics have given the phrase 'publish or perish' a new meaning: publish or lose your job! Of course this is a harsh simplification, which does not account for all the support and development opportunities universities offer their staff (e.g. supervised writers retreat weeks with feedback from experienced authors), but it does help to illustrate how important publications are in the world of academia.

However, unless you are completing a doctorate by publication, which we will look at in more detail in Chapter 8, you usually do not need to publish anything to be awarded your doctorate. Nevertheless, due to the increasing importance of high-quality publication output for universities and their staff (which determines funding and career promotion), as well as the increasingly competitive postdoctoral job market, the pressure to publish will increasingly be recognized at the doctorate level. As such, it is likely that in the future doctoral students will require at least one or two publications (either published or accepted for publication) for the successful completion of a doctorate degree. Of course there are many other reasons why you may want to publish and these are discussed throughout this chapter.

Types of publication outlet

In general there are two different categories of publication outlet with distinct features: books and journals. As for journals we distinguish between:

- academic journals;
- practitioner journals;
- hybrid journals;
- trade magazines;
- conference papers;
- working papers.

A book-style publication, on the other hand, can take the form of:

- self-authored book;
- edited book;
- chapter in an edited book.

Academic journals are the publication outlets most commonly targeted and discussed during doctorates, since doctorates are completed in an academic context. So, for purposes of generalization and simplification, it is fair to say that most people in academia refer to academic journals by default when talking about publishing. If they do not specify, assume they are talking about academic papers.

Academic journals publish papers based on high intellectual standards, which are ensured via a double-blind review process using peer referees (see p. 93 for more information on double-blind reviewing); hence these journals are also often referred to as refereed journals. Papers and articles presented in them have to be connected to the existing literature in the area and report state-of-the-art research that was conducted in a rigorous way to reveal unique and interesting results, which advance our knowledge of the phenomenon under investigation. Of course there are various types of paper that can be published in academic journals, such as:

- theoretical (e.g. conceptual paper etc.);

- empirical (e.g. research paper, case study etc.);
- review pieces of work (e.g. literature review, viewpoint etc.).

Put succinctly, theory articles focus on theory-building and development, empirical papers present findings from research, and review papers focus on summaries and critiques of the existing literature. Although most papers in academic journals include a section on practical implications, academic journals are often criticized for lacking significant practical relevance.

Practitioner journals are journals designed specifically for a practitioner audience written in the language of the field. The papers have to be of high impact and relevance with direct application to practical issues; there is less of a focus on theoretical development and research may be less rigorous or original. These types of journal are especially popular in disciplines that operate closely to the market or the practitioner world, such as marketing, operations management or human resource management. In fact, it is not uncommon for papers to be co-authored by practitioners and academics, for example based on consulting projects or industrial studies that have been conducted (see pp. 91–92 for more information on authorship rights). These journals are often criticized for lacking empirical and theoretical rigour. Indeed, practitioner papers rarely try to make a contribution to theory.

Hybrid journals are those journals that bridge the academia–practice division by presenting academic papers based on rigorous academic work to practitioners. Often it is a translation of academic research into practical implications or adaptation of theory into practitioner terms without using academic parlance. Normally these types of paper start off like a normal academic paper, with strong theoretical and empirical basis phrased in academic terms and strongly tied into the academic literature; the focus diverts in the second half of the paper, where the focus is very clearly on the practical implications of the paper, that is what this 'academic jumble' means in practice and how practitioners may benefit from the research. The audience tends to consist of practitioners with a strong research interest and academics with a strong practical focus.

Trade magazines are very different from the other three, most obviously because they are not a journal, but a magazine. Trade journals generally offer brief highlight reports and research summaries rather than extensive academically or practically oriented papers. However, since these types of magazine have strong readership consisting of a wide variety of people in the industry (academics, researchers, managers, consultants) and has large distribution lists, often reaching tens of thousands of people, it offers the opportunity for high exposure. However, the decision about what is accepted for publication in trade magazines tends to fall entirely to the editorial team and publications in these types of journal and thus more often than not do not count in the publication quota or for performance-related pay scheme in academia.

Conference papers and posters are more often than not a summary of ongoing work in progress rather than finalized papers, and hence best thought of as a working paper of high quality and standard. This is ensured through a double-blind review process similar to academic journals that, however, tends to be applied in a less rigorous way, since the aim of a conference is to attract a variety of topical contributions and provide an outlet for dissemination, as well as feedback. In general conferences provide great opportunities to get constructive and valuable feedback, which stimulate further work on the paper and thus tend to bring about significant improvement in your paper. In short, conferences are about sharing and developing ideas. For you this means that as long as the paper you submit to the conference fulfils certain basic requirements, your paper will be accepted into the conference programme. Of course there are some conferences and conference streams that are more competitive than others, so it pays to be informed. Conference papers are usually published in proceedings in written (a thick telephone-style book) and/or electronic format (a CD or DVD). More information on conferences follows later in this chapter.

Working papers are papers internally published through a university (generally, but not always, your own). These paper submissions also tend to go through a single or double-blind review process before being accepted into the paper series. The advantage of undergoing this process is that you get valuable feedback on your work and are able to advance your ideas further; similar to a conference paper. Hence, working papers are often a starting point for a 'proper' publication in an academic journal. Since most university paper series have their own ISBN/ISSN number, it also enables you to protect your work from being hijacked or plagiarized by having it 'pseudo-published' at an early stage in your doctoral process. We thus encourage you to use this kind of infrastructure at your university not only to protect your intellectual property but also to advance your ideas and writing skills. It is a perfect opportunity with a good balance between effort and achieved outcome that also prepares you for the publication process of high-quality journals (see p. 93).

Whereas some people view **book chapters** as similar to journal papers, **books** and **edited books** definitely will not be seen this way. They differ from journal papers in various aspects:

- appearance;
- length;
- content structure;
- underlying process (e.g. handing in your proposal to the publisher, negotiating the terms of publication, delivering chapters to certain deadlines etc.).

Since writing a book usually tends to be a very time-consuming and demanding process, we do suggest you leave this until after your graduation – for most people book authorship tends to be too much of a distraction during their doctorate. View it from this angle: your thesis is a book in itself; hence there is no rush (or capacity) to write another one. However, authoring a book chapter for an edited book might be a good idea, especially if it is focused on the topic of your doctorate.

Unfortunately, edited books are *edited* by a certain scholar and unless you are invited to submit a chapter for this book, you probably will not even be aware of it. At this point it will prove useful to have a senior supervisor who is well respected and connected within the academic community and gets invitations from various colleagues in which they may ask you to participate.

Decisions involved in publishing

Behind every successful publication lies an informed decision-making process. In the following section of this chapter, we discuss the following key decisions you will have to make on your way to a successful publication:

- whether to publish or not;
- where to publish, that is which outlet (journal v. book) to choose;
- which specific journal to target;
- with whom to publish, that is whether it is a sole or joint piece of work.

When thinking about publishing, the critical decision you need to make is whether you actually strive to **publish**. As with most things in life, publishing during your doctoral process comes with advantages and disadvantages. As already mentioned, doctoral researchers generally do not need to publish to satisfy the requirements of their degree. However, this does not mean that you should not try to publish, at least in the form of working or conference papers. In fact, there are many good reasons for making efforts in this area and there is much to gain.

As publishing is highly competitive, getting a publication is an achievement in itself. It recognizes that you have made an original contribution to your discipline and that the knowledge you discovered is relevant enough to be published within your discipline. This is not only very rewarding but more importantly will also help you to defend your thesis in your oral examination (see Chapter 10). By publishing, you demonstrate that parts of your thesis are original and comply with rigorous academic standards. This will allow you to refer to your own work in your thesis (do not go over the top though!) and help support your work.

Furthermore, as we have already touched upon, your time as a doctoral researcher is a period of professional training – in most cases training to become an academic. In this context writing papers will have a twofold effect. First, you will learn how to write scholastic publications, thereby improving your academic writing skills to a degree that is considered sufficient to publish. Secondly, writing a paper will force you to think through your work very carefully, since journal papers have to transport a great deal of information in a very concise way, thus helping you to reflect, focus and structure your ideas.

This is easier said than done and will require some trial and error loops. Related to this is another important fact: journal papers usually follow a similar (but very condensed) structure to a thesis. Having a paper accepted for publication in an adequate journal means that you could use the manuscript as a basic foundation for your thesis or a chapter in your thesis – you 'just' need to expand the work.

In addition, publications increase attractiveness to employers, both in academic and practitioner fields, although it should be noted that publishing is currently much more important in academia, as jobs will be given to the most suitable applicants based on their research and publication record. Of course the fact that you have not published does not necessarily mean that you will not find a job in academia or that your research is not important or interesting. Indeed, it may just be that the research was not well presented or topical at that time, or that you did not have a mentor who encouraged you to publish. Whatever the case may be, from our point of view it is advantageous for you to try to publish – personally and professionally (see also Andrew's story below).

Nevertheless, publishing during your doctorate can also be seen as a 'waste' of thesis time. It is very easy to get caught up in the publication process of writing, submitting, rewriting, resubmitting or being rejected and aiming for another journal (more on the publication process in the subsequent section). Furthermore, doctoral students often use paper writing as an excuse to sit down and actually write their thesis because writing a short paper of 20 pages seems less daunting than a thesis of 300 pages. This, however, is only an illusion. From our own experience we can tell you that it is a lot more difficult to write a concise journal paper – which has to entail all the major arguments of your thesis anyway – than writing a few hundred pages on the same topic. We suggest you get this straight sooner rather than later because the deadline for submitting your thesis will approach faster than you expect. The key is to find the right balance between paper writing and thesis writing, and making the most out of your publications.

Publishing – a worthy distraction

I always saw my doctorate as a job with certain duties, such as doing research, writing my thesis, teaching but also writing papers and trying to publish in adequate journals. Although it can be an additional burden – looking back at the endless hours spent at writing papers and later revising them in accordance with the comments of the reviewers – I never saw it as such. Whenever I lacked the motivation to work on my thesis chapters, I tried to write something else – either a journal article, a working paper, a little literature review or just a concise summary of my ideas – in order not to feel guilty about wasting thesis time.

My first drafts were heavily changed, corrected and rewritten by my supervisor who co-authored most of my work at that time. However, towards the end of my doctorate, my academic writing skills had improved so much that my supervisor hardly edited any of my work anymore, that I increasingly produced sole authored work, and that I also found it increasingly easy to write the chapters in my thesis. It was very rewarding to build a few hundred words up to a few thousand words and knowing that they wouldn't have to be rewritten at a later stage. When you reach that stage in the process, you'll know what I am talking about and how good it feels.

And don't forget: Having two papers on my research topic published in quite highly ranked journals in my area before I even submitted my thesis gave me a really good feeling for the viva. I was quite confident that I would pass, since I have found my place in the academic community and made the required contribution to knowledge. I would say it takes away lots of the usual nervousness before the big showdown and all your efforts and hard work will pay off at this point at the latest. I'm very happy I chose to publish.

Andrew (graduate in business)

The next decision you will need to make is **where to publish**, that is which journal to target. We have already reviewed different types of journal outlet. Remember, it is important to aim for the right journals. If you are keen to stay in academia, it is important for you to publish in a decent academic journal; the higher the journal rating, the better. However, if you desire to return to or enter the practitioner world after your doctorate, it might be better to target practitioner or trade journals to demonstrate your awareness and knowledge of problems and issues relevant to industry.

So, think about what you want in the future (more on alternative career paths in Chapter 9). If you are not sure, we suggest you try to publish in a variety of journals, which also demonstrates the flexibility of your writing skills by being adaptable and satisfying different journal requirements; of course not all the papers will be relevant to your future employers but at the very least it demonstrates versatility.

After you have selected the type of journal you would like to write a paper for, you then have to **select the specific journal** in your research area you will target. It is important to do this as early in the process as possible, since you have to tailor your paper to the journal's requirements (each journal usually offers author guidelines that can be downloaded and/or printed). As mentioned above, the journal should ideally be of high quality and recognized within the academic community in your particular discipline.

A good starting point to find an appropriate journal could be the internal journal league table of your department and/or university. Here, a great selection of journals relevant to your department, faculty and/or university is ranked according to their importance and reputation. However, since this evaluation is subjective to your specific university (journal league tables of other institutions will look differently), you should also refer to more objective guides, such as the Social Science Citation Index (SSCI), which is an index measuring the number of citations of a certain journal and thereby calculates its related impact factor, that is a proxy of the importance of a journal to its field. Unfortunately, the SSCI only shows results for the most important and more established journals and if you are a student writer, you may want to aim a little lower than that (at least at the beginning).

Another good option for publication is a special issue of a journal. You usually find out about upcoming issues through the Call for Papers (CfP) available directly on the publisher or journal website or included in newsletters (e.g. from the publisher, from academic bodies and institutions etc.). The advantages of special issues are:

- they have a quicker turnaround from paper submission to publication compared to scheduled issues that normally have a long pipeline of papers;
- they specifically focus on a certain topic;
- they accept a larger number of papers on the topic per issue compared to a regularly scheduled issue, which generally increases the changes of having your paper published.

The specific criteria outlined in CfP thus enable you to be more specific in your targeting of journals. CfPs generally provide a number of research areas and issues to focus your contribution on. However, competition in special issues is usually stronger than in scheduled issues, which makes special issues challenging but also highly rewarding.

Another decision involved in publishing is whether you would like to produce a **joint publication** or an **individual piece** of work. There is no one best way to approach writing and both options have strengths and weaknesses. However, research by the Council of Graduate Schools (2004) suggests that the laboratory-based sciences, where students are generally integrated into a research team, are conducive to collaborative publication, while students in the social sciences and humanities tend to pursue their research individually and thus are more likely to produce individual pieces of work.

A joint publication means working with someone else who, in most cases, mentors you and provides you with their experiences. This is especially important for early career researchers just starting down the publication route. More often than not, this will be your doctoral supervisor. However, you may also like to collaborate with other academics, inside and outside of your department/faculty/university, or even with practitioners. We do not want to advise against this but we would like to sensitize you to the fact that this might become a political issue since you are not a fully independent academic yet who creates all research, knowledge and papers in isolation (see Chapter 7 for more information on the issue of politics).

Nonetheless, having a co-author from your department/faculty/university does not necessarily lead to a harmonic relationship. The main issue of joint publications – especially between supervisor and doctoral student – is authorship. Although each university should have a set of regulations and guidelines on good practice and ethical standards of joint publications, in many cases these are not mandatory and their adherence will not be strictly controlled. This often leads to the consequence that, despite doing major bits of the work involved in the paper (i.e. not only writing but also data collection and analysis, literature review etc.), the doctoral student ends up being the second author of the work or moves even further down the author list. This is not uncommon and whether you are happy to accept this practice depends on you (see Daniel's story below who shares his experiences on this).

Thus, we strongly recommend that you are clear about authorship questions at the start of your collaboration to avoid any 'publication rows'. Indeed, it is best practice to set out the terms of authorship prior to writing the paper by specifying who does what and when. Remember, this is often a negotiation and may become open to negotiation again at a later point, if contribution differs to that laid out in the original agreement.

Writing an *individual piece* demonstrates that all the work is your own and 'sole authored papers' are certainly attractive because they demonstrate skill. However, they are also more difficult and less enjoyable, since you do not have a collaborator to run ideas by and motivate you to drive the paper forward. The key lesson to take home is that you need to think about what you want and write papers strategically, with clear aims and direction, in order to be successful and get published. At this point we strongly recommend to read Barley's (2006) paper on what makes a paper interesting. This will be a good starting point for you when you write papers for highly reputable journals.

Feeling like a lemon – Fighting about authorship

Looking back at my time as a doctoral student and the painful experience I made at the beginning of my 'publication career', I would either say don't publish at all or do it yourself. However, I am also aware that as a young and motivated first year research student you probably have neither the necessary writing skills nor the knowledge of the publication possibilities in your area, including conferences, journals etc. At least I didn't have any.

So, the first time my supervisor approached me with the idea of writing a paper for a conference I was delighted and very enthused about it. I envisioned my name being printed on top of a paper in black and white . . . awesome! However, this feeling vanished pretty quickly when I found out that despite the paper being focused solely on my research and conceptual ideas, as well as being mainly written by me (my supervisor contented himself with editing work), my name came second on the top of the paper, right *after* his. When I saw that, I couldn't believe it. There may be some people who don't mind about where on a paper their name appears, as long as the name is on the paper at all but I always felt very strong about this subject.

I always thought (and had assumed) the person doing most of the work would be first author. Anyway, I thought I was being petty, swallowed my pride and let it go. When the same situation occurred a few months down the line when we were aiming for a journal paper, I drew the line. In fact, this time around, it was even worse: We used my literature review, my data (which I collected in endless experiments without any assistance whatsoever from my supervisor), the concept I had developed – And to top it all off, I had written the whole thing. I felt like a lemon being squeezed for publications and got the impression that my supervisor was just looking for a quick and dirty option to gain some publications to support his career advancement.

I decided to take a stand and we ended up having some heavy discussions about authorship and who deserves what. In the end, the issue got resolved to my satisfaction and I retained first authorship. Luckily I had some very good experience with other co-authors later on and can thus be a bit more well balanced in the advice I present here: Develop your writing skills, familiarise yourself with the publication environment in your area and discuss all issues about authorship with your co-author upfront.

Daniel (graduate in environmental studies)

The publication process

In this section we explain what is meant by publishing and the steps it involves. We thereby aim to demystify the publication process and take the fear out of it for young researchers like you.

Once you have written a paper (and this is an iterative developmental process that takes time), you will have to submit it to a journal for consideration. As described above, you should have already selected a journal prior to writing the paper, in order to tailor the paper specifically to the requirements of the journal. Generally, journal papers are either submitted through an electronic manuscript system or emailed directly to the editor in charge (the email address will be available from the journal website). There are still some journals that require paper-based submissions but these are becoming increasingly rare. Once submitted to the journal, the paper tends to go through a multiple step process, which is depicted in Figure 5.1.

After your paper is submitted, it then goes through a thorough review process. In most instances, the editor or someone from the editorial team is the first person to read your paper. They act as a filter and screen out papers deemed inappropriate for publication in that journal. Decisions are made on the basis of suitability to the journal, originality and quality of the paper, topic relevance and format. At this point, submission may either be rejected directly by the editor or sent out for peer review (in trade magazines, and some practitioner and hybrid journals, submission may also be accepted at this point).

The peer review process often utilizes a double-blind format, where two to

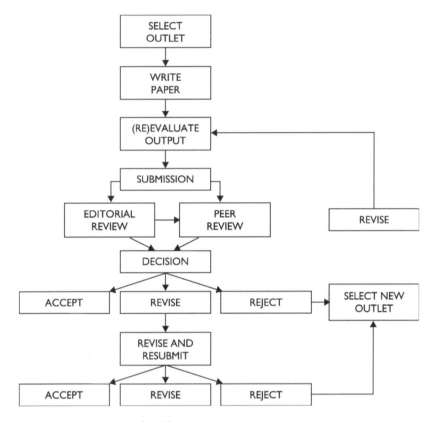

Figure 5.1   Depiction of publication process

five experts in the field will review your paper – the reviewers will not know who you are and you will not know who the reviewers are, hence the notion of double-blind. This is by far the most commonly utilized review format and the one you are most likely to encounter. However, in order to encourage account-ability and increase the recognition reviewers receive, sighted-open peer reviews are being trialled in some disciplines and journals with some success.

This part of the review process can take anywhere between three to twelve months. A good turnaround time is three months and many journals will aim for this in order to shorten publication timelines. However, the average review time is about six months. *Note*: If you have not received a decision about your paper after six months and have not been contacted by the editorial team, it is acceptable practice to get in touch with the editor and request an update.

The editor then reads and collates the reviewers' responses to your work and, based on their feedback and recommendations, decides which decision to make with regard to publishing your paper. The three basic categories of decision are:

1 accept without changes;
2 revise and resubmit (either minor or major changes);
3 reject.

Immediate acceptance is extremely unlikely and most authors thus hope for a revise and resubmit with minor changes. However, major revisions and rejections are very common and it is thus not unusual to engage in various loops of revision and resubmission. Minor changes usually require slightly rewriting and restructuring your paper, whereas major changes can go as far as reanalysing existing or collecting new data.

Most resubmissions will require you to make a number of changes to your paper based on the reviewers' suggestions. Remember that you can accept or reject the reviewers' individual recommendations (as a word of caution, if you choose the latter, remember that you are 'fighting' experts in your area, so the onus is on you to make sure you have strong empirical and theoretical justification for this decision). Once you have made the improvements to your manuscript, you need to offer a formal response to the reviewers. This generally takes the form of a letter and involves responding to each comment, criticism and recommendation the reviewers made. You will be required to outline all the changes you made to the paper (and why) in order to allow your editor and reviewers to trace the progress of your work. Last but no least, you may find it helpful to write your letter in several sections: response to the editor (in the case where the editor has asked you to amend or address certain issues in your manuscript), response to reviewer 1, response to reviewer 2 and response to reviewer 3. Remember to anonymize your response!

Top journals often have acceptance rates ranging from 1 to 10 per cent and have turnover times (time from submission to publication) of up to three years, which means that you will need to be resilient and patient if you want to persist at publishing. We honestly believe that every paper has potential and can find a home somewhere – it is just about framing the paper appropriately and placing it in the hands of the right editor. If you can do the latter, you have won half the battle already.

Remember that even the best papers are not always published in the highest ranked journals, since publication in top journals often depends on the right contacts and a solid publication history (also bear this in mind when doing your literature review as many good papers that will help you to develop your unique concept/framework will be published in lower-ranked journals).

Last but not least, you need to remember that publishing carries considerable lead times with it. Generally, the higher ranked the journal is, the longer the lead times will be. Once submitted, the multi-phasic review and revision process means that a publication takes 12–18 months to get accepted in a good journal. However, much depends on your ability to address the reviewers' comments and rework the paper. The quicker you are able to resubmit the paper, the quicker a new review process can be started. You also need to know that, once a manuscript is accepted, it can take up to another year to appear in print. So, if you want to publish during your Ph.D., it would serve you well to remember that there are no 'quick wins' when it comes to publishing. You must plan ahead and make sure that you start to build a publication pipeline – one in press, one under review and one in progress (or multiples of each).

Conferences

Another media for transporting your research and gaining valuable feedback are conferences. As mentioned above, conferences are a great opportunity to get constructive and valuable feedback on your work, which stimulate significant improvements and the advancement of your ideas and concepts. Often papers are presented at conferences before being submitted to a journal for the first time. In addition, the question and answer session that is usually held at the end of a paper presentation helps prepare you for the all important viva at the end of your doctorate career. Going to a conference means considering various issues, such as which conference to go to, where and how to get funding, how to act at conferences, how to deal with negative feedback at a session and so on. In this section we briefly look at the decisions and steps involved in going to conferences and conclude with some key messages drawn from the conference experience of various current and former students we have talked to.

Going to conferences: decisions and steps

Similarly to publishing, you have to decide first whether you want to attend conferences during your time as a doctoral researcher or not. Despite problems you may face with regard to conferences, such as struggling with funding or paper acceptance, we strongly recommend that you consider going to at least one conference in your doctoral career. Conferences can be very enjoyable, wonderful learning experiences and provide opportunities for you to receive valuable feedback from people interested in your field, which can help you to advance your work. Plus, since conferences tend to move every year, you could end up going to some conferences in some really nice places!

Whatever the reason is that you are thinking about applying for a conference, we firmly believe that these benefits of paper submission and conference attendance far outweigh any negative issues you may encounter at the conference itself. Although we know students that have not been to a single conference and still succeeded in producing a high-quality thesis, we consider this sideline to be an elementary part of your professional development as a doctoral researcher. Conferences are definitively something you should engage in.

The same conference usually takes place annually or biannually at alternating locations. We suggest you focus on conferences in your discipline and research area because these will produce the most relevant high-quality feedback and thus prove most useful to your future work. We also suggest that you start with a small to medium-size national or European conference in order to get used to the process before embarking on big international flagship conferences, such as Academy of Management Conference or the Annual Convention of the American Psychological Association. Also do not forget smaller (doctoral) conferences, workshops and seminars that are highly focused on certain topics – they will often enable more interaction in smaller groups due to a limitation of delegates and introduce you to up and coming people in your discipline.

You can find out about relevant conferences by asking your supervisor or peers in your department; they should know about these conferences, since they have been researching in your area and discipline for quite some time. Another option is newsletters of academic bodies, such as the European Institute for Advanced Studies in Management (EIASM), which entail CfPs, generally with a direct link to a conference website. On these websites, you can get further information including:

- topic of the conference;
- available conference streams;
- submission requirements;
- potential bursaries;
- awards;
- dates and deadlines;
- location.

Before you apply to the conference by submitting a paper for presentation, you need to sort out the often annoying but important issue of funding. Of course the most obvious option will be your supervisor. Every member of staff has a yearly research budget that can be used exactly for purposes such as conferences. So, do not hesitate to ask for support. In some universities the faculty or departments have central budgets that can be used to support doctoral students for conferences. We suggest you get familiar with all funding options that are internally available at your institution and apply.

Also do not forget to ask for discounted conference fees and funding options (e.g. scholarships) directly from the conference organizers. Sometimes societies and funding bodies like the Economic and Social Research Council (ESRC) or the Engineering and Physical Sciences Research Council (EPSRC) also offer support. Just make sure you consider and exploit all available options before – in the worst case – either not going to the conference or self-funding attendance. There is often a lot more support out there than people realize. It just takes a bit of initiative and persistence to find your way through the funding jungle.

In order to participate in a conference, you will have to submit a conference paper and present it at the conference in one of the sessions, which are usually organized by topic. In most cases your acceptance into the conference will be based on your abstract, either short or extended, that you are required to submit. However, there are conferences that will require you to hand in a full paper straight away. As mentioned above, conferences also engage in a double-blind review process, even though it often is not applied as rigorously as in academic journals. In case of acceptance you will normally have to submit a full paper (unless the acceptance was based on the full paper already). Either the paper or the abstract will then be included in the proceedings of the conference.

Some conferences do offer separate doctoral and early career tracks, which often take place before the main conference, and, unless you are planning to submit two or more papers, you will then have to decide whether you would like to present your paper in a mainstream session or within the doctoral track (you also need to be aware that most conferences have restrictions on submission and thus only let applicants submit a maximum of two or three papers per conference round).

If you are going to your first conference, presenting your paper in the doctoral track (if offered) is not a bad idea. The audience will probably be smaller and have a higher portion of doctoral students than in one of the main tracks. As such, these sessions are very useful as training platforms and enable you to get used to the standard conference format (i.e. paper presentation and feedback session) before jumping into mainstream presenting. On the other hand, the feedback you will receive on your work from fellow doctoral researchers may be less rigorous than the feedback you would receive in a main session. Experience can (but does not always) matter as you can see from John's story below.

In addition, you should use the infrastructure provided by your department/faculty to practise your presentation skills continuously while doing your doctorate. These are core skills you will need throughout your career regardless of whether you are aiming for academia, consultancy or industry. This can include presenting your work at research away days, research colloquia or research in progress meetings (dauntingly abbreviated as RIP).

These RIP meetings or seminars are also an important part of your doctorate and can almost be seen as sidelines in themselves. We thus suggest you take them seriously and prepare yourself for them as if they were big conferences. Regardless of where you present, how it is funded and what the focus of your paper is, it is important that you remember to enjoy the experience too. Have fun and make it a memorable experience.

The guy I wanted to kill – My first conference presentation

I was excited – I was going to my first conference and only in my first year of my doctorate! And on top of all, it was at INSEAD, one of the most prestigious universities in Europe. What an opportunity. What I didn't know at that time, INSEAD located in Fontainebleau – apart from being in France – is in the middle of nowhere and definitely too far south of Paris to make the trip during the conference. Never mind, at least I had time to focus on the academic part of the conference, I mean that is supposed to be the whole idea of going to conferences, isn't it?

I got some good advice from fellow students – I was well prepared and dressed the part. OK, INSEAD here I come. At the registration on the evening before the conference, things started to go wrong: I found out that my presentation will be in the very first session on the very first day! I mean, on the very first conference day people tend to be motivated and actually listen to the speaker; not like the last session on the last day when half the delegates have left already or enjoy some time off before going back home. I couldn't sleep properly that night and felt the urge to go through my presentation again and again. I must have looked like a zombie the next morning in the session.

Nevertheless, I managed to deliver what I thought was a solid presentation; not reading from my script, speaking loud and clearly, establishing eye contact with the audience, and demonstrating expertise in my area. Everything was nice until the question and answer session. For some time nobody spoke, then an interested listener posed a question. I was petrified and unable to focus on what he said – Was that actually a question or was he just criticising my work? I felt personally attacked and imagined myself bushwhacking him in a dark corner on the way to the conference dinner that evening. But luckily I also found an ally who liked my work and supported me in my approach and the research I was doing. From then on, everything went smoothly and I regained my confidence.

My next conferences went well because I learned not to take the criticism to heart. I know it is difficult because our research projects become our little babies but nevertheless, it is important that you filter the received feedback – save the valuable stuff and ignore the rest!

John (final year student in politics)

Key messages

Drawing on the experience of various doctoral students who have attended a wide variety of national and international conferences around the world, we have put together a list of key messages summarizing their comments:

- *Go to conferences in your field (big is not always good)*: do go to some big conferences in your field to get a better feel for different types of conference but do not neglect the smaller conferences and workshops. Although the smaller sessions might at first glance not look so prestigious or exciting, these will often be more specific and therefore also more relevant to your research. It will also give you the opportunity to introduce yourself to the right network of people – people researching in your area, who share your interests.

- *Always check for funding*: Never pay for a conference if you can avoid it and always check for student discounts and rates – most major conferences will offer both of these. Funding is available internally from your university, your school and your department, and externally from the conference organizers, subsections, societies and funding bodies like the ESRC. Remember to apply for all the relevant doctoral awards. You may also want to check for 'early bird' booking discounts, for registration fees and travel, which can significantly lower the overall conference cost.
- *First impression matters*: Dress and act the part. You are at a professional conference, so present yourself professionally. You are a student but you do not want to be seen as a student – you want to be seen as a peer, so make an effort!
- *Negative feedback is good and questions you cannot answer are okay*: Everyone is scared of their research being received badly but at the end of the day it is important to remember that flattery will get you nowhere. If you want to progress your work, you need people to take an active interest and review your research in detail. This often means that points of critique will be raised, some difficult to bear. Try to stay positive, that is do not take it personally, and focus on the learning and development you will be able to gain from it. And, in the case of a rare personal attack, remember, if you can see the difference between this and constructive feedback, so can the rest of the audience. Shrug it off – there are mean people everywhere!
- *Submit a high-quality paper*: Although the review process for conference papers is not as strict and thorough as for academic journals papers (they are trying to attract and include a great variety of topics), try to make an effort and produce a high-quality paper. We recommend this because a good and interesting paper published in the conference proceedings may actually attract an invitation to publish a fully developed paper in a special issue of a leading journal (look out for announcements in the call for papers).

Teaching

Being one of the main pillars in the 'business model' of a higher education institution, teaching is as important a doctoral sideline as publishing and going to conferences. Especially for those of you who opt for the academic career path (see Chapter 9 for more information on the alternative of an academic career), teaching skills and experience will be a great asset to you, since teaching forms a large part of your job description.

Indeed, universities often want to see both theoretical and practical teaching experience in their applicants. If you plan to stay in academia, the sooner you start to learn these skills, the easier it will be for you to start practising the profession of being a lecturer. And, what better training can you get than teaching from time to time during your doctorate? Of course, you can also engage in teaching for reasons of funding your doctorate studies (see Chapter 6 for more information on the option of using teaching for funding your doctorate via either part-time work or a teaching assistantship).

Especially those doctoral students who are offered scholarships by their department/faculty/university are in return often required to teach or support their supervisors and departments with teaching-related duties. The quantity and level of teaching you have to engage in depends entirely on faculty or departmental policy but it would be as much as six hours of work per week, which is the maximum number of hours allowed by the research councils and also in line with the guidelines recommended by the national postgraduate committee. In other countries, such as Germany, you are most likely employed as an assistant of a professor for doing your doctorate, which automatically involves teaching duties.

Teaching work is not strictly limited to lectures though and this is important to know, since it will impact on the time commitment you will have to make. Teaching can also involve tasks such as:

• holding office hours;
• tutoring students;
• administering exams;
• running seminars for undergraduate and postgraduate students;
• marking assignments and exams;
• providing lab assistance;
• performing various other administrative duties.

In the case of giving lectures/seminars/tutorials on the undergraduate level (doctoral students are generally less likely to be involved in teaching at the postgraduates level), most UK universities that adhere to good practice and high-quality standards require teaching staff to at least enrol in – if not complete – a teaching certificate programme. If you do not possess one by the time you have to enter the classroom and teach, you will be able to gain the required certificate for teaching and learning in higher education institutions through the professional development possibilities at your university (see p. 120).

Networking

'Networking' is another one of those abstract terms people use that can mean a thousand things. As a doctoral candidate, think about it as a collection of your private and professional relationships; in other words, your professional and social network. Relationships can act as priceless resources before, after and during your doctorate. As previously touched upon in Chapter 2, having connections can make the application process less daunting and help ensure that you are placed with the supervisor of your choice. During your degree, the people you know can help in numerous ways, including getting access to participants or proofreading your thesis. After completion, your network can help you hear about open positions and research opportunities or publish papers to name but a few.

For these reasons and more, building and maintaining relationships is crucial. In this section we thus discuss types of contact, value of contacts, how to build an efficient network and utilize it effectively, the role of professional bodies in networking, and conclude with some thoughts on how to avoid potential contact traps. If you want to read more on this subject, a good starting point might be D'Souza (2007).

Types of contact

As a doctoral student, you will come into contact with quite a lot of different people, including managers, consultants, academics, friends and family. All these groups of people form a valuable part of your network, although addressing slightly different issues.

Industry contacts such as managers and consultants can help facilitate access to industry resources, for example including access to:

- companies and organizations;
- participants;
- financial funds;
- use of technological equipment.

You may have built contacts already without being aware of it, for instance during internships, previous employment or through family relations. These contacts are useful before, during and after your doctoral degree. They are particularly important when it comes to conducting the empirical part of your study. For instance, students in natural sciences often receive funding to do their doctorate from a collaborating organization, which has an interest in the outcome of the project, for example to get a patent on a technical solution. Similarly, having good contacts in industry can increase your attractiveness as a student since your research process may well be facilitated by this contact and you bring these contacts into your supervisor's network. Both of these are very attractive elements. After your doctoral degree industry contacts do not lose value either. They can help you hunt for jobs, either by passing information to you or by offering a recommendation, and may support potential grant applications, which highlights the relevance of your research to industry, something that funding bodies tend to like.

Academic contacts are also very good. Before your doctoral candidature, they can help you by sharing information and supporting the application process, as well as helping to formulate research ideas. During your doctorate, academics can offer you valuable feedback, review papers, support grant applications, provide assistance in seeking funding or paid work, and/or help you develop an academic career. Once you are enrolled, good relationships within your department are crucial. Of course, relationships outside of your department are also important as they allow you to get another perspective on issues and to extend your professional network. After your degree, these relationships remain important, even if you exit into industry, hence you may like to keep in contact. For instance, they may be your referees in the job application process, provide career advice, review future papers, keep you informed about opportunities, support grant applications and so on.

Friends and family are often seen as a bit of a 'warm and fuzzy' category because they are an important source of social support. However, this should not blind you to the additional value this network can offer you; in fact, it is very similar to the other two. Friends and family can be a source of funding, advice and contact into industry as well as academia. It is important for you to remember that just because you do not know these people in a professional context, you can still, however, approach them with professional issues.

This leads to our final point – do not forget that each individual in any one of these three groups has their own network, which you can potentially gain access to and exploit if you know the individual well enough. We call these 'secondary contacts' and they should not be forgotten about either. If your father's best friend is the Chief Executive Officer (CEO) of BMW and you happen to be doing research in the automobile industry, he may be able to get you access to the organization. Why not give it a shot? When it comes to networks, you need to think outside of the box but always act with tact.

Building and maintaining relationships

Throughout your doctorate, there are two main ways of building relationships:

1 through personal contact;
2 through professional bodies.

Personal contact is established through courage and hard work. You come across a lot of people throughout the duration of your degree and will seek contact with some of them. This could be because they made some interesting comments at a conference you went to, because they wrote some of the papers that align with your theoretical ideas, because they work in an industry that is attractive to you or a multitude of other reasons.

It is easy to establish contact with someone you meet by simply having a quick chat and exchanging business cards (this is a very powerful tool; make sure you have some in your pocket – but do not undervalue yourself by referring to yourself as 'student'; call yourself 'doctoral researcher', and make sure the business cards are official ones from your institution and not from the category do-it-yourself).

You may also establish contact by 'cold calling' – sending letters, emails or making unsolicited phone calls. This is a lot more difficult but may be necessary if you are unable to meet them another way and do not have any mutual contacts. Especially, academics are actually receptive to this kind of contact, so do not shy away from getting in touch with people you want to be in touch with.

The second and complementary way to build a network is by interacting through **professional bodies**. For this purpose and more, we strongly encourage engagement with professional bodies. Professional bodies form the cornerstone of disciplines; they support and thus should be supported. We would therefore expect any student to join at least one membership body, generally based on their affiliation and/or research interest.

There are many benefits of joining membership bodies; speak to your supervisor about which would be most suitable for you. Professional bodies or societies often have receptions at conferences where you can network and meet other people working in your area, and also have listserv distribution lists, where you can receive and send emails about core issues in your area.

Always remember also to link into the student network (and this goes for professional bodies, conferences and your own university) – these students may all be small potatoes within their respective fields now but they are also the bright minds of tomorrow. You will see many of them growing alongside you and becoming strong allies. So, make sure you create a balanced portfolio of contacts in your network, that is a healthy mixture of small people and big names.

Maintaining relationships is actually much more difficult than establishing contact. It is pretty hard work that requires determination and commitment. The key is actually to stay in touch. To just get a business card at a conference is just not enough to form lasting professional relationships. You need to stay in touch after the event; this may be casual social contact, chatter about upcoming conferences, discussion about research ideas and/or mutually reviewing each other's papers.

Whatever the case may be, if you lose touch, you will be forgotten – so stay in touch or do not bother getting in touch. Professional relationships and networks are no different from personal relationships. They are based on mutual respect, trust and like. Offer these things to your partner and you have the basis for a strong relationship. Apart from actual contact and communication, the key to a productive relationship is staying clear of the following 'contact traps':

1 Do not let others take advantage of you.
2 Do not take advantage of others.
3 Do not exaggerate or overwhelm your contact.

As straightforward as these ideas may seem, many students fall into the trap of doing endless 'free work' for a peer, supervisor or senior colleague without ever reaping any benefits from the relationships. Ensure that you only do what you want to do and what is sensible. When the relationship starts to become only one way, try to readdress it or devolve it (see also Chapter 4).

Of course this does not mean you should not do favours for anyone and always look for payback. No, relationships are about taking and giving – if you want people to give you favours, you will need to give favours too. The second point is about not being a user yourself. As doctoral students, many people will respect and even look up to you. Give and take, do upon others as you would have them do upon you, and do not exploit any good-heartedness or nativity you encounter. You get what you are given in life, so make sure that any relationship you have is well balanced. Do not make promises and commitments you cannot keep; this will only lower you in your colleagues' esteem.

Professional development

Good universities give you plenty of opportunities to engage in professional development throughout your doctoral degree. In this section we discuss some of these opportunities, how to access them and which opportunities to seize and which to best leave untouched.

Opportunities

Development opportunities come in several guises. For one, the university may well offer you financial support through a yearly personal development fund. This money is set aside to foster your professional development and can generally be spent for any part of your professional development including conferences, membership body fees, qualifications and so on. In addition, the university may offer professional development courses and workshops.

These types of event may be general and targeted at a large audience group (e.g. how to write research proposals, how to publish, how to be assertive, presentation skills etc.) or specific and focused on a selected few (e.g. how to communicate negative findings in biomedical engineering to your sponsor, how to do multi-modal regression analysis etc.). These types of lecture or workshop tend to be one-offs, can be internal or external, and the quality of them varies widely. However, these courses and workshops are also a very good source of training for the soft skills and competences necessary for your postdoctoral career (see Chapter 9).

Finally, universities may offer support with professional and practical qualifications or offer them through their own staff development institute. These commonly include postgraduate certificates in teaching in higher education that are increasingly required for any teaching purposes at a higher education institution in the UK (see pp. 100, 120), accreditation with professional bodies such as chartered accountancy status and sometimes even higher education degrees (e.g. the Master of Business Administration, MBA).

Access

Access to most of these opportunities is managed via Staff Development Centres, which are now commonly part of good practice in UK universities. If you do not know what is available at your university or what type of developmental activities other doctoral researchers engage in, we suggest you book an appointment with an adviser and find out how you can best tailor your doctorate degree and all the development opportunities it offers to your needs.

The second most common source of opportunity is through your department. Most departments have guest speakers and departmental lecture series. These are very interesting since they are tailored specifically with your department's interest in mind which, as discussed in Chapter 2, should align closely with your own interests and work. Your department may also offer funds in addition to those allocated to you by the university and this is worth speaking to your supervisor and/or Head of Department about.

Finally, professional bodies and societies often put on courses and lecture series, which may be of interest. Put your name on the listserv and attend courses that are of most interest to you.

Balance

What you should do and should not do really depends on why you are doing a doctorate and what you hope to achieve by doing this. So, unfortunately, we cannot present a black and white checklist of 'things to do' in this section. Just remember that – as with most things – the key is achieving a good balance between your sidelines and your Ph.D., that is actually doing research and writing the thesis.

Do things in moderation; do not do too much and do not do too little. This will facilitate personal growth without overwhelming and distracting you from your degree. It will also turn you into a versatile flexible researcher, who will appear attractive to a number of potential employers. If you try to grab every development opportunity you come across with both hands, you may also end up with a profile that is too versatile and lacks focus (this is aside from the fact that you may well feel overwhelmed). Focus on things that interest you and have direct relevance to what you are doing and where you are heading.

Exchanges

There are also opportunities to spend periods of your doctoral degree at other institutions in the UK and abroad, for example as Visiting Research Fellow or Visiting Scholar. Generally an exchange lasts from three to twelve months, with you completing parts of your doctoral requirements abroad (mainly collecting and analysing data and/or writing up). There are opportunities that are cyclical, coming up every year, and those that are sporadic as the need arises.

If you are interested in doing an exchange, keep your ear to the ground and find out which arrangements your university has. They may already have partnerships with other universities to facilitate this type of transfer and cross-fertilization. Even if it does not, there may well be people at your university who are aware of these types of opportunity and can help guide you through the application process. Like so many things in academia, exchanges are often competitive and you will need to invest in the process if you wish to be successful. Opportunities are also announced via professional bodies, societies, forums, and formal and informal networks. And, if nothing else, working at another institution for a while will enable you to extend your network further. Read for yourself what James has to say about his visiting scholarship.

On the road as a visiting scholar in Norway

I believe most PhD students go through periods when life feels monotone and inspiration and creativity are tending towards zero. Two years into my doctoral studies my office at uni had become my home. This was where I spent most of my time, where I had the majority of my meals, where I hung out with my friends, and where we drank our pints moaning about our students and supervisors. It was great, but I felt it was time to leave – I went on leave as a visiting scholar.

So how do you make this happen? I do not think there are any particular rules. Throughout my PhD, I had maintained contact with the university where I got my masters degree. Of course, not everyone has such contacts from the beginning. I think going to conferences is a great way to make new contacts (conferences are much more about networking than actually getting comments on your work). Use this media to talk to scholars in your field and get them interested in your work. A great alternative to establishing your own network is of course to use your supervisor's network. Once you have established contact, I believe it is quite easy to get a position as visiting scholar. As long as the host department isn't in urgent shortage of office space, and above all, doesn't have to make any financial commitments, it takes very little effort to get a visiting scholarship.

In my case, convincing my home department was the main challenge. As with many things in life, I guess it is always easier to leave than to be left. My home department was concerned that I wouldn't fulfil my teaching duties and my supervisor was worried that I wouldn't come back. After some diplomacy and a few compromises I got my 'go ahead'. Promising that the leave would lead to a boost in research results was a very useful argument.

Six months in a different environment was indeed good for the progress of my research. Inspiration was boosted by the challenge to show the new department how eminent my research project was. This was a great opportunity for networking and building my own trademark. A couple of weeks after my arrival I got the opportunity to give a seminar about my research project. Several senior faculty members attended and shared their thoughts on my work. This was much more fruitful than any conference I've been to. Whenever I had a question, my future colleagues knew my project already. In my view, that seminar was the basis for establishing a whole new network of academic colleagues that I could learn a lot from. Also, all of them are potential future co-authors, colleagues, references in research or when applying for jobs.

Remember that the PhD is not only about becoming a super expert in your field. It is a substantial part of your life and it should be fun and interesting (your future employers will probably agree). It always takes some effort to break the patterns of everyday life, but it usually pays off very well. Going as a visiting scholar for some time is a good way to do it!

James (final year student in business)

6

Finances

Scholarships and bursaries • Self-funding

Ideally, you would not have to worry about this issue and some students are lucky enough not to have to. However, finance is a serious consideration for most postgraduate students. Being a postgraduate student implies that you have already spent three to seven years in higher education. This places a substantial constraint on resources, especially since students normally are not able to work full time while enrolled in a doctorate degree (generally three to four years), which means that they are on limited income. At the same time, however, a postgraduate degree can be very cost-intensive, not only in terms of tuition fees and research costs (which may not be fully funded) but also in terms of living costs, including accommodation and sustenance costs (e.g. food, clothes, travel to work – but not 'extras' like entertainment costs and holidays).

Given the importance of these issues in student life, this chapter discusses the various ways students can fund their studies, including opportunities for self-funding (through teaching or research assistantships as well as part-time work) and other funding (through scholarships and bursaries, whether it be internal from your university/department or external from a public or private funding body).

Scholarships and bursaries[1]

When you first start looking into scholarships and bursaries, you will probably find it a frustrating and overwhelming experience. Although it seems straight-forward, you cannot expect to be able to rely on a single comprehensive guide to doctoral funding, largely because no such guide exists. This means that you will need to find out the information yourself and, since there are diverse funding bodies, your search will need to be widespread, which means that it will be both laborious and time-consuming. Indeed, a range of organizations including public, private and non-profit organizations fund research within the UK. It is this diversity and information overload that often makes it dif-ficult for students to know just where to start looking. However, a good piece of advice is that universities (specifically career services) often offer a collated list of funding opportunities which, though unlikely to be 100 per cent com-prehensive, give you a good starting point for your search.

To serve as a helpful starting point for your queries about funding source, we distinguish between three general types of scholarship:

1 scholarships and bursaries provided by the department/school/university you are enrolled in (internal funding);
2 scholarships and bursaries provided by an external governmental funding body (e.g. research councils, educational trusts etc.);

---

[1] This section was prepared with help from Frances Meegan (see Acknowledgements, p. xiii).

3 scholarships and bursaries issued by an external private organization (generally associated with a specific research project; called private sector funding).

We now give examples of funding available for each type of source. Keep in
mind that this is not a complete list of *all* doctoral funding opportunities but
rather represents a comprehensive overview; in other words, this section is
meant to act as a guide to help inform your own search.

Scholarships, bursaries and grants: the basics

Before you make an application for any form of internal and external funding,
you need to ensure that you are eligible. Eligibility criteria and other requirements are usually strictly applied by funding bodies, so there is little point of
applying if you do not meet them (otherwise you waste valuable time learning
about a funding scheme and countless hours preparing application documents
in vain because no matter how good your application is, you will not be
awarded the funding). Eligibility is generally assessed on the basis of a range of
criteria, which commonly include:

- nationality and/or country of residence and/or country of first degree;
- age and gender;
- area of study (field and discipline);
- institution you are enrolled in;
- scope of funding (e.g. fees, maintenance, other expenses etc.);
- duration of funding (e.g. first year only, 3+ years etc.);
- exclusivity, that is whether other sources of funding can be held at the same
  time?;
- deadline, that is whether your doctorate needs to be completed within a
  certain time?

While some sources of funding are available at any time throughout your
doctorate and you can apply for them several times throughout your degree
(generally every year), some sources are only available when you first start a
doctorate, which means that you cannot reapply if you are unsuccessful the
first time.

The decision about whether you receive funding is usually based on a variety
of factors in addition to the eligibility criteria. If you are eligible, the award of a
scholarship depends mainly on the quality of your research proposal, which is
essentially your doctoral research proposal or your first year qualifying report
edited to suit the requirements of the funding body (see also Chapter 2). Funding bodies generally use a panel of experts to evaluate this proposal against
criteria of relevance and feasibility. The core questions will be:

- Is this a valid and reliable way of conducting research?
- Are they capable of conducting this work in the allocated time?

- Do they have adequate support (e.g. expert advisers in the department)?
- Will the work produce (theoretically and practically) relevant results?
- Is the topic in line with funding body priorities?
- Is this a timely and important topic?

Ensure that you make these issues explicit in your proposal.

Although there are some forms of funding that exclusively cover tuition fees, in most cases funding will also cover (basic) living costs and provide a (small) annual budget to cover research expenses. The research budget can generally be used for expenses related to data collection and analysis (e.g. travel to data collection sites, lab equipment, transcribing), for conference and workshop attendance, to buy books and pay for journal subscriptions, and to cover professional membership fees.

Last but not least, you need to be aware that funding – and this is true for both internal and external forms of funding – is often explicitly linked to the institution you are studying at (see criteria above). As such, a change of university (e.g. if you choose to change supervisor as discussed in Chapter 4) will often lead to a loss of funding. This is not a cruel way to tie you to the university; it is actually based on sound reasoning. Your proposal partially got funded based on the expertise within your department, which you will no longer be privy to once you move institutions. As such your move constitutes significant risk to funding bodies, who cannot guarantee the quality of work or supervision at the new institution – for better or worse, this is a risk they are often not willing to take. However, this does not prevent you from applying for funding again once you have moved to your new host institution. Additionally, there may also be funding opportunities at the new institution.

More general information on funding opportunities can be accessed via the following sources:

- *Higher Education and Research Opportunities* in the UK (HERO) (www.hero.ac.uk)
  Hero markets itself as the 'UK's official gateway to higher education and research information'; the agency is supported by UK higher education and research organizations.
- *National Postgraduate Committee* (NPC) (www.npc.org.uk)
  NPC is a charity that seeks to advance postgraduate education in the UK; it deals with issues affecting postgraduate students.
- *ResearchResearch* (www.researchresearch.com)
  ResearchResearch is a global database of academic research jobs and funding opportunities.

University and departmental funding

Many UK universities and departments offer studentships, scholarships and other kinds of bursary to students enrolled in their doctoral programmes.

Information about these opportunities can be gained via the university websites, research degree programmes and student support services. This is often the best way to access the information, since individuals at these institutions are often able to provide the most comprehensive information about these types of funding opportunity. However, in order to increase the potential pool of applicants, university funding may additionally be advertised via the following web channels:

- www.jobs.ac.uk
  Check out the 'PhD studentships' section.
- www.prospects.ac.uk
  Search for 'Postgrad study'; explore the subsection 'Funding my further study'.
- www.postgraduatestudentships.co.uk
  Found under 'PhD and other doctoral funding'.
- www.timeshighereducation.co.uk
  Classified as 'Studentships'.
- www.jobs.guardian.co.uk
  Search for 'Education'; look for studentships in the 'Research' subsection.
- www.studentmoney.org
  Look under 'Search for funding'.

Doctoral students who are offered scholarships by their university or department are often required to do some teaching, research and/or related activity in return for the funding. However, as opposed to teaching and research assistantships (see below), where the commitment may be substantial, the teaching and research load you take on as a funded student is relatively light and usually does not exceed six hours per week.

Some universities also offer a small grant to each doctoral student on the programme that is at your disposal for expenses related to your doctorate, for example conferences (fees, travel expenses etc.), data collection and analysis (e.g. interviewing, transcribing etc.), stationery, thesis binding and so on. For example, at the university where we studied this was £275 per year for every doctoral student, no matter whether you were self-funded or on a scholarship. Although these funds are generally available on an annual basis, it is important to note that unspent funds cannot be carried over into the new academic year. The philosophy is – spend it or lose it!

Public bodies and institutions

There are a number of public bodies and institutions that sponsor research degrees. In general terms, there are five key public sources of external funding:

1 research councils;
2 higher education funding councils;
3 UK government departments;

4 educational trusts, charities and foundations;
5 specific funding for overseas students.

The scope of each of these funding organizations differs dramatically. While some fund research across a range of areas, others only provide funding on specific science or humanity topics. Research funding organizations run schemes tailored to their particular objectives. Each type of grant, fellowship or award will have associated information about the type of funds available, who is eligible and how to apply. Some will allocate lump sums of funding to the university or department (which then selects the best candidates), while others will require applications to the sponsor, either directly by the individual or via the university.

In what follows, we list some principal sources of funding bodies in each of the five categories to enable you to access further information directly from the funding body. It is also important to note that in most instances funding would go to a university department or research group, not to an individual student. This is especially true for research councils, higher education funding councils and government departments, but can apply to all sponsors. Generally, lump sums are paid to the institution and then funds are transferred to the student on a monthly basis (although universities sometimes opt for bi or tri-monthly payment instead).

1 Research councils

Research Councils UK (RCUK) (www.rcuk.ac.uk) is a strategic partnership set up to champion science, engineering and technology supported by the following UK research councils:

- Arts and Humanities Research Council (AHRC) (www.ahrc.ac.uk)
- Biotechnology and Biological Sciences Research Council (BBSRC) (www.bbsrc.ac.uk)
- Engineering and Physical Sciences Research Council (EPSRC) (www.epsrc.ac.uk)
- Economic and Social Research Council (ESRC) (www.esrc.ac.uk)
- Medical Research Council (MRC) (www.mrc.ac.uk)
- Natural Environment Research Council (NERC) (www.nerc.ac.uk)
- Science and Technology Facilities Council (STFC) (www.scitech.ac.uk)

Generally speaking only UK and European Union (EU) students residing in the UK are eligible to apply to research councils for funding, except in the case of specific schemes for international students (see below). The AHRC and ESRC invite applications from students via the university. Other research councils give resources to the university to select which students should receive awards.

2 Higher education funding councils

Through the Department for Innovation, Universities & Skills (DIUS), parent organization of the higher education (HE) funding councils, the UK's HE funding councils provide significant funding for university-based research in England, Wales and Scotland.

- Higher Education Funding Council for England (HEFCE) (www.hefce.ac.uk)
- Scottish Funding Council (SFC) (www.sfc.ac.uk)
- Higher Education Funding Council for Wales (HEFCW) (www.hefcw.ac.uk)
- Department for Employment and Learning, Northern Ireland (DELNI) (www.delni.gov.uk)

3 UK government departments

Central government departments are a major source of research funding within UK HE. Among the biggest are the following:

- Department for Business, Enterprise and Regulatory Reform (BERR) (www.berr.gov.uk).
- Department of Health (DoH) (www.dh.gov.uk)
- Department for Environment, Food and Rural Affairs (DEFRA) (www.defra.gov.uk)
- QinetiQ and dstl (previously Defence Evaluation and Research Agency – DERA) (www.qinetic.com)
- DIUS (www.dius.gov.org)
- Department for Transport (DfT) (www.dft.gov.org)

Responsibility for overseeing public sector scientific research lies with the DIUS and the BERR (formerly the Office of Science and Innovation, OSI, within the Department of Trade and Industry, DTI), and the UK Chief Scientific Adviser (CSA). The Office of Science and Technology is also charged with maintaining the excellence of the research base, promoting the exploitation of research results, and monitoring and influencing the UK's participation in international research.

4 Educational trusts, charities and foundations

Although lots of these types of source exist, there are some drawbacks: They are not always easy to locate, more often than not offer only small amounts of money, are usually very precise about what the money can be spent on and have very limited eligibility criteria. However, they can be a useful source for additional funding (commonly referred to as 'top up funding'), or to support travel and other specific activities related to your doctorate.

As a starting point you can use the following agencies and links, which offer information on Educational Trusts, Charities and Foundations:

- Association of Charitable Foundations (www.acf.org.uk)
- Directory of Social Change (www.dsc.org.uk)
- Funderfinder (www.funderfinder.org.uk)

A selection of specific educational trusts, charities and foundations that might be of interest to you are listed below:

- Leverhulme Trust (www.leverhulme.ac.uk)
  The Trust emphasizes individuals and encompasses all subject areas to support of research and education.
- Emslie Horniman Fund (www.therai.org.uk) (under 'Grants')
  Promotes the study of the growth of civilizations, habits and customs, religious and physical characteristics of the non-European peoples and prehistoric and non-industrial man in Europe.
- Wellcome Trust (www.wellcome.ac.uk)
  Funds research to improve human and animal health.
- Wenner-Gren Foundation (www.wennergren.org)
  Offers a range of funding for Ph.D. work in anthropology.
- Royal Economic Society (www.res.org.uk) (under 'Grants, fellowships and prizes)
  Economics departments can apply for funding for junior fellowships that are offered each academic year.
- Open University (www.open.ac.uk)
  UK distance learning university that also carries out and funds a number of research projects.

5 Specific funding for overseas students

If you are an overseas student undertaking a doctorate in the UK or thinking about enrolling, funding arrangements tend to be different. In addition to checking out the funding sources listed in this section, you should also check with the Ministry of Education or Education Department in your home country, as well as foreign councils and embassies for available funding. General information on funding for overseas students is also available from the British Council (www.britishcouncil.org and www.educationuk.org).

Other relevant sources for funding for overseas students are:

- Overseas Research Students Awards Scheme (ORSAS) (www.orsas.ac.uk)
  Provides funding to pay the difference between the international student tuition fees and the home/EU student tuition fees.
- Commonwealth Scholarship and Fellowship Development Plan (www. csfp-online.org)
  Open to Commonwealth citizens permanently resident in any Commonwealth country other than the UK.
- Fulbright Commission (www.fulbright.co.uk)
  Awards for US citizens to study, lecture or research in the UK/EU.

- Aga Khan Foundation (www.akdn.org)
  Provides scholarships for postgraduate studies to outstanding students from developing countries.
- Great Britain–China Education Trust (www.gbcc.org.uk)
  Awards available to Chinese students accepted to complete a doctorate in the UK.
- UK–India Education and Research Initiative (UKIERI) (www.ukieri.org)
  Offer funding for science and technology projects jointly funded by the Department of Science and Technology, Government of India and UKIERI.
- Dorothy Hodkin Postgraduate Awards (DHPA) (www.rcuk.ac.uk/hodgkin/default.htm)
  The DHPA brings outstanding students from India, China, Hong Kong, South Africa, Brazil, Russia and the developing world to the UK for Ph.D. study.

Find out below about Peter's very specific experience with his scholarship.

Sometimes you have to take chances – How I got my funding

Having missed out on several deadlines to apply for funding – both internally and externally – I was investing in my career by paying the tuition fees and other living expenses myself in my first year. It actually took quite a lot of time to find out about the right sources of funding in my area and whether I was actually eligible to apply. Enthused by the good news of being able to apply for bursaries, I started looking at the specific guidelines on the websites.

What helped me to write the actual proposal was to look at successful applications of fellow doctoral students. While they were not in the exact same field, their submissions helped me in structuring my proposal in terms of how much of the word limit I should use for my literature review, the methodology section and for my project timeline. Due to the importance of the proposal, which was about more than just passing and failing, I invested a lot of time in drafting it. After receiving a fair bit of input from my supervisor, I submitted the proposal on time to the funding body.

From the submission phase, I went to the waiting phase. And here comes the howler: Based on the official information of the funding body, I expected an answer in the first two weeks of August. So, I decided to book a holiday in France starting at the end of August (still leaving some buffer time in case of a delayed answer). Moreover, France is not at the end of the world, which meant that I could get back to London any day if necessary. When the announced period passed, I was quite disappointed by the fact that I had probably not been awarded the studentship. However, hope dies last. Hence, before going on holiday, I asked two colleagues and good friends to check the letterbox at my flat once a week and see whether a response arrived.

When I received a phone call from one of my friends with the good news that

I received my letter of acceptance I was overjoyed. However, my delight flew away when they told me that the answer was due the very same day! Damn, I couldn't believe that I was awarded with a scholarship, which I will not receive because I was such a donkey and left for holiday instead of waiting for a definite answer. There was not much I could do, so I decided to take chances. I asked my friends to fax the documents to France, signed and faxed them to the funding body (although original documents were explicitly required). Fortunately for me, it worked out fine and I could hand in the original documents later. I received the first payment in October.

My key message in terms of applying for scholarships is:

Be aware about the guidelines of what is needed to put into a funding proposal. A funding proposal is similar to a research proposal, it needs to contain what type of problem is addressed and how you are planning to address this problem methodologically. It needs to become clear that your research project is feasible within the timeframe of a Ph.D., which is usually three years. Deadlines may seem to be an obvious thing to consider when applying for funding. However, you really need to consider deadlines not only when applying for funding but also in responding to the funding body by sending a signed copy of the confirmed contract back to the funding body (don't go on holiday during that time).

I would also like to send a message of encouragement to those who do not receive funding straight away – You usually are able to apply year after year for funding. Hence, if you are not awarded it first time around, DO apply again! Your chances will definitely be higher than if you don't apply.

Peter (final year student in marketing)

Private organizations

A multitude of private sector companies offer opportunities for funding. This could either take the form of the company sponsoring your degree (employee sponsorship), the company offering you sponsorship in return for some research work or patent rights (research sponsorship), or the company offering scholarships in goodwill (corporate social responsibility). Since the companies are varied and scholarships are often offered on an opportunistic basis, it is not possible to provide a comprehensive overview here. However, some of the private sector organizations that have offered postgraduate studentships in the past include:

- British Telecom;
- BAE systems;
- Simul8;
- Dytech;
- IBM;
- Metso.

Opportunities depend on the research field and the nature of the work. From our experience, corporate sponsorship is most common in applied fields like engineering, the natural sciences and computer sciences, while they are less likely in the humanities and social sciences. You always have to think, 'What's in it for the company?' (See Daniel's case example in Chapter 4, p. 71, for the types of issue involved in a private–public partnership.)

Self-funding

Not all of you will be able to enjoy the advantages of being funded by your department/university, a government body or a private organization. If you are unable to obtain funding but are still keen to complete a doctorate, you will need to find an alternative solution. If you are lucky, you will either have enough savings to get you through the three to four years of completing a doctorate or your family will be able to carry the – not insignificant – costs for you. If this is not you, you will have to think of appropriate ways to fund your doctorate yourself. In what follows we introduce you to some alternatives, which may work for you. According to the Council of Graduate Schools (2004), doctoral students in the humanities are more likely to hold teaching positions during their degree than those in other fields, while those in physical sciences, engineering and maths are more likely to hold research posts.

Teaching/research assistantships

Teaching is not only a great source of teaching skills and experience for your future academic career (see also Chapter 9, and Chris's story on p. 121), but potentially also a source of funding for your doctorate. **Teaching assistants** generally receive funding from their university/department in exchange for taking on teaching duties, but you may also find yourself teaching at a different university to supplement your income. Regardless of whether you teach at your home institution or not, you need to be aware that teaching work is not strictly limited to time spent actually teaching classes, as there are a host of other responsibilities associated with teaching. As a teaching assistant you are likely to be responsible for a complete undergraduate module in your discipline (doctoral students are less likely to be involved in teaching at the postgraduate level, although this also occurs in some cases), which involves additional tasks such as having office hours and offering one-on-one or group tuition, administering exams, running seminars and tutorials for the students, marking assignments and exams, and providing lab assistance, as well as various administrative duties (which might include replying to countless student emails and uploading materials on e-learning forums).

As already explained in Chapter 5, most UK universities adhering to good practice and high-quality standards require teaching staff to enrol in a peda-gogic teaching programme (in case you do not already possess one). This is especially true for teaching assistants who occupy a full teaching position within the department. Although this is an excellent opportunity for profes-sional development, which is generally sponsored by your department or uni-versity, you also need to be aware that a teaching certificate will impose an additional workload on you, which you will need to fit in to your timetable. Moreover, as a teaching assistant you will be officially employed by the uni-versity, which means that you have to pay taxes on your income (unlike studentships that are generally not taxed).

The teaching load teaching assistants carry varies vastly. Although research councils and the National Postgraduate Committee generally recommend that doctoral researchers teach a maximum of six hours during term time, this may well be exceeded on a teaching post. If you are considering going down the route of a teaching assistantship, we thus recommend that you carefully review the terms of your contract in order to avoid unpleasant surprises and unfulfilled promises. This is especially true in terms of exactly specifying the tasks that fall into your responsibility and your remuneration for those tasks – you do not want to get yourself into a position where you either end up doing stuff you are not paid for or cause bad feeling for resisting to carry your share. You might also find it helpful to talk to other doctoral students in your department who have engaged in teaching duties in order to get a better understanding of the situation and whether you would be happy to take on such a post.

Research assistantships are similar to teaching assistantships in many ways, and are also seen as welcome sources of funding for a doctorate. As the name implies, as research assistant you will be dealing with research-related issues, that is collecting and analysing data, writing reports, and drafting papers and grant applications and so on. Research assistantships have both long- and short-term benefits. First of all, the skills and know-how you obtain through a research assistantship will also be a great asset to you (especially, but not only, if you are considering an academic career) in the long term. Secondly, being a research assistant may also be beneficial for you in the short term, that is support you in your doctorate – in terms of funding but also in terms of progress, if the research project you are working on is related to your thesis topic. As a researcher, you may be able to use some of the data, or utilize the contacts to facilitate additional data collection. You will also become better and more competent at doing research, which means that a research assistant-ship may prove to be more advantageous than a teaching assistantship.

On the other hand, being a research assistant can require substantially more time investment than teaching. Because the work is mostly project-based, it is often more complex and integrated and hence cannot be clearly scheduled like teaching duties. There may also be issues around authorship on papers or related issues, where you do much of the work but are not involved in the conceptualization and evaluation of the data, thereby not qualifying for some of the most rewarding benefits. We suggest you take time to consider your decision and carefully weigh the pros against cons. For example ask yourself:

• Can I use part of the work for my doctorate which would make the workload more acceptable?
• How much work is required and how much will I get paid?
• What kind of work will I have to do, for example only analysing pre-collected data, or collect data myself (which means getting in touch with potential contacts)?
• Will I be involved in writing papers on the research outcomes and also granted authorship?

Just as is the case with teaching assistantships, contract conditions vary widely and you need to specify the details in advance. In general you will receive a full year contract involving a certain workload. Make sure that the work you are required to do can actually be done in the allowed time you get paid for (and that you still have time for your doctorate!). There are often (but not always) opportunities for contract renewals, so look into these options before you commit, otherwise you may face funding issues again in your second, third or fourth year.

Teaching/research assistantship – A good starting point for an academic career

My PhD was financed by a teaching/research assistant bursary, which involved the delivery of lecturers to undergraduate students in my area of expertise, and to participate in ongoing research projects alongside my PhD research project. The bursary gave me a monthly salary which was more than what you usually will receive from other PhD bursaries (such as EPSRC or school bursaries) and it covered my student fees. People often do ask me why I didn't do my PhD the easy way, i.e. answering one substantial research question and doing nothing else for three years.

First and foremost my motivation for doing a PhD was to become an academic. While a PhD in itself might be the entry ticket, it often isn't sufficient. Employers in particular at higher ranked universities and business schools do not only look at your PhD, they also look at what else you did during and alongside your PhD. Being involved in additional research projects not only helps to further qualify you as a researcher, but also to learn the ropes of publishing. If these research projects fall into your area of research (which I highly recommend), it helps you to raise your profile as an expert for a certain area of research.

Another aspect is teaching. While running tutorials might help you have your first teaching experiences, delivering an undergraduate/postgraduate course is a completely different story, and as such is taken much more seriously when you apply for jobs in academia. If your teaching falls into the area in which you are doing research (which I highly recommend), it might also help to cross-fertilize your research. Engaging in teaching and collaborating on research projects with others also has indirect benefits, as they are much more willing to help you, support you, and provide you with information research and teaching-wise, which you might not receive otherwise.

Having been quite positive about assistantships so far, obviously there are also downsides, which you should consider. The process is much more time consuming than doing it the easy way (e.g. it took me 4 instead of 3 years to finish my PhD) and you are less flexible (if you have to teach a course at a certain time, you can't just fly abroad for two or three weeks to negotiate access or solve a problem with the organisation in which you are collecting data for your PhD). Last but not least, teaching is stressful and exhausting, particularly at the beginning when you are not used to it. It depletes the resources you need to enjoy working on your PhD research project (e.g. don't think that when you have taught 100 students in the afternoon that writing on your PhD in the evening will be a pleasant undertaking).

Having said all that you will have to decide whether this is something for you or not. I myself would do it again, and not only because it led to various attractive job offers even before I have finished my PhD, but also because I have enjoyed it. Isn't it boring to stare at your laptop and see the same research question for three years?

Chris (graduate in mechanical engineering)

If you feel that neither teaching nor research assistantships are exactly what you are looking for in terms of funding your doctorate (or maybe parts of it because you receive some funding from elsewhere), then you might want to consider engaging in other forms of part-time work.

Part-time work

In this section we draw on part-time work in the proper sense of its meaning (due to the amount of time required and the quite fixed time schedule, we do not consider teaching and research assistantships part-time work in its specific meaning). When it comes to part-time work, we can basically distinguish between:

1 academic-related work (e.g. teaching, research, marking exams, invigilating undergraduate and postgraduate exams, library or sports centre etc.);
2 non-academic work (e.g. bar tending, translating, transcribing, consulting etc.).

Generally, we conform with the views of Phillips and Pugh (2000) that it is better to do something related to academia than to work endless hours behind a bar – although there is no shame in that either. The advantage about work in academia is that it generally helps build your CV and tends to be better paid. Pay for casual teaching and research-related work varies widely, usually based on module or project content, but generally ranging from about £10/hour (low end research work) to £60/hour (premium rate). This hourly rate may or may not include preparation time. The good thing about casual teaching or research work is that you do not have a fixed commitment or wage, which means that you can be more flexible about which work to take on *and* will also be paid for each hour you work.

The downside of part-time work is that it can be difficult to get enough money to cover all your expenses, often resulting in students being forced to take on several jobs at the same time (as for example described in the case story by Samantha below). This will ultimately lead to a vicious circle of less time for your doctorate and lower quality of life. Hence, as suggested by Samantha, it is sometimes better to wait until you are financially ready to do a doctorate.

Self-funding – Lower quality of life

To be honest, it is a quite unpleasant experience to pay a great deal to do a Ph.D. because the financial pressure can be very high. Paying for your Ph.D. yourself doesn't only involve tuition fees, but also accommodation fees and various other expenses for your living. After I blew all my savings within my first 2 years of my Ph.D. (the UK is really expensive!), I was holding down three part-time jobs to try to keep above water. Ultimately this led to a lower quality of life.

After a few years in academia, I figured out that there are plenty of opportunities to get funding but whether you'll get funding or not is often not down to what you're capable of or how good your research is, but who you know or who you work for. However, a good research proposal and in-depth understanding of relevant theories does help a great deal. Therefore, you definitely should work on developing an attractive research proposal, while on the other hand trying to get to know the right people in your area – this may well improve your chances of getting a scholarship or other types of funding.

Unfortunately, I feel that there is often a hidden but common mentality among academic staff that self-funded students are not as good as those who are funded. This might not be true but often seems that way. So, in short I can say: Don't pay to do a Ph.D. unless you have sufficiently exploited all other options to get funding. Get to know someone in the area you're interested in and apply for funding. Convince them through a good research proposal that your work is worth funding. Don't rush into doing a Ph.D. Sometimes it is better if you wait until you're financially ready.

Samantha (final year student in medicine)

From our point of view, a sensible compromise could be to fully concentrate on your doctorate during term time (maybe very casually complemented by some teaching work) and engage in part-time work between terms as:

1 You will be able to get better paid jobs, especially in industry, because of the longer time period you will be available; hence, you will earn more money than if you engage in casual part-time work during the term.
2 Spending more time on getting practical working experience (e.g. through industrial internships, small consultancy projects etc.) will prove beneficial for your future career, regardless of whether you choose industry or academia (see Chapter 9).
3 During the term you will be able to fully focus on your doctorate and eventually will make better progress without being distracted and interrupted by part-time work.

However, an essential prerequisite is that you are disciplined enough to be effective and productive during term time, thereby enabling you to make sufficient progress to allow you to spend the time between terms in employment.

UK employment and international students

While most international students know what it takes to study at a UK institution, they are not always equally aware of what it takes to work in the UK. The good news is that, if you have been awarded a study visa (which is a basic condition for studying in the UK and means that you have the permission of the UK Border Agency, formerly called *Border and Immigration Agency*, to live and study in the UK) and are studying in the UK for more than six months, you are likely to have authorization to work in the UK subject to certain conditions:

- You can work up to 20 hours a week during term time.
- You can work any number of hours during vacations (any period where you do not have classes, revise for exams or do academic work, for example complete a dissertation).
- You can take up industrial placements as part of your course and do course projects with an employer.
- After course completion you can work full time until your student visa expires or for a period of four months, whichever is sooner. This excludes permanent positions.

Note: These conditions apply to any paid, unpaid and voluntary work – you can get additional information on working as a student in the UK from the British Council website (www.educationuk.org) in the section on Study Advice (Immigration and Work). They also offer a useful leaflet entitled 'Find your way to work' (published by the Department for Innovation, Universities &

Skills at www.educationuk.org/downloads/work_in_uk.pdf). If an employer is concerned about your right to work it might be helpful to show them this.

You can start work without a National Insurance (NI) number but you will need to provide one to your employer soon after you start. We suggest that you make an appointment with your local Jobcentre Plus Office for an interview as soon as you have a job offer. You can locate your local office at www.jobcentreplus.gov.uk/JCP/Aboutus/Ouroffices/index.html. Remember that you may also be liable for NI and tax reductions, so the money you earn is not always the money you take home. Currently, any earnings over £105 per week are subject to NI deductions (these are generally deducted from your pay by your employer on behalf of the UK government). Depending on your total earnings in the tax year (which goes from April to April of the following year), you may also be liable for income tax deductions. Currently, anything over £5,225 is liable to be taxed. Up-to-date information can be found on the HM Revenue and Customs website (www.hmrc.gov.uk).

Finally, it is *your* responsibility to ensure you adhere to the conditions of your visa. Not doing so is considered a violation of immigration law and can be taken seriously. Make sure you understand the terms and conditions of your visa to avoid unnecessary hardship.

Own resources

As mentioned above, if you are self-funding, the best case scenario is either having enough savings to cover all your expenses during the three–four years of your doctorate or having a family who is able and willing to support you financially. If this is the case, consider yourself lucky, as you will not be forced to engage in part-time work. However, you may wish to choose to get involved in a variety of projects to increase your postdoctoral employability (see also Chapter 9). Whatever you decide and whichever route you choose to explore, we wish you good luck on your journey!

7

Politics

*University structures • Why politics happen • Early warning signs
• Avoiding messy situations • What to do once you are caught up in politics
• Using the political game to your advantage • So – what's the verdict?*

Politics are part of life whether you are studying or working, so it should come as no surprise that universities are often a minefield when it comes to politics. Or at least that is what it feels like when you are low in the hierarchy. In this chapter we introduce and work through some of the more sensitive and politics issues students may encounter during their doctorate. We begin by introducing departmental and university hierarchies, groups and relationships.

University structures

If you want to understand hierarchies and power structures, it is important to understand a few things about the university you are studying at: the general structure, the staff structure and its operational committees. The structure differs from university to university, just as it does from organization to organization. However, there are a few core principles that apply universally. These are explained in the following section of this chapter.

The generic university structure

Generally, higher education institutions consist of three layers as shown in Figure 7.1:

- executive board;
- academic schools/faculties;
- departments.

The executive board of the university goes by a number of names and is sometimes called the senior management team (SMT), the university senate, the chief officers or the university council. Regardless of which name is assigned to the function, the executive board of the university is responsible for the vision, strategy and governance of the university. They are for all intensive purposes the leaders of the university and members generally include the chancellor, vice chancellor (chief executive), pro-vice chancellor, deputy vice chancellor, chair of the board of governors, university secretary (registrar) and the finance director. This executive structure is generally underpinned by academic boards and governance committees, for example exam board, teaching board, research board and so on (*Note*: This is a simplified view of the university structure and often the 'strategic' and 'governance' sides of the interface are managed separately in practice).

The next tier of the organization tends to focus on the academic structure of the university and includes the schools or faculties, which are each represented at the academic board. Usually each faculty/school is headed by a

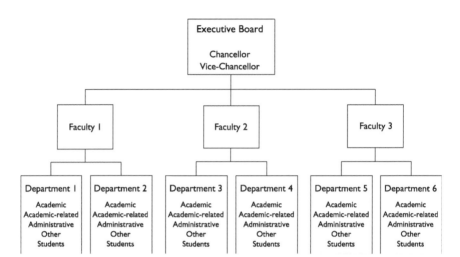

Figure 7.1 Example of university structure

dean, a deputy dean and a research director as the most common 'executives'. However, there are also functions that have responsibilities across faculties such as the directors of undergraduate, postgraduate and doctoral studies.

The lowest tier consists of the departments or academic (research) groups within each faculty that represent the lowest form of structural governance. In order to make things even more complex in most universities, you will also find separate research centres or institutes that are often interdisciplinary in their nature (if not across faculties) and are headed by a director who also belongs to a department or academic group, at least formally.

Finally, this outlined generic academic structure is of course supported by administrative personnel on all hierarchy levels either in central functions such as finance, real estate, human resources, communications and so on or decentral functions such as programme coordinators that are school-specific.

Staff structure

In addition to this organizational structure, there are distinct groupings at universities and it is important to understand these to get a sense for the hierarchy and roles that express themselves in any organization. These groups include:

- academic staff;
- academic-related staff;
- administrative staff;

- other staff;
- students.

Academic staff comprises of professors, readers, senior lecturers and lecturers (or if you use the US-related classification systems – professors, assistant professors and associated professors; see Table 2.3 in Chapter 2) – the big wigs.

Academic-related staff consists of research fellows, research assistants, teaching fellows, teaching assistants and associates as well as lab technicians. This can include senior and junior members of the university.

Administrative staff includes office staff, personal assistants, secretaries and research administrators. Administrators are often thought as junior staff, since they are not academics; however, they have a lot of expert knowledge about the university processes and procedures, guard the diaries of the 'big wigs', and may even administrate accounts – so, do not be fooled, they do have a lot of power.

Other staff around the university includes catering, estates and cleaning staff, that is people who help to run the university smoothly.

And, finally, we have **students**, undergraduates and graduates learning at the university. Sadly, being a student firmly places you at the end of the food chain. This is because you need a lot from people (time, advice, supervision, resources) but do not have a lot to offer in return. For better or worse, you will be seen as a bit of a drain. Of course being a doctoral researcher is a little bit different, which is part of the difficulty. Doctoral students are unique and do not fit into any of these categories perfectly because – although they are students supervised by academic members of staff – they also often engage in academic-related activities such as teaching or research support. Hence, as a doctoral researcher you are somehow stuck in the middle, that is caught between two hierarchy levels within the academic structure of the university.

Why politics happen

Politics are a part of university life because resources are highly desired but very limited. Thus people try to gain the power to influence decision making in their favour. It is really about who gets what, when, why and how, and so power is something that is visible in all interactions. Politics are a normal and natural part of everyday life. People will try to influence each other in a number of different environments and situations, which is fine. The problem is that sometimes people try to push too far and gain too much, and will use unfair means to advance their goals. Often this means trying to influence other people's behaviour in ways that they do not like; in other words, getting them to do what they don't want to do. Unfair methods of persuasion usually include:

- bribery (generally by withholding financial and knowledge resources until compliance is achieved);
- manipulation (making someone think they have to comply).

These unwarranted means can then be used to make people do things they would not otherwise have done, things they either do not want to do or do not believe they should do. This may lead to people feeling vulnerable because they are being taken advantage of. All this would not be such a problem if you – as a doctoral researcher – were not pretty much at the bottom of the chain of command and hence most likely the victim of such unfair methods and behaviour by your superiors.

However, at this point it is very important to distinguish between politics and favours. You may do things as a favour to someone out of the goodness of your heart or to contribute to your department. This is fine and in fact some-thing you should do as part of good collegiality and organizational citizenship behaviour. Overall, you are part of this 'organization' and should demonstrate your commitment. It only becomes problematic if you are forever giving favours and never benefiting from them and are starting to feel that the con-tributions you make are far outweighing the benefits you receive from being part of the department, if you receive benefits at all. If you no longer wish to make these types of contribution but are coerced into it one way or another, something is wrong.

Nonetheless, we hope this brief discussion helps to illustrate that it is a thin line between cooperation and coercion. Try to make sure you stay on the right side of it because when things go wrong, they tend to get ugly. Scrupulously being taken advantage of or wrongly accusing someone of abusing their power are two things that are not going to go down too well. So we advise you to mind your own business, stay out of politics and power games, and focus on your work, that is research and writing your thesis. However, we are also aware that as a doctoral researcher you are expected – if not required – to contribute and commit to your department, which brings you on the slippery slope of depart-mental and university politics. Based on our own and other students' experience, in the following sections we want to provide you with some guidance on how you can avoid being involved, and what your options are if you do get involved.

Early warning signs

Power and politics are interwoven into the fabric of universities, so it can be difficult to see where politics start and where you are likely to get yourself into trouble. It is especially hard for newcomers to the organization to tell which scenarios leave you susceptible to being taken advantage of and which topics and situations are sensitive. You are likely to know very little or nothing about the work context and the history and relationships of people you work with, which makes it difficult to judge when things are about to go wrong. However, the more you get involved in your department the more important it is that you recognize if and when you are on the political stage. There are some tell-tale signs that politics are at work:

- *People distance themselves from a certain issue*: Do you ever feel like you have hit a brickwall? You raise a topic or ask a question and people start to look around the room uncomfortably or change the topic? Well, if people distance themselves from an issue or will not discuss a subject, there is a reason. People not wanting to get involved is a clear sign that something political is going on – they probably know something that you do not know, so unless you are very savvy, we suggest you stay out of it too.
- *Things look too good to be true*: Have you ever been offered something (maybe part-time work or a co-authorship) at conditions so good that it made you wonder why there was no competition? Remember, people do not just give up a good thing. You may not see the 'strings attached' but they are probably there. When things get sugar-coated by means of excessive compensation, it should peak your suspicion. Certainly, there are good deals out there; just make sure there are no ugly surprises.
- *Unexpected things happen and situations play out differently than you expect*: Has a professor suddenly left the department without much notice? Or have regulations around a certain issue suddenly changed? Were you surprised at an outcome because 'everyone knew' something was going to happen and then nothing did? Or that a certain person did not get appointed even though they were qualified for the post? Well, that is probably the force of politics you feel. We recommend you distance yourself from the situation before you get pulled in.
- *There is evidence of favouritism*: Did you ever witness anything that really surprised you; for example, John got the job when Susie seemed more qualified and had more experience? Or the time that Donal got the bursary although his proposal only got a C? Well, that is probably the influence of power you feel – and it is likely to provoke a reaction somewhere. Someone is looking out for someone else and probably for good reason. Do not stick around to find out what that reason is. If you do, you are probably already too close for comfort.

Politics are messy and difficult to uncover; you will need good instincts and a feel for people to really understand what is going on. Thus, whatever happens, the best advice we can give you is to trust your intuition. If it feels wrong, do not do it. It is often better to lose out on a good deal than to get caught up in a mess. In the following section we discuss and explain how to avoid these situations.

Avoiding messy situations

Think of yourself as a little fish without teeth in a big pond full of other fish. Survival of the fittest dominates and a shark is on the approach. If you want to survive, you are going to swim away as fast as you can. Swim, swim, little fish, swim! It is the same in politics. Lots of people are involved and some of them are pretty aggressive and will not stop short of getting what they want.

Unfortunately, being a student makes you a tiny little fish and you are unlikely to be able to sway things in your favour. In case you have not picked up on the core message of this chapter on departmental and university politics yet, let us outline it right here: do not get involved! And if you do manage to get involved, dig your way back out as quickly as possible. Politics are very sensitive and convoluted, which makes it very difficult to deal with them and creates the very real potential for the situation to get messy. So, stay out of it as best you can. Do not let others involve you and refuse to side with people publicly. Staying neutral is the best you can do.

If you are not sure whether a situation is politically charged or not, take some time to assess what is on offer. Take the following advice:

- Never ever let yourself be backed into a corner or forced to make a decision straight away. Any ethical person will give you time to consider your decision when making a credible offer.
- Take the information or offer away to digest using something like other work commitments as a pretence to explain your inability to make a decision straight away.
- Take all the time you need to give the issue due consideration and do not let yourself be pushed to make unqualified and immature decisions.
- Do not let others sway you into doing something you do not want to do. This also means, not making any promises if you are not sure that you can keep them. This will unnecessarily expose you to the influence of power and politics. And people will use it against you, be assured.

Sometimes it also happens that political players will try to pull you onto their side. In other words, they will ask you to support something that you either know very little about or could place you in an awkward situation. As a student you have the great advantage of being able to play the 'innocent' or 'naïve' card. You will often be underestimated and, although this can be very frustrating, you can also use this to your advantage. If you detect some tensions around an issue, pretend you do not see what is happening. If the person will not let you get away with giving no answer and continues pressing you, explain that you have not had time to inform yourself adequately or to form an opinion but that you will get back to them. This will ensure that you do not transform into public enemy number one by being pushed to support a controversial view about the department. It will also buy you some time to consult with more experienced (and trustworthy) colleagues about what you can do in this situation.

What to do once you are caught up in politics

Whoops! – didn't you read the first part of this chapter? Only joking, it is much easier to fall into political traps than most people think. In fact, *that* is the easy part. The difficult part is climbing back out of the trap. In this section we talk you through some of the common strategies for defusing political situations, including pulling back, finding allies and offering alternatives.

Escalating and withdrawing

If you do not think you can come 'trumps up' in a political game, the best thing to do is to withdraw. There is no shame in admitting that you are in over your head and rather than getting more entwined into a web of politics, it is often better to retreat. That is not conceding defeat, that is being clever. So, if you get into a situation that has more depth than you originally anticipated and there are nuances you do not understand, we suggest you opt for a calm retreat. If it is about being a member of a committee or group, resign expressing regret and providing valid reasons like alternative commitments and personal reasons. This does not mean you should back out of commitments you make; if you have committed yourself to an administrative role, you should continue with it if possible, otherwise you will be letting down yourself and those around you.

This is only specific to politically sensitive situations you cannot rise to and that are likely to land you in more trouble than they are worth. If the situation is more complex than that, then speak to the person or persons involved as soon as possible and explain that you are unable to continue your involvement. Again, justify your decision and explain that you are otherwise committed. This is what Sarah in the following situation should have done a long time before the issue came to a head. Unfortunately for her, it was not done and so the conflict escalated.

It all started to go wrong when . . .

. . . my supervisor promised me a full scholarship. All I would have to do is help her on some research projects and she'd make sure I'd always have funding. One hand washes the other, right? I was up for that, no problem. I was wondering why everyone else wasn't doing it too – But, hey, beggars can't be choosers. And so I grabbed the opportunity with both hands. The problem is that I did the research work and never got the funding. And because I was doing the research work, I didn't have time to do the paid work I really needed to do to fund myself.

I was faced with a couple of terrible choices: Stop the research work and lose any chance of ever getting the funding *and* pissing my supervisor off (who, by the way, signs off all my coursework and decides whether I'm ready to sit my viva or not) or continue the research work and risk flunking out of my doctorate degree due to financial reasons. Plus the various options in between. GREAT. I had no idea what to do.

I was so new to the university, so naïve, I'd fallen right into a big political trap and had no way of crawling back out without messing myself over or making a big mess of my professional life. Fantastic. I didn't know what to do; I had no one to turn to. So I did what most people would do – I shut up and put up. It seemed like the safest thing to do and I really thought things would turn around. Every day I just kept hoping that the funds would come through. I hoped and I hoped and I hoped. But the day never came.

A year and a half later, I had to act. I was no longer in a position to make it work. Grinning and bearing it was getting me nowhere. I sat down with my supervisor and told her exactly how I felt. It was really bad. I didn't hold back, she didn't hold back. All the animosity and resentment that had built up over the time and the sense of injustice I had been struggling with came to the surface and were fully expressed. I complained, I made accusations and I yelled. She made it clear that she thought I was really ungrateful and didn't understand the 'due processes' of the university. She said she had invested a lot in me and was shocked by my 'lack of respect'. She yelled too.

It was the worst possible scenario and I walked out of the meeting not only knowing that I would never get the funding but also knowing that I had just lost my supervisor. Whether or not my supervisor ever told anyone else what happened in that meeting, I don't know. But I do know that nobody wanted to supervise me or come near me for a long time. It took me days to pull myself together, weeks to be able to face the department again and months to get my doctorate back on track.

Eventually I had to change departments, adjust my research topic and work very hard to pull through *without* funding. Looking back that was the hardest time of my life – If I could do it all over, I wouldn't have ever agreed to such an informal agreement. I knew I needed the money, so I should have either fought for it from day one or delayed my doctorate until I had secured the funds to support it. Had I stood my ground, I think things would have never escalated the way they did. My supervisor and colleagues would have respected my decision and I would have never had to go through what I did. My supervisor wouldn't have had to either.

Sarah (graduate in civil engineering)

It is also noteworthy that it is generally not good to voice your political concerns openly. Politics are sensitive and expressing your perception of them will likely cause friction for a number of reasons. First of all, you may be the only one who is aware of the situation, causing unnecessary concern and grievance. Secondly, the person or people involved could get offended by your perception, which they may see as inaccurate and based on ill judgement, further intensifying the situation you find yourself in. Thirdly, by expressing a conflict to others, they may seek to avoid you in order to stay out of the conflict. This appears to have been the case in the example above, where nobody wanted to get involved with the student out of fear of getting associated with the 'troublemaker' and placing themselves in the middle of the conflict.

Seeking support and allying

Nobody likes being alone, especially when faced with controversy and conflict. If you wandered into a political minefield and any move you make may lead to a detonation, it could be useful to take advantage of existing allies or to try to make new friends. You are a little fish and what you want matters relatively little in the grand scheme of things. However, there will be people that are genuinely interested in seeing you succeed (e.g. your supervisor, close colleagues, peers) and increasing your numbers might help in giving your opinion more weight. Appeal to these people for help, advice and support. This is what Laura in the following story did. She did not know how to deal with the situation and so employed the help of her supervisory team in resolving the matter; in this case very successfully.

Thank Goodness that's over

Someone in my department was being excessively friendly to me. It was completely innocent but inappropriate and it made me feel uncomfortable. I didn't know if I was imagining things and misperceiving another person's kindness for something else or if my intuition was right and I was in over my head. I didn't know what was going on or what to do – I didn't like being around her anymore and that's difficult when you're working together.

The whole situation was really political. It was a minefield and I felt like I was heading for disaster. Part of the issue was that this colleague was working with me on a fully funded project – No longer working with her might have meant losing the project work *and* the associated funding. Whatever would happen, I was pretty sure I would be asked to leave the project. After all I was the one with the problem, right?

I was in a bad situation and didn't know how to get out of it. So what did I do? I faced it full on. I went to my supervisors and told them what was going on. I was as honest as possible and explained the situation. I made a point of making sure everyone knew that nothing inappropriate had happened. I didn't want them to think that I was throwing (very serious) allegations around and making accusations. Instead I explained that I felt uncomfortable about the closeness of the relationship and didn't know how to proceed without hurting my colleague's feelings and creating more discomfort in the team.

My supervisors were very supportive and understanding; they stepped in and sorted it out for me. I was pulled off the project and reassigned to another one, with the same hours and the same funding arrangements. The situation was really well managed by my supervisors, who explained the transfer through staff shortage on the second project. One of my supervisors also reminded everyone about the importance of departmental relationships and appropriate conduct between staff. Since it was done some time later in the context of a departmental meeting, with no reference to me or my situation, no suspicions were raised.

I'm really glad I said something. It was a critical issue for me and a core distraction from my work. If I hadn't said anything, I might still be feeling uncomfortable and spending time wondering about the awkward relationship rather than actually doing what I came back to university for – My doctorate!

Laura (graduate student in philosophy)

Running a scenario by another person can get you valuable advice and also helps you think through the situation carefully, analysing its elements. Having others lend you their ear and judgement can be very useful. However, often actions speak louder than words, and a bit more may be required to release you from your political predicament. For instance, while a colleague may ask you to share your office with his research assistant, your supervisor, who happens to be a professor, may be usefully employed to oppose this suggestion. It is much more likely that your colleague will yield to a professor's wishes than yours. It is the law of the hierarchy. After all, denying a professor can put them in hot water politically, something they are as keen to avoid as you. All of this goes back to having good relationships based on mutual trust and respect. See the section on 'Networking' in Chapter 5 (p. 101).

Compromises and alternatives

Sometimes it is not possible to avoid or withdraw from politically difficult situations. In scenarios where this is the case, we suggest making compromises and coming up with alternative solutions, which are less difficult or damaging to you. For instance, if you feel unable to commit to something you have already agreed to, it may be very difficult or even impossible for you to pull out without causing bad feeling. Say, for example, you have promised a professor to help with 100 hours of data collection. If you now leave the project, they are going to have to find someone else who is qualified and willing to replace you at relatively short notice. This may not be possible and could jeopardize the project.

Consequently, pulling out may not be an option (these types of thing result in what we call 'political suicide' because they destroy your credibility in the department/faculty/university and make things progressively more difficult for you because people cannot trust your words and actions). There is far less likely to be a negative feeling if you explain your alternative commitments, alongside your awareness of the difficulty this creates for the professor and consequently offer to meet them halfway by continuing involvement in the project at 50 per cent of the previous commitment. Often that is the right thing to do because it is the fair thing to do. It also cuts the resentment and difficulty out of the equation and thus resolves the situation more effectively.

Negotiate and fight

During your doctoral career you might find yourself in tricky or even messy situations that you were not able to avoid. And now that you are in the middle of it you cannot withdraw, you cannot or do not want to find allies, and making a compromise will be disadvantageous to you, not because it seems like a defeat but because you are involved so deeply that you would lose on all fronts. The only option you have left is to stay and fight, trying to negotiate the best terms you can get.

A situation where this is quite common is the clarification of authorship for joint publications. As we already discussed in Chapter 5, it is more often than not the case that existing codes of practice are ignored or not strictly applied. This has the effect that doctoral students at the bottom of the academic hierarchy are sometimes facing pressure from their superiors who want to be named as first authors no matter how much they contributed to the joint work. Whether you are happy with this is totally up to you (you might be happy to be on a paper at all because you could not publish it alone) but in general we recommend that you stand up for your rights – people will try the same the next time again if you do not take action the first time.

So, withdrawing is not a good option as you might end up being a kind of 'ghostwriter' for someone else otherwise. Of course ideally it helps to clarify the terms of authorship in advance but in reality things often run differently and in many cases the paper is written already before you start thinking of the order of names to appear on the paper.

Authorship is a difficult issue and one which academics often disagree about: Should you foster students to become independent academics and allow them first authorship, or is it a case of credit where credit is due? Hence, this is a good situation in which to use your diplomatic skills, for example by offering compromises and alternatives maybe in the sense that first authorship should alternate for the next joint piece of work.

Another situation in which the exit strategies for politically sensitive situations described above might not work to your advantage is when the bottom line is in jeopardy, that is when your financial well-being is at risk. This could be a similar case to Sarah, our graduate in civil engineering, who never received the promised scholarship. In general this applies to all situations where you are asked to do additional work for individual people or your department as a whole, for example research, teaching and so on, and are promised financial compensation for your efforts but your requests fall on deaf ears when it comes to collecting your money. Because you have lots to lose your best option in these situations might be to face the situation by negotiating and fighting. This is what William in the following story did when he discovered that his department did not want to pay him the promised amount for the teaching he had done for them.

Gentlemen agreement . . . no thanks!

I always thought UK is the country of gentlemen and that people will keep their word. I was proven wrong! It was quite at the beginning of my Ph.D. when my department was seeking my support. Due to the illness of a member of staff they needed someone to take over her teaching for an undergraduate module. Since none of the other staff members could fit this particular module in their timetables I was assigned to take over the lectures.

I was flattered to be trusted with such a high responsibility without even possessing the necessary teaching certificate. Most of my doctorate colleagues only taught tutorials and seminars and I was going to teach regular class lessons to students. I felt special, closer to being a member of staff than being a student. However, the initial euphoria disappeared quickly. Looking back, the biggest mistake I made was that I didn't insist on a written contract. They gave me their word and promised me to pay me for my efforts with the usual rate. Maybe I was too naïve or credulous at that time but I trusted them. Overall we were in the country of gentlemen, right?

Things had to proceed quickly since business as usual had to be provided to the students. Hence, I focused on my new task trusting that everything will sort itself out at the end. Since the module was restructured by the former lecturer I had to prepare the weekly slides, set and mark assignments as well as the end of term exam. All this was quite a distraction and a major disruption to the progress of my research. Nevertheless, the teaching was rewarding mainly due to the positive feedback I received from my students at the end of the term.

That is also when the odyssey of my troubles began. After being asked how many hours I roughly spent on the module I was told by the Head of Department that I won't be able to be paid the full amount since it would involve extremely high costs for the department. I was shocked. I didn't know what to say. It felt even more wrong since I helped them out of a tricky situation thereby neglecting my own studies. And I trusted them. I was fooled and that pain stuck deep.

I almost couldn't sleep that night but went back to see the Head of Department the next day to tell him that if they don't pay me I would refuse to engage in any kind of teaching related activities for the rest of my Ph.D. He didn't accept this at first but eventually we started negotiating about the amount of hours I spent in total. It was a tough discussion but I decided to be strong and insist on my rights.

At the end, I was paid for the time I spent on marking all the exams as well as for the contact hours with the students (i.e. lectures, tutorials, office hours) but I had to wait for my money until 5 months after the end of my teaching. And frankly speaking, the amount I received was far less than people receive with a teaching assistant contract although teaching a complete undergraduate module was the same effort for me. In the following years of my Ph.D. I became very careful when it came to helping out my department with teaching related work.

William (graduate in chemistry)

Using the political game to your advantage

The problem with political scenarios is that there are no straightforward answers. Things are not black and white. A lot of what happens and how you respond to it depends on perception and behavioural nuances. That is why people skills are crucial when looking to avoid political disasters and some people are really good at dealing with people. And, if you think that is you, you may just be able to use politics to your advantage. However, beware, you are about to start playing with 'the big boys'.

So, remember to proceed with care – pride comes before the fall! There are ways to be clever about it and play the game, and there are people who are able to use their diplomatic talent to gain some advantage over potential 'competitors'. This can include being looked upon more favourably when it comes to departmental bursaries or scholarships, assistant positions, funding for conferences and so on. In this section we give some tactical advice for the brave among you who think they can compete in the jungle.

This is not a section for the faint of heart. Where politics are involved, things are bound to get messy. The main strategies for getting what you want include bluffing, undercutting others and holding out for better offers. Each of these is described below in the context of the related advantages and disadvantages.

Bluffing

Bluffing is an age-old trick people use – and we concede that it can sometimes help get you out of a difficult situation and/or help enhance your position. Some individuals are very skilled at putting on a poker face and telling their 'opponent' that someone else is offering them a better deal to push up the offer currently on the table. However, we strongly advise against this tactic, especially for students. The problem with playing people off against each other is that they may well catch on to what you are doing and, unsurprisingly, people do not like being played for fools. In other words, this method can seriously backfire if you are not careful – before you get involved, think about what you will do if someone calls your bluff.

Undercutting others

The other thing people do when they want to come out on top is to trump or undercut their rivals. Offer the seniors a better deal and they are likely to take it. This could mean demonstrating that you are more qualified or trained for a job, that you have more knowledge or intellectual power or that you have more experience. On the other hand, it can also mean that you will work more or accept lower pay and fewer benefits. Of course, this means stepping on others' toes, and will make you pretty unpopular pretty quickly. It also does not tend to earn you respect within the department.

Hold out for better offers: negotiation tactics

This is probably the least offensive political move but depending on your negotiation skills can lead to drastic results in your favour. The basic premise is to refuse deals until they are sweet enough to accept. Of course this is a bit of a zero-sum game. If you hold out for too much or for too long, you may well end up with nothing. But if you play it clever, you can end up with a decent deal. And this is mainly due to your negotiation skills. Remember, people will try to get the most they can at the lowest cost.

The key points for you to consider when trying to increase your benefits through negotiating can be summarized as follows:

- Gather as much information as you can about yourself and the other party.
- Always make the first offer and make it extreme (to anchor your aspiration).
- Immediately re-anchor if the other party opens with an outrageous offer.
- Make larger concessions early and smaller ones later on.
- Make bilateral not unilateral concessions (i.e. do not negotiate with yourself by making two concessions in a row without an intervening concession by the other party).

More information on negotiating can be obtained from Fisher et al. (1981).

So – what's the verdict?

Politics are a difficult, messy business. If you can avoid them, do not get involved. It is not worth the risk because more often than not you will end up drawing the short straw. If you do get involved unintentionally, make sure you make a clean exit or, if that is not possible, do a bit of damage control by avoiding getting pulled in even deeper. Last but not least, if you do want to play the game, make sure you are well informed, well prepared and proceed with caution.

8

Alternative routes to a doctorate

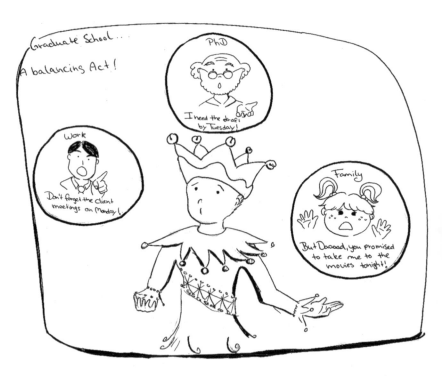

Part-time, distance learning and mature doctorates • Overseas and international doctorates • Executive or professional doctorates • Doctorate by publication

If you feel different from other doctoral students, then this chapter should be of particular interest to you. In this chapter we discuss some of the issues arising if you do not fit the mainstream full time on-site doctorate model. We review part-time and distance learning research degrees, overseas and international student life, executive or professional doctoral degrees, and the doctorate-by-publication. This chapter covers some of the main challenges faced by individuals pursuing a doctorate in a non-traditional way and is thus dedicated to people that fall into the 'different from the rest' category. Remember, different does not have to mean difficult.

Part-time, distance learning and mature doctorates

At most UK universities the doctorate is designed around the traditional three-year full-time model (a notable exception is the Open University, which operates entirely on a distance learning model). As such, certain assumptions are inherent in the model, which means that you may face some challenges if you opt for the part-time and distance learning route.

The first thing you will need to do is to find a way to absolve the first year research training modules (see also Chapter 2) that are part of most research degree programmes. These courses are usually taught in block seminars, either one day a week for two terms or several weeks in succession. As you are not based on site and quite likely also have other commitments to juggle, you may find it difficult to attend. If you cannot find the time to attend, find out about the support mechanisms your institution offers to circumvent this problem – it is likely that they have encountered this issue before and a satisfactory solution may thus already exist (e.g. video files of the lectures, a distance tutor, mentoring programme etc.).

As you become more involved in your doctorate, you often experience some role pressure as a result of balancing your regular job duties and your doctoral research. Do not underestimate this issue; part-time students often have to be far more disciplined than full-timers in order to survive their doctorate. You will need good time management skills to work out a schedule that allows you to fulfil your daily duties and find time to work on your research. Unfortunately, for most people this will mean sacrificing evenings and week-ends. As this can create some strain at home, make sure you discuss these issues with your spouse and family ahead of time, so both of you have realistic expectations about what doing a doctorate really means.

Once you have resolved the time management issue, you will need to start thinking about other practicalities. It is not uncommon for people to find it difficult to pick up their work where they left off, especially if some time has passed since they last visited it. Hence, it is important to introduce some routine into your work schedule and avoid unnecessary distractions – regardless of whether you follow a daily, weekly or monthly routine, consistency is crucial. Also, as a rule of thumb, the more frequently people are able to engage with their work, the more effective they will be, as they keep the research at the fore of their mind.

Being away from university often also means that you have less personal contact with your supervisor. You may find it difficult to access them remotely when you need advice and guidance, depending largely on their goodwill. You also will not have access to some of the more convenient ways of interacting, like being able to just stop by your supervisor's office to ask for advice on an urgent issue. In addition, you may sometimes feel left out of the loop, as you will not necessarily know what is going on in the department or the university. (Just like in any other organization, many of the interactions at university are informal and knowledge is shared implicitly. As such, not being there physically may mean that you end up missing out.)

However, there are ways in which these issues can be managed successfully, especially if you have a good relationship with your supervisor. You could have quarterly face-to-face meetings and bi-weekly or monthly conference calls (using VoIP programmes like Skype or MSN messenger means keeping the cost down and having access to a video conferencing facility more or less free of charge). Talk about both the research and the department to make sure that you stay in touch with what is going on. In addition, we recommend trying to attend key departmental meetings like research away days to ensure you remain linked into the departmental network.

Perhaps unsurprisingly, it is particularly mature students who opt for the route of part-time and distance learning. There are many reasons students may choose this path but often it is due to the personal situation, for example being married with children and financial responsibilities (see John's story on p. 145), which carries inherent issues with it. For one, you might find it challenging to connect with your peers, who tend to be younger, lead a different lifestyle and have different interests and conversations. Well, let us help you alleviate some of your concerns – none of this was a problem for John, who is a good friend of ours despite being in his 50s. Be open-minded and you may be surprised who you connect with.

Another cliché you will have to contend with is the assumption that mature students are more resistant to supervisory guidance, especially if the supervisor is younger than their student. This does not have to be an issue and you may indeed complement each other – you bring the work and life experienced to the table, and your supervisor brings the research and academic skills. Remember, you are entering new territory and your supervisor is helping you understand the lay of the land. Your interaction may need some fine-tuning, especially if you are your supervisor's first mature student, but this is no obstacle for a constructive long-term relationship; rather it presents an opportunity for learning and enrichment (for both of you).

You may have been away from the academic world for a while, so will need to prove yourself intellectually, that is demonstrate that you are capable of producing a quality piece of research with up-to-date methods and concepts. This may be challenging at first but is also a very rewarding growth experience. Do not let your age or life situation be an obstacle; according to Phillips and Pugh (2000) the oldest doctoral graduate is an Australian, who was awarded his degree when he was 89. If an 89-year-old guy can do it, we are sure you can too!

Two case examples from international part-time students are shown below. Each has their own story to tell, so we will let them tell it.

Part-time is nothing for whiners

In my case it was necessary to do the degree part-time. I am a mature American with a supportive wife, two near-adult offspring, and a supersized Californian mortgage. Therefore denying my family two to three years of income just so I can endow myself with the title of 'doctor' would be a bit irresponsible.

Actually, in my case it would have been possible because my wife is a nuclear physicist with a robust income. But that also provided some of my motivation – I'm a plumber! Parties can be a drag. People would ask my wife: 'What do you do?' – Her response: 'I run calculations for the proton accelerator at (insert expensive hospital name here).' Then the inquisitive guest would turn to me and ask 'What about you?' – My response: 'I'm a plumber.' You can see the surprise in their eyes. I want to be able to say 'I'm Professor of . . . at . . .' so that I can be just as intimidating as she is! I am motivated but must retain some shred of my (macho) dignity by providing income for my family, meagre as that contribution may be. Perhaps this seems all too familiar to you. So, how do I survive?

Secret 1: Suck it up!
When I finally arrive home after a day of working as a drain surgeon I peruse the e-journals, collect and organise data, pound on my laptop; in other words for an hour or two after work every day I suck it up. Weekends are something for people who were smart enough to get their education behind them while they were young, they don't exist for me. I can hear you say 'oh that sounds like loads of fun'. Well if you want to have fun, grab your game controller and slaughter some aliens, don't do a PhD. If you choose to inflict a PhD on yourself while holding a job fun becomes a distant memory. Remember: Quick pain is better than slow pain. The quicker you can put this PhD affliction behind you, the quicker you will get to the fun part. For me the fun is seeing students squirm in the classroom: 'Pop Quiz!' – What will a PhD provide for you? Look forward and aim for a quick finish.

Secret 2: Well meaning friends and family are the enemies of my PhD
On occasion I will be in the groove of grinding something (almost) intelligent into the computer and my beautiful wife will enter my study . . . It would be best if those unplanned interruptions can be avoided, I'm not strong enough but you should try. Friends are those non-family members I used to hang out with. I'm not all that social so friends were a dispensable luxury in my previous life. But if you are normal, this will be a real problem. Just remember that every minute you waste with friends is another minute your dissertation waits. If as a part-timer you can avoid friends, great, you might actually finish before you retire. Little children! What can I say? Mine are at least old enough to wipe their own butts and blow their own noses, so this is a trial I do not have to endure. If you have demanding pre-school curtain crawlers, God alone can help you finish your dissertation.

Secret 3: Realise that the TV is the devil
Keep in mind that as a part-timer your enemy is the clock. It's a relentless, soulless enemy that must be defeated daily. Nothing is a greater time sucker for me than the television. 'Honey, the game is on'. AARGH! Three hours gone! Avoid it at all costs.

Secret 4: Never give up, never surrender
That was Tim Allen's tagline in the Star Trek rip-off movie 'Galaxy Quest'. It is often a tiring and discouraging task to cram a huge amount of data into my petulant laptop and have something intelligent, let alone academic, emerge. Perseverance is a necessary character trait without which no part-timer will ever finish. Not having the sense to know when to quit is a good thing for the part-timer.

Secret 5: Don't do a part-time PhD
By now you will have noticed that this is written in the present tense. In other words, I'M NOT FINISHED YET. Five years and I am ABD (that's All But Dissertation if you're not up to speed on PhD lingo yet). But I will – Assuming I'm not delusional. However, if I had it to do over again I would have figured out some way to do this full time.

John (final year student in politics)

Of course each learning experience is unique, especially when it comes to distance-learning. Here is another viewpoint.

Being part-time is about taking initiative

Doing a PhD part-time and at a distance is quite a different experience from that of a full-time resident student. No quick knock at your supervisor's door for a brief question or exchange of ideas, no getting solace from the fact that there are two other students pulling an all-nighter in the room next door because their deadlines are looming, just like yours . . . If the PhD in general is a very lonely experience, doing it at a distance is even lonelier. Especially when you're balancing job, family, kids, among other things.

One of the most important hurdles I think is discipline and time-management. Once I learnt to establish some self-discipline, found out when I was most effective (peak productivity levels), and committed to some set work times that work best with my weekly routine, I found that I was getting my work done – on time. Moreover, I found that trying not to go without working for long stretches of time was best since it always took a long time to get going again after a long break.

The worst part of the long distance experience is the long waiting times. You send stuff to people for feedback and then wait . . . and wait . . . and wait . . . You're not sure when to send a reminder, how much to insist, why there's no sign of life, etc . . . It gets a bit awkward sometimes. But you learn to insist and fight for your needs and rights. You do sometimes get into some awkward situations though, so consider yourself warned!

Because of the isolation of the long distance experience, added to the slow pace of a part-time program, you do sometimes feel left out and have no idea what's happening in that part of the world (let alone the department and the university!). I have learnt that you always have to take the initiative to make contact with as many people as possible, keep yourself updated on news, and make a point of meeting with as many people as possible when you visit. That helps some.

Finally, if the whole PhD experience didn't also have its rewards, no one would persevere through its challenges and isolation: Nothing like the exhilaration of getting a good piece of writing done after hours and hours of research and hard work; nothing like the satisfaction of a very tough Professor telling you that your work is of very high standard; nothing like getting closer and closer to your goals . . .

Anne (final year student in language studies)

You might also want to read about Unwin's (2007) reflections on supervising distance-based Ph.D. students that provides some further information on dealing with particular challenges of distance learning doctorates.

Overseas and international doctorates

As an international student, you have to think about a few additional issues. This especially includes finding a way to cover the high student fees, and the possibility of culture shock and homesickness. Financially, the student fees are important to consider for a number of reasons. First of all, since international student fees are not subsidized by the UK government, they can be up to three times as much as UK/EU student fees (international postgraduate students will pay on average £10,000 per year for fees alone, and on top of that have to calculate around £8,000 per annum for modest living expenses). Secondly, there tend to be fewer scholarships for overseas students, thus competition is fierce (see Chapter 6). You also need to be aware of stereotypes that suggest self-funded students are not as good as their peers (see Samantha's story on p. 123 of Chapter 6).

In addition, as an international student you will often be far away from home. This not only means that you are prone to get homesick and miss your family and friends, but also that you come from a culture quite different to the UK, which could result in culture shock (Dodge, 1990; Oberg, 1954; Schumann, 1978). Culture shock occurs when there are significant differences between your home culture, where you were born and raised, and the host culture, where you live at some point during your life. It can be quite a difficult and lonely experience, generally associated with feelings of discomfort and even displeasure at cultural norms.

According to Oberg (1954) there are three phases of acculturation: the *honeymoon phase*, which is a romantic period of infatuation with the wonders of the new culture and the excitement associated with the change; the *dissonance phase*, in which differences between the countries become fatiguing and you long for a return to known habits and accepted norms; and the *acceptance phase*, in which you develop routines to cope with the new culture and adjust, no longer finding the norms and habits of people in that culture surprising. After having been emerged in a new culture for a significant period of time and having acculturated, some people also experience a 'reverse culture shock', which is the process of adjusting to one's own home culture (for a brief summary and some coping tips see www.bbc.co.uk/dna/h2g2/A2848359).

Cultural differences that students often struggle with surround norms, the taken-for-granted assumptions and habits in a culture. For instance, unlike the more collectivistic Asian cultures, the UK has a very individualistic culture, which takes some time getting used to. You will be expected to be independent, both in thinking and in action. The greater good of the group is considered but the focus tends to be on individual achievement. Develop your own ideas and new concepts, be critical about your work but also evaluate the suggestions your supervisor makes (see Chapter 4).

In addition, the way people engage tends to be much more personal, with lots of facial expressions, hand gestures and some bodily contact. As much is transmitted through nonverbal communication like facial expressions and body language, and many things are implied rather than externalized through in conversation, it can be difficult for non-native speakers to pick up on all of the meaning the speaker seeks to transmit. In addition, handshakes and shoulder pats are common ways of congratulating and praising individuals. If you are not comfortable with certain forms of bodily contact, you need to make this explicit from the start, both to avoid uncomfortable situations and to avoid offending your counterpart.

It is also common for you to be on a first name basis with your supervisor and other members of your department. This informality does not change the nature of your relationship but is something you should be aware of to avoid being caught off guard. If you are in doubt about how to address your conversational partner, start by using their formal title – they will often ask you to use their first name (and as a general rule it will then be okay to continue using the first name for the duration of the relationship, with some exceptions, e.g. around students).

Moreover, many of the comforts will be taken away from you – different language, different food, different fashion and different social interactions. You will need to challenge your own assumptions and, although a very powerful learning experience, this can be difficult at times and make you long for home. Most students experience some problems in getting settled and making contact, which is absolutely normal. Be patient and allow yourself some time to adjust. However, there are ways to facilitate the process, for instance by researching the UK prior to your arrival. If you feel that your language skills are inadequate for a postgraduate degree, we suggest you do a language course to polish up your English. Universities often offer pre-course language sessions, which are invaluable ways of refreshing your skills – tempting as it may be, avoid falling into the trap of befriending only people from your home culture. Take yourself out of your comfort zone and force yourself to speak English out of hours – an easy way of doing this is to make friends with English people or foreigners that do not share your mother tongue, for example by engaging in societies and activities like sports.

There are also various norms about working life that you need to be aware of. Most British institutes of higher education in the UK operate non-discrimination and equal opportunity policies, which means that individuals from all backgrounds (cultural, religious, ethnic), ages and genders have an equal right for promotion based on their qualifications and experience. If you are from a male-dominated culture or from somewhere where women and men have distinct roles, you may find it surprising. If you are uncomfortable with any part of the interaction, you need to raise it with your supervisor as soon as possible – cultural factors are very salient in the UK and no one will take offence to a polite request for adapted ways of interaction because something opposes your cultural or religious beliefs. (We know people who will not shake hands with members of the opposite gender due to religious reasons – They often opt to wear gloves or bow instead – most of the time people will willingly help you accommodate your beliefs in a UK cultural context).

Of course being an international student also carries many advantages with it – living abroad is one of the most broadening experiences you can have. You will have the opportunity to learn about another culture, hone your language skills, make friends from all over the world and also be able to share parts of your culture with others.

How I acculturated

Being a foreigner in the UK isn't unusual. Indeed, the majority of students and faculty in my department are foreigners, and I think that adds greatly to the richness of my PhD experience. However, challenges can sometimes arise when different cultures meet. For instance, you may not always be sure how you're coming across and whether others fully understand you (or not).

When I arrived in the UK for the first time, after a 10 hour flight from Thailand, I was overwhelmed. Everything was different from what I expected and what I was used to, so it took me some time to adjust to the new situation. Food, living standards, infrastructure, people: Everything was different. I felt like the loneliest person on earth, having just been violently torn out of my comfort zone. But I knew I could rise to the challenge, so I decided to stick it out.

When I attended my departmental induction, I tried to make contact with PhD colleagues who were in the same situation as me. We spent a lot of time together, sharing our hopes, fears and expectations. This was crucial for me as I discovered that everyone felt pretty much the same way I did – I was no longer alone! I quickly decided to stay on campus not just because it was more convenient for me to organise but also because I knew it would help me avoid isolation. Looking back this was the right thing to do. Over my four doctoral years, I lived with people from 13 different nations and learned a lot about other cultures. It was great. However, I also didn't want to lose touch with my own culture, so I joined the Thai society at my university – I met lots of great people and made lifelong friends.

Based on what I've learned, I can only advise you: Don't isolate yourself and don't be sorry for yourself. Be open and take initiative to meet new people and discover new things, even if it is very difficult for you and you don't feel comfortable. Every beginning is difficult but don't let this put you off, as the payoff can be great. Doing a PhD in the UK was one of the best experiences of my life!

Christie (graduate in public management)

Executive or professional doctorates

There are many reasons why someone with a successful career would like to engage in a doctorate. This could be due to high academic ambitions, to facilitate company progression, or even to enable a career change. Professional doctorates are very popular, as they give individuals the tools and techniques to grow both personally and professionally. Indeed, they are often marketed as 'career propellers'. It is about staying ahead of the game by gaining the knowledge, skills and abilities to implement best practice.

Often executive or professional programmes are more flexible than regular postgraduate programmes, in acknowledgement of the fact that professionals tend to maintain their employment alongside their research degree. It is exactly these issues that create the stereotype that professional degrees are less rigorous than regular full-time degrees but this does not necessarily have to be the case. As with any degree, it is what you make of it. There is a minimum required level and a desirable level – you need to decide what is right for you at that stage of your life.

In this respect the professional doctorate can be seen as an alternative to the traditional Ph.D., as it provides the opportunity for professionals to gain a doctoral degree. Fink (2006) provides a basic comparison between the Ph.D. and the Professional Doctorate as can be seen in Table 8.1.

Table 8.1 Comparison between Ph.D. and Professional Doctorate (adapted from Fink, 2006)

Criterion	Ph.D.	Professional Doctorate
Orientation	Process driven Researcher seeking academic training	Outcome driven Practitioner seeking qualification
Content	Context of discovery Focus on discipline	Context of application Focus on workplace
Outcomes	Thesis New knowledge Wide dissemination / application	Project reports Advanced practice Narrow dissemination / application
Process	Entry through research Specific research training Individual	Entry through experience Applied action research Collaborative

The Doctor of Business Administration (DBA) is probably one of the most prominent examples of a professional doctorate. According to Perry and Cavaya (2004) it is a professional doctorate for managers whereas the Ph.D. is a professional doctorate for academics. Despite this distinction, the DBA – or other degrees such as Doctor of Psychology (DPsych), Doctor of Science (DSc), Doctor of Education (EdD) or Engineering Doctorate (EngD) – are equivalent to the Ph.D. in most respects, for example all must make a contribution to knowledge and be rigorous in their research approach. However, the major difference between a Ph.D. and a Professional Doctorate seems to be that the Ph.D. focuses strongly on the development of new theory in a particular discipline by preparing candidates to conduct highly specialized research whereas the Professional Doctorate focus on the novel application of theory in order to advance business practice through research-based management (see www.professionaldoctorates.com).

The great thing about professional degrees, with the exception of flagship programmes like the MBA is that the courses tend to be small, even smaller than the regular doctoral programme. As such, there is much opportunity for interaction with professional and teaching staff. However, because of the nature of being experienced and mature practitioners, professional doctoral students face various challenges. Though some are the same as for distance learning and mature students, others are specific to professional students with prior work experience.

One of the main challenges for professional students that enter the doctorate life from practice is to get used to the different lifestyle and routine that comes with doing a doctorate (see also Steve's story below). Usually you will not find fixed working hours as in a company and there will be no boss who tells you what you have to do (unless you have a very demanding supervisor; see also Chapter 4). As a result, you will have to define your own work tasks and schedule deadlines yourself, which is easier said than done if you are not used to it. Effective time-management is the key (see also Figure 3.1 in Chapter 3).

Meetings usually will not be arranged by online calendar (e.g. MS Outlook, Lotus Notes, Meeting Maker etc.); instead you have to make an appointment with your supervisor by phone or email. Overall, the atmosphere in academia is more laid back than in industry or consulting. But be careful not to be fooled by this. You need to work just as hard. Furthermore, you may need some time to get used to the bureaucratic university system, which requires more time to get things done. Try not to let that frustrate and demotivate you. How you can survive your time as a doctoral student is explained by Steve in the following story about doing his Ph.D. in the UK.

When it rains it pours – Doing a Ph.D. in rainy England

Before my Ph.D. I worked in consulting in the US. One day I saw my older colleague trying to sign a document and noticed his right hand shaking. He couldn't control it. I wanted to avoid burning out like that so I decided to do something else. The alternative was pretty obvious – working in global headquarters of Company X, I noticed that not only was I the youngest, but also that everybody in the senior management had a PhD. So I decided to get one. A couple of weeks later I accepted a scholarship from England, crossed the pond and picked up the research topic from my M.A. thesis.

I tell you – it *was* a change. Imagine you work in one of the most competitive industries in the world and then you move to one of the most laid-back places possible – academia. Then add plenty of politics behind the curtains, mind-boggling admin and general reluctance to change. What you get is the summary of my two-year-and-four-month-long Ph.D. and explanations for the title – from slightly stressful, my life changed to stressful. Let me tell you why.

When you are used to hard work, deadlines, down-to-earth approach, and professionalism, the world of academia looks pretty much like anarchy. Your email account doesn't have enough space, nobody uses online calendars, every email has a different topic, filing of documents is non-existent, deadlines are virtually unknown, free-riding dominates. Setting up a conference call is akin to mailing 95 theses to Schlosskirche in Wittenberg, Germany. I could go on for ages. You know how it works. If not, you will.

How can you survive? Well there are two options, either you succumb to the temptation and become a typical member of the academia or you fight back. I tried the former (sweet sweet times) for a couple of months but then decided to do it properly. Old habits from consulting kicked in. I started commuting to the office every day and worked late, weekends included just like in consulting. I organised all the emails, setting up the date labels, filling systems, etc. Every article I read was filed in a special folder, titled and marked. I set up the database of references and updated it regularly. I invested time in learning statistical and typesetting software so that I could redo any document in minutes by simply compiling the code.

Oh, and I forced myself to create CD backups of everything every week. With daily backups of stuff I was working on currently. Remember, always backup! There are two kinds of people in the world – those who do backups and those who do not (but will!).

I managed to submit my Ph.D. before the deadline. Got a list of publications, updated my CV. And you know what? I'm going back to consulting. Academia is not for you when you are young, ambitious and used to hard work. It will just stress you out.

Steve (graduate in economics)

Doctorate by publication

For some time, scholars (e.g. Halstead, 1987) have recommended for the UK doctorate system to move away from the traditional 'one-piece-research' because evaluating academic competence on the basis of one piece of research is unrealistic (Phillips and Pugh, 2000). This is even truer in a time where business and society change more quickly and frequently than ever before, and it is incredibly important for research to remain responsive.

Hence, building a doctoral degree on a series of smaller projects, generally realized through separate publications, can be a valuable alternative route to the traditional model. Proponents of this approach argue that this not only better inducts doctoral students to the academic world but also enables them to learn and improve the craft of doing research gradually (there is a saying in academia that your doctorate is the worst piece of research you will ever do).

In addition, by running several different projects simultaneously, you also increase the likelihood of producing publishable work results (and to do so more quickly). This is something that is very important for a successful career in academia (see also Chapters 5 and 9); so why not start early? Apart from the positive effect of getting publications, it also spreads your written workload across your time as a doctoral researcher, rather than with the thesis, where most students are tempted to leave the writing until the very end of their doctoral career.

A doctorate by publication is in essence exactly what it sounds like – research results have to be published in recognized academic journals in order for the degree to be awarded. It is quite common that you begin by targeting good national journals and then increasingly build your profile. In later stages of your doctorate you will be expected to demonstrate your ability to publish in journals of international excellence. Generally the requirements each publication you produce needs to satisfy are well publicized. Most institutions require two to five publications of various standards.

Since doctorate by publication is a fairly new model in the UK – as opposed to Scandinavian countries and Germany where this mode is much more common and widely implemented – there are few opportunities to pursue this model in a UK context. In addition, there is no one standardized approach, which means that if you choose this model you need to expect regulations to vary between universities. Do not let this put you off. We think it is definitely worth considering this alternative route, especially if you want to stay in academia after graduation. Having a couple of papers on your CV will only benefit you. However, as you will see from Adam's story below, you have to make sure to inform yourself about the existing regulations and requirements at your institution.

My experience of undertaking a Ph.D. by published work

The published work route is still a relatively unusual way to a Ph.D. in the UK and this is an outline of my experience of it. The first item to consider is that most published work regulations (and the regulations will be different across universities) restrict those that can undertake this route. At my university the route is available to former graduates of the university (after a time lapse of seven years) and academic staff who have been in post for a minimum of three years. This restriction of three years in post did present a dilemma for me in deciding whether to pursue a traditional route (which I could begin immediately) or wait 3 years and then pursue the published work route.

In my case I initially chose to pursue the traditional route but changed to the publication route when it became clear I had sufficient papers for that method. The timescale for my Ph.D. experience is as follows:

- Year 1 Appointed in post as a lecturer.
- Year 4 Preliminary submission made to Quality and Standards Committee (QSC).
- Year 5 Letter confirming QSC agrees prima facie case made for formal submission of PhD by published work.
- Year 5 Original submission of Ph.D. to 2 external examiners.
- Year 6 New submission of P.hD. following feedback from external examiners.
- Year 6 November 2007 Viva with 2 external examiners completed successfully.

The preliminary submission made to the QSC consisted of a short statement outlining the main theme of the submitted publications (10 published papers in total). An outline of 1000 words plus the submitted publications can then be sent to the external examiners no less than 6 months after the QSC decision. Unfortunately the external examiners felt the 1000 word limit for the synopsis was too low to allow them to properly judge the submission. This led to the university amending the rules regarding the Ph.D. by published work to allow a greater word limit and a new submission was made in May 2007. This was accepted by the externals and a viva was finally arranged for November 2007.

In summary reflections on my experience are:

- Make sure you know the rules for this route at your university.
- Don't assume that you will finish in the minimum time (6 months). 2 years is more realistic and, if you are new to your post it may take up to 5 years.
- Make sure you have an experienced supervisor who can advise on the suitability of your publications, the format of your submission and suitable external examiners. This route is much less prescribed than the traditional route, so get good advice.

Adam (lecturer in operations management)

9

Career paths and strategies

The academic career • The industrial career • The hybrid career • The undecided career • Active career development • Being aware of stereotypes

Doing a doctorate does not only qualify you for a career in academia; it also qualifies you for a career in industry. No matter which route you choose after your doctorate, you should try to decide as early as possible. We know – easier said than done! Still, thinking about this and planning ahead will allow you to shape your doctorate in the way that best suits your future career path. In this chapter, we give some examples of alternative career options and discuss the related doctoral strategies.

We focus on *academic careers*, concentrating on research and teaching; *industrial careers*, including company employment and consultancy, and also touch upon working in government institutions and non-profit organizations; *hybrid careers* that try to combine academic and industrial career paths; and finally also include a section for those who have not quite decided what their career will look like. Before we conclude, we offer a summary of the most relevant activities for actively developing your future career.

The academic career

There are many reasons to do a doctorate but one of the most common ones is the desire for a career in academia. Most academic positions (and there are still a few exceptions) have a doctorate as an entry requirement; in other words, you need a doctoral degree in order to get a foot in the door. This means that if you are serious about a career in academia, whether it be research or teaching-oriented, you are required to complete a doctorate. Of course there are different types of academic career, each with its advantages and disadvantages, and unique requirements. We discuss them in two parts: fellowships, which include research and teaching positions, such as the postdoctoral (postdoc) fellowship, and full academic lectureships.

Fellowships

A fellowship is one of the most popular routes into academia. It is generally a time-limited appointment, normally one to five years, which is based on certain needs and requirements. For instance, a fellow may be hired to work on a specific research project or to do a set amount of teaching on a course. Alternatively, a fellowship is sometimes used as a preparatory post to give individuals a period of time to trial and prepare for a full academic post.

It is important to note that fellows are generally not considered full academic staff – they are generally classified as academic-related or research/ teaching staff, which carries slightly different connotations than being full term. In addition, there are different types of fellowship and these can roughly be grouped into three broad categories:

1 research fellowships;
2 teaching fellowships;
3 postdoc fellowships.

Before describing each of these, it is important to distinguish between fellowships and associate posts. The key difference is that fellows tend to have a doctoral degree and associates do not. This generally also means the former receive more responsibility and have a higher pay grade.

Research fellowships are very popular in academia. Being a research fellow basically means that you are employed by a university to work with an academic research group, generally on a specific project, for a set period of time. Research fellowships tend to last one–five years, and are on average two or three years long. It is contracted work and – depending on internal/external funding – fellowships may be renewed or extended after a set period of time. It is worth clarifying this point with your employer in advance.

Research fellowships can be funded by the university and/or department themselves but more often than not are funded by a research council (e.g. the ESRC, EPSRC or RCUK). Fellowships tend to be advertised as full-time jobs and involve an applicant going through a rigorous recruitment and selection process. Sometimes the individual may also be asked to contribute to grant writing, teaching and tutoring prior to and throughout their employment with the university. If this is something you are keen to avoid, make sure you carefully review the fellowship obligations before making a decision about whether to apply for the post.

Research may be limited to a specific research project or fall within a broader research area. It may also be focused on one part of the research process such as data collection, lab experiments and so on or touch all aspects of the research process – from conceptualization to data collection, data entry to analysis, as well as report and publication writing. Conditions also vary in terms of ownership over data and involvement in research publication. If these issues are important to you, and they may well be if you decide to stay in academia, then make sure you are well informed about the conditions before accepting a fellowship post.

Research fellowships are a useful first step onto the academic career ladder because they make you a member of university staff and as such give you a relative gentle introduction into the professional world of being an academic. They help you to learn about departmental and university processes, while giving you the opportunity to conduct more research (hopefully in an area that you are very interested in) and boost your publication record.

If you accept a post at the university where you completed your doctorate, it also provides a period of relative stability without a period of upheaval and disruption, as would be associated with a move to a new institution. A research post is also a great way to get a realistic job preview without making a long-term commitment; you may well decide you love academia but if you do not, this gives you a clear exit date, which can offer a nice clean break from academia.

Teaching fellowships are also popular, albeit probably slightly less common than research fellowships. Teaching fellows are contracted by a university to do a set amount of teaching per academic year (although this can sometimes also be assigned on a pro-rata or term basis). Teaching-oriented fellowships often aim to replace a faculty member on sabbatical, paid academic leave, or to take over teaching load while the department seeks to fill an empty academic post. Since teaching fellowships tend to be created to satisfy a specific need within a department or university, they tend to be shorter than research fellowships, normally only one or two years in length.

Again, fellowships may or may not be renewable after the set contractual period. Teaching fellowships are likely to be funded by the university and/or department themselves but may also be indirectly funded by a research council, through fEC (full Economic Costing), a procedure that allows academic staff to buy out their teaching time in order to enhance engagement on research projects. Teaching fellowships are also advertised as full-time jobs (if you are only helping to teach a module or contracted for a part-time number of teaching hours, it means that you are either a teaching associate or contract teaching staff); as such, teaching fellowships involve a full selection process.

Depending on experience, teaching fellows may or may not be asked to prepare their own teaching material. Inexperienced members of staff are more likely to be eased into a post by being given material, which has been prepared in advance. However, the fellow will still be expected to significantly redraft and reshape the work in order to offer a comprehensive learning experience to the students.

People taken on as teaching fellows are often also expected to have a pedagogic teaching qualification like the Certificate of Learning and Teaching in Higher Education discussed in Chapter 5. If you do not already have this qualification and are seeking to become an educator at a higher education institute, you will likely need to complete it while doing your fellowship. Universities tend to set a certain time limit for having completed the qualification, generally within two years of joining the university.

Teaching fellowships are similar to research fellowships in that they are contractually driven and conditions can be diverse. Although teaching is generally limited to a specific academic group (e.g. strategic management), it may also extend to a faculty (e.g. business school). If it is important for you to stay in one area or discipline, then make sure you understand the boundaries of your teaching. It is also important to know whether the teaching encompasses related responsibility like teaching boards and other administrative tasks. Regardless of where your interests lie, we suggest you review the obligations of the fellowship post before deciding whether to apply for and/or accept the position.

Teaching-oriented fellowships also allow you to step onto the rungs of the academic career ladder, thereby offering you first-hand knowledge about the world of academia. Since a teaching fellowship is a relatively short-term commitment, it does not bind you to any one individual, department or institution for long and is a great way to gain some initial postdoctoral experience without stepping too far outside your comfort zone.

A **postdoc**, the third and final type of fellowship we discuss here, is a research or teaching fellowship, generally with better terms and conditions than regular fellowships, aimed directly at people who have very recently completed their doctoral degree and are on the job market seeking a post for the first time. They tend to be 'breakthrough' posts that give promising young individuals the chance to experience academia and help prepare them for a full post. Read on and see what Darren has to say about it.

Why does everyone want a lectureship? Being a post-doc is great!

I'm in the third year of a two-year post-doc and love it. You're probably wondering how I managed to do three years on a two year contract – Well, I actually extended my post-doc. Post-docing is a great way to get experience in a relatively protected environment. You're generally part of a small research team and are pretty much shielded from office politics. Being 'contract staff' means that you don't have to invest as much as everyone else and (more important) that others don't expect you to either.

Sure, there are some drawbacks. Lack of continuity and job security could be an issue for some people, I suppose. However, I'm at a stage in my life where that isn't important to me – Plus, I trust the people I work with and know they would give me plenty of notice if for any reason they couldn't extend my contract. The way it is right now, I'm in a pretty good place. I have flexible working conditions and am well on my way to being a career academic. And a quick word of warning for the slackers among you – I don't work any less than a lecturer. I am contracted to work 40 hours per week but like most serious academics actually work closer to 60. The difference is in the type of work that I do – My focus is on research and publishing, rather than teaching.

And, yes, for you cynics out there – Doing a post-doc is a choice. I'm not just doing it because I have to. In fact, I've been offered a lectureship several times (and turned it down). I could be lecturing right now – But what's the rush? I've got a fantastic research project, which puts me in touch with some very diverse and interesting people, I've got a fantastic mentor, I've got a light teaching load and am working on top level publications.

I seriously couldn't imagine a better start to my career. I now have the time to research, which means acquiring data sets and building my 'publication portfolio'. Having a light teaching load allows me to focus almost exclusively on research, which helps to intensify the experience I bring to the table in contract negotiations. And in the long term I will be well placed for promotion because that is not based on length of tenure but achievement – So whilst it may take me longer to reach the academic career ladder, I should be able to move up it faster. I have several enviable datasets that will produce papers for

> years to come and I have fantastic industry contacts. In short, my post-doc is the cornerstone of my career.
> So, before you sign on the dotted line, ask yourself – What's the rush?
>
> Darren (graduate in psychology)

Lectureships

Most people who choose to stay in academia after their doctorate undoubtedly strive to become lecturers or even senior lecturers. This may be because they love to teach or because they love to research, or both. Regardless of why people strive to become lecturers, it is a tremendous achievement to be raised into the rank of full academic staff. However, it is often difficult to reach this step right after completing your doctorate and additional experience is often required. Specifically, this entails a certain number of research publications and a set amount of teaching. The emphasis on research and teaching varies based on the university.

Universities with a strong research focus tend to seek out candidates with publications in top-level journals, while teaching universities look for individuals with qualifications, experience and expertise in teaching. However, regardless of which way the scales are tipped, it is always good to have a balance of teaching and research activities in your portfolio. This leaves you with the greatest flexibility when making your ultimate career choice.

A general rule of thumb is that the better your publications, the better the university you can strive to seek employment with. Most highly ranked universities will expect to see at least two or three low and medium-level publications or one high-level publication (these can be 'in press', which means that although they have been accepted for publication they have not appeared in print yet). However, lower-ranked universities tend to be satisfied with one minor paper or may not require any publications as a prerequisite for a lectureship at all. See the section on publishing in Chapter 5, pp. 83–96 for more information on this topic.

A lectureship is the lowest rung on the ladder to a full academic career. Most universities will begin you on a time-limited commitment – three to five years – and then interview for a tenure (permanent) post based on your individual development over this time. While receiving tenure does not fundamentally change anything in a lecturer's role, it does mean additional stability and specifically job continuity. As such, it is highly desirable and people strive to get tenure. This is why you will often see lectureships advertised as 'tenure track positions'. However, it should be noted that the tenure system in the UK is very different from the US, where tenure is much more sought after and also much more difficult to attain.

So what does a lecturer do? Responsibilities vary from university to university but generally fall into three main categories:

1 research;
2 teaching;
3 third stream activity.

Research is almost always synonymous with publishing and bringing in research income. As such, it is a lecturer's responsibility to bid for research funding from funding bodies, generally by the means of research proposal and grant applications. This brings substantial income to the university, something that has gained importance in recent years, with the conclusion of the Research Assessment Exercise (RAE; see Chapters 2 and 5).

Hence, lecturers are expected to conduct high-quality research that advances knowledge, which is then disseminated through publication. This is often related to taking on and supervising doctoral students in order to investigate new research areas or explore existing ones in more detail based on new ideas.

Academics may also be asked to take on research-related administrative roles including acting as a research convenor, becoming a member of a research group or institute, coordinating student research and/or being part of a research committee such as an ethics approval board. Much of the research work an academic engages in constitutes professional development and often leads to professional advancement. As such, many career academics are very focused on research and give preference to it above any other activity – based on the motto 'publish or perish' (see Chapter 5).

However, a second and equally important pillar of academia is **teaching**. Teaching is the 'bread and butter' of academia because it is in essence how academic wages are supported. There are different aspects to teaching, including:

- module design;
- lecture preparation;
- teaching (lectures and often tutorials);
- contact hours;
- marking;
- administrative work.

Most academic staff will be expected to do at least some teaching throughout the year, with notable exceptions being individuals in senior administrative positions (e.g. Head or Dean of School) and staff on sabbatical (paid time off, generally to engage in research).

Teaching loads vary from university to university, school to school, department to department. Teaching-oriented schools will expect staff to do more teaching than research-oriented schools. Staff at UK universities generally teaches between two and six modules per year. This might not sound like lots of work to you but do not forget the additional preparatory work necessary. As a rule of thumb, at least two hours of preparation are required for every one hour of teaching – this may vastly fluctuate depending on experience level, expertise in the area and number of times a module has been taught.

Administrative posts are also demanding and include exam board, teaching committee and a number of other posts across the school and university. The more junior you are, the more administrative posts tend to get assigned to you. Although teaching is undoubtedly an important part of academia, the increasingly pressured and demanding academic environment has created a situation where some members of staff may begin to see teaching as 'standing still', that is filler work that distracts from the developmental work that moves their career forward, namely research.

Last but not least, academics have recently taken on the task of **third stream activity** (a term popularized by the Higher Education Funding Council for England, HEFCE; see Quotec, 2007). Third stream activity came about as a result of wanting to encourage HE institutions to put their cutting-edge research and teaching to use as a means of promoting corporate innovation, competitive advantage and public value benefits. Some see it as the academic version of the 'corporate social responsibility' and 'giving back' activity that industry has been engaging in for years. It is about:

- using academic research to advance knowledge that can be used in practice, for instance, finding ways to sustain local business, to reduce pollution in the area or to increase dialogue about a core issue;
- making research meaningful and offering practical benefits to the community;
- increasing visibility of research and raising the university's profile.

Although much potential undoubtedly exists in this area, both in terms of adding value and building important community contacts, academics may feel too overloaded to engage with this third and final theme appropriately. This is something currently being worked on and enhanced in the UK.

Read how Carly managed to become a lecturer.

On becoming a lecturer

Becoming a lecturer was one of the easiest decisions I ever had to make. Actually, to call it a decision is already a bit of an overstatement. After having finished my undergraduate studies in Biology I spent two years working in consultancy. During this period I started missing the intellectual challenges of academic life and felt that I needed to return to university. I then started a MSc program and became so involved in my dissertation research project that I didn't hesitate for a single second when my dissertation supervisor offered me a place on the doctoral programme. My answer was an automatic 'yes', both to the Ph.D. and to the academic life.

Despite also having gone through all the lows that are an unavoidable part of the process, I never considered swapping academia for a job in consultancy after completion. If I wouldn't have found a position at a university, eventually I would have had to try that route but that was always my second (or third . . .) choice. Luckily it didn't come to that as I was offered a position in my department a few months before I submitted my thesis. People say that having your first lectureship in the same place you graduate entails both advantages and disadvantages. On the positive side, the adaptation is usually much smoother, as you already know 'how things work' and are familiar with the culture of the place. The negative side is that your transition to member of staff is usually harder, as other staff are likely to keep thinking of you as a doctoral student. I don't think this has really been an issue for me.

Concerning my new responsibilities, I can only say I am enjoying almost every minute! I had already taught one of the modules I am responsible for this year, so that gave me quite a lot of confidence at the beginning of my teaching year. The experience with the students has been very rewarding and it is really good to be able to combine the two aspects that I liked about training – transmitting information to others and the interpersonal contact – with my research. I am doing what I always wanted to do and that makes me really happy.

Carly (graduate in biology)

Doctoral strategies for an academic career

Academic work is basically founded on three main pillars: (1) teaching; (2) research and publications; and (3) third stream activity, including consulting and related activities. In order to thrive as an academic, we suggest you try to gain some experience in all three areas during your doctorate.

Getting together a solid publication record is crucial for becoming an established academic. The notion of 'publish or perish' was already explained in Chapter 5 and when you work on becoming an academic you will experience the very essence of its meaning. The earlier you start thinking about papers the better. Having two or three decent papers published, in press, or accepted for publication by the time you finish your doctorate will make you more attractive for lectureship posts.

However, publishing is only one requirement. It is basically the output of doing research in which you also need to be an expert. This not only involves knowledge in your research area and expertise in various methods and techniques for data collection and analysis but also some experience in grant writing, which is also an important part of doing research (no money, no research!). If academia is your ultimate goal, try to get involved in these things during your time as a doctoral student. If striving for this type of post, it is less important for you to finish your doctorate quickly than it is for you to bring relevant experience into negotiations. A different strategy could be to use a postdoc to build your publication portfolio and gain some further teaching and research experience (see Darren's story on p. 160 above).

Just the same, teaching experience is essential if wishing to become a professional scholar. If you already know that you want to travel further along the academic road after your doctorate, we suggest you try to get involved in teaching and teaching-related activities (see above) during your doctorate. You should also use the opportunity to obtain a qualification for teaching in higher education, which is now a prerequisite for being a lecturer at a UK university. Although you will also be given the opportunity to obtain such a Teaching and Learning Certificate during your first few years in the profession, it is valuable to have one when applying for such a post as this takes some of the load off at later stages.

Teaching requires communication and presentation skills that you can build by teaching students in classes, and also presenting and 'defending' your research findings and ideas at conferences and workshops. So, use that medium to improve your communication and presentation skills. In addition you can use conferences to disseminate your work to a wider audience and get feedback on it (see also Chapter 5).

The third element of academic work is applying your theoretical knowledge in practice, for example through consulting projects or some kind of community engagement activity (see above). You will certainly have plenty of opportunity to pick up this type of work throughout your doctorate – whether it be private research contracts or bits of consultancy work. These often come in through your research group and/or supervisor, so make sure you remain receptive to these opportunities.

Further information on pursuing an academic career can be obtained in the following sources: Ali and Graham (2000), Baxter et al. (1998) and Grant and Sherrington (2006).

The industrial career

What is a prerequisite in one area may make you 'overqualified' in another area, and this is often true for a doctoral degree in industry. Although there is no doubt that a doctorate may sometimes be an advantage in industry (mainly at later promotion stages), this is not always the case. It may actually be that having a doctorate means you are overly qualified and leave employers wondering why they should employ you on a higher pay grade and not just take a fresh-faced graduate instead (especially at the beginning of your career). In the worst case, you may be treated and paid like someone with an undergraduate degree, something you may find difficult to understand and hence deeply frustrating.

Having said that, a doctoral qualification does not prevent you from having a successful industrial career and may actually help you to progress through the career rungs more quickly. There are three basic routes you can take if you want a career in industry:

1 company employment;
2 consultancy;
3 government (like) institution.

All three certainly have advantages and disadvantages and offer different kinds of lifestyle as explained below.

Company employment

Entering the industrial job world via company employment generally offers you two alternative models: either becoming a specialist in a particular area, for example chief engineer for mechatronic drives, or a generalist involving management and leadership functions. In order to become a specialist it is better to start directly into a specific position within a certain functional department of the company. Through various job rotations (but staying within similar job descriptions), you will gain relevant and very specific experience and competence, eventually developing into a specialist in a certain area.

On the other hand, if you are aiming for a management position it might be advisable for you to enter a traineeship or management programme for young professionals. Although smaller and medium-sized companies (especially medium-sized) have established such programmes and initiatives over the past few years in order to better compete in the battle for talent, it is still more common in larger companies. This also creates a different kind of choice: shall you work for a smaller (often referred to as SME) or a bigger (often referred to as blue chip) company? Again, there is no right and wrong choice; it depends entirely on your preferences.

Working for a big company not only looks good on your CV (most people will know the company) but also gives you the opportunity to link into its international network. On the other hand, you may end up being just another cog in the wheel, having limited responsibility, flexibility and influence. In SMEs hierarchies are usually flatter with more responsibility and power delegated to employees at the lower levels.

However, we still encourage you to select your first job carefully to ensure it meets your needs. If it is not quite what you imagined, you can always reinvent yourself – you are not bound to one company or one job for the rest of your life; finding your dream job early on just makes everything a little bit easier.

Whatever you do, do not sell yourself short. Do not take the first job offer you get and make sure you end up in a position that reflects your education and experience. This may involve demonstrating to your future employer that you gained valuable working experience relevant to the company during your doctorate, for example through consultancy projects and so on (see 'Doctoral strategies for an industrial career' on p. 171). This initial discussion is crucial, since it will be difficult to negotiate changes in your working conditions later on.

So, when you find a suitable job with an acceptable company (that should offer you good opportunities for individual development and promotion), we recommend that you stay with them for at least two years. It is an important learning phase for you, as most early career training programmes take six–twelve months to complete, and it is important to have some stability while going through this process. It also demonstrates to future employers that you are serious about this type of work and can stay with a company for a relatively long period of time. Since training constitutes a significant financial and time commitment on behalf of the employer, they are unlikely to be pleased if you depart after six months or one year, that is before their investment has paid off. Hence, although there are national differences, changing jobs frequently can have a negative impact on your future career. Employers may think that you are not loyal and will run off as soon as something better comes along – unsurprisingly, given the significant investment employers make in their staff and the competitiveness of the labour market, they are often not willing to take this risk.

Consultancy

Consultancy seems to be in vogue at the moment and is very popular in all kinds of industries and industry sectors. It seems like everyone wants to be a consultant these days, with the term being expanded to a variety of different areas. The term is used broadly – you can be a 'business consultant' or a 'medical consultant', but also a 'car sales consultant' or 'make up consultant'. The list goes on.

Of course with a doctorate, you will be aiming for a professional more management-like consultancy role. In that context, consultants are expert advisers that help individuals and organizations, generally the latter, to improve a specific area or element (e.g. a process) of their organization. In practice, this could include business improvement and cost-cutting, workforce professionalization and skill enhancement, and expert advice on individual cases, as is common in the medical profession.

Whichever role you adopt, the pressure is on. You are paid for your expert judgement and as such are also expected to act like an expert from day one. There is no 'settling in' period or friendly advice from colleagues – more often than not, you will be thrown in the deep end. If that is a challenge you would love and an environment you would strive in, consultancy is for you. Basically, there are two types of consultant:

1 external consultants;
2 internal consultants.

Although the former is more popular, the latter is also increasingly in style with large corporations, who prefer to keep their experts in-house. Some companies are actually bringing their consultants back in-house (something known as in-sourcing). However, the worlds of internal and external consultancy are not too far apart. Indeed, they tend to do similar work and approach that work in a similar way.

Consulting brings a certain image to mind. Constantly on the go, travelling all over the country or world, staying in hotels more than their own home, with a suitcase always packed, and ready for 'deployment' whenever the mobile rings. Consultancy is a peculiar form of employment. You go where your clients are. That means that:

- you do not have a fixed set of work colleagues you work with on a daily basis;
- you do not have an office to call your own;
- your laptop is your best friend;
- you have a mobile office on your phone (or, more likely, your PDA or BlackBerry);
- you have several different access cards and IDs;
- you know the best coffee places and restaurants at most airports and train stations.

Travel makes days and evenings long, especially Mondays and Fridays, and project work means tough deadlines, which could involve working through the weekends on occasion. Although this paragraph really caricaturizes consultants, many of these conditions will apply. If you enjoy an intense working environment where you stretch yourself almost on a daily basis and if you thrive under pressure (eustress), you will love consulting – there is no business with a steeper learning curve.

Depending on your ambitiousness and lifestyle aspirations, you may choose to work for a different type of consultancy – either big or small – or even seek self-employment. The big international consultancies tend to be well known and respected, thereby attracting large clients, lucrative contracts and offering very competitive pay schemes. However, they are also very demanding and often operate on principles of 'dog eat dog' or 'grow or go' competitiveness. Small companies tend to retain their clientele through strong relationships, bespoke service and highly focused expertise. The working environment also tends to be more personal, with you working closely with a number of individuals within the consultancy and thus getting to know your colleagues well. However, small consultancies do not tend to have the same budget for pay and development as large firms and as such do not tend to be as competitive in what they offer their employees.

The flipside of the coin is, of course, self-employment. If you like to be your own boss and are ready to embrace what this means in real terms, you may wish to steer away from company employment and offer your services on a one-to-one basis. If you choose to go down this route, you need to be aware that it is a difficult path to travel. You need to have credibility with clients. This means strong experience, good skills and abilities, a range of industry contacts and impressive interpersonal skills. You need to be well rounded and able to address the diverse needs of clients.

In addition, consultancy has attracted substantial criticism in recent years. Industry representatives and management scholars criticize the extortionately high cost of consultancy work, including rumours of overcharging and mis-charging, low quality of advice and service, vague project plans, poor return on investment, questionable ethical practice – notably dependency creation (i.e. creating dependency on consultancy expertise in such a way that clients cannot take the work forward themselves), and using standardized 'off-the-shelf' packages rather than offering individual advice. In response to this, many large reputable consultancies have engaged with the topic of corporate social responsibility and now guarantee clients a 'value-add' service. In other words, consultants will only accept and execute projects that will allow them to add value to an organization.

Consultancy is a profession with high burnout (job exhaustion) and turn-over (job attrition). Few people stay in consultancy for long; generally invest-ing a few years at the start of their career in order to earn good money, gain relevant experience and propel their career (see Steve's story below). Some people also use it as a mechanism for changing profession, spending a few years in consultancy while reshaping their career trajectory. This reflects some of the advantages of consultancy, which includes strong autonomy in decision making. Indeed, some might even argue that junior people are given too much responsibility and latitude in a consultancy context. But if you love demanding work, you will see your share of challenges in consultancy.

More information on pursuing a career in management consulting can, for example, be obtained through Wetfeet (2006).

It is about time for some action: Joining a consultancy after graduation

For a long time I wanted, or at least could imagine, staying in academia after graduation. After all that was the whole point of doing a doctorate and going through this hassle – Or at least for me it was.

However, some time around the end of my second year as a doctoral student, I got fed up with the endless reading and writing involved in doing research. I'd managed to publish a couple of papers in good journals and had gone to various international conferences. So, there was no challenge in that anymore. I felt the need to escape the laissez-faire and isolated world of academia. I was sick and tired of begging people for interviews and to fill in questionnaires so I could have some data to work with. No, I was ready for the real thing – Real business meetings, real impact.

The problem was that for most graduate jobs in industry I was far too overqualified with a PhD – that's why I ended up in consulting. At least you get paid well for working late and travelling around the world. If you like hotel rooms, this is the ideal job for you. I could build on my initial project experience and, as opposed to other industries, publication experience and abilities are welcome here as well. There is no job with a steeper learning curve than consulting. The motto is 'learning-by-doing' and project work is part of your life, almost from day one.

My personal opinion is that academia is not for you when you are young, ambitious, eager to work hard, and trying to turn the big wheel. Not to mention the money. However, you won't have the freedom to do as you please that you have in academia, and this can be very tempting as well. So, I guess, as with most things in life, you got to look deep inside yourself and make a choice. I opted for industry but that doesn't mean that I can't imagine going back to academia in a few years.

Chris (graduate in mechanical engineering)

Government institutions and non-profit organizations

Government institutions and non-profit organizations are unique organizations. Government agencies are driven by public and political agendas, while non-profit organizations typically focus on satisfying one specific social need, thereby reinvesting any profit in satisfying this need, rather than gaining profit themselves. Essentially, a career in government or the NFP (not-for-profit) sector is like any other job in industry. The difference is that instead of working for a commercial organization, you work for a government department or a charitable organization.

The nature of these organizations means that they have low margins and thus need to keep costs down, something especially true for NFP organizations. This has implications for the way these organizations are run and ultimately the conditions of employment. Civil servants, individuals employed full time by the government (and there are often also civilian contractors who work with government), tend to have a lower pay grade than they would in industry. However, they tend to have very good benefits, including a strong pension, good job security, a generous allowance of vacation days, a working week of less than 40 hours. The workload is similar to that working in a company (although some people might disagree with this point, arguing that civil servants experience less pressure than their industrial counterparts since they are not subject to the same commercial pressures).

These conditions are similar for charitable organizations with the exception that many employees are actually unpaid volunteers who are doing this work pro bono, that is free of charge. Of course this is a completely different scenario and not something we can cover in this book due to space restrictions. If you are a paid employee with a NFP organization, your workload and working conditions will vary widely depending on your organization. However, in general, these will be better than industry conditions, albeit this likely reflected in pay and benefits. The work is very rewarding, since the organization (just like the government) seeks to satisfy public value and social goals. It has been suggested that the nature of the work in the government and NFP sector tends to attract a certain type of individual, namely those with a higher social consciousness.

Interesting, there is also an observable effect, termed the revolving door principle (see Maxwell, 2001), which sees people moving from civil service into industry and back. Thus, choosing one path does not restrict you to this path forever. More information on careers in government and related professions can, for example, be found in Axelrod-Contrada (2003).

Doctoral strategies for an industrial career

If you are going to start working for a company after your doctorate, publications and research experience are most likely to be less important than in academia. Publications could be valuable in terms of increasing your industry profile and certainly will not put you at a disadvantage. This is especially true in consulting where increased visibility is attractive.

Teaching also brings useful skills with it in terms of presentation and interpersonal competence; however, it is not likely to be directly relevant. Nevertheless, in industry you need to be credible and convincing if you want people to take you seriously and invest in you.

What is important if you seek a career in industry is not to spend too long doing your doctorate (otherwise you may be too old) and to have some practical experience, preferably some time spent in industry. This is similar for the three alternative industrial routes we described above. People in industry tend to be highly sceptical of people in academia, who they see as abstract intellectuals with little real world relevance; often the attitude is that academics teach without having any real experience, which partially invalidates their efforts: 'Go out into industry, you know, go do something useful for a while'.

So, if you wish to go into industry or return to industry, it is important to keep a foot in the door. Ensure you have relevant experience to take to the table. You will certainly have plenty of opportunity to pick up this type of work throughout your doctorate – whether it be private research contracts or bits of consultancy work. These often come in through your research group and/or supervisor, so make sure you remain open to these opportunities.

Also remember to keep your industry knowledge and qualifications up to date. The last thing you will want to do after completing your doctorate is to do an expensive three-year professional qualification. It is important to know that there are often developmental funds that can help you facilitate efforts in this area. Make sure you explore all the extra employment avenues and educational support facilities your university offers.

The hybrid career

Hybrid careers are those careers that combine principles of academia with principles of practice; in other words, they try to merge industry and academia. This includes, for instance, scientific, academic or research-based consultancies, as well as scientific bodies and councils, and various professional research institutes. The diversity of jobs that constitute a 'hybrid' career means that we cannot discuss each in detail here. However, if you are interested in alternative careers, we suggest that you speak to your career adviser (generally universities provide this as a free service to students and alumni), who will be able to provide you with much more information about this topic.

In general, hybrid careers demonstrate a little more flexibility than industry jobs but less than academia (see Jennifer's story below). Autonomy in decision making tends to be high, the intellectual challenge strong and ethics positive. Diversity of work and workload very much depends on your employing organization but again lies somewhere between academia and industry. Pay, promotion and vacation days tend to reflect workload.

The life after the Ph.D.: A post-doc with the Center for Applied Research[1]

The Center for Applied Research (CAR) is a global, not-for-profit institution based in the United States, with various branches in Europe and in Asia. CAR's mission is to advance the understanding, practice, and development of leaders for the benefit of society. Founded in the late 1970s, CAR engages in leader development and research. As such, it caters to a broad audience.

I joined CAR in 2006 on a two-year post-doc contract and moved to continental Europe. My boss sits in our headquarters in the US, but I also have a mentor in Europe who gives me advice and visibility inside and outside the organisation. As a post-doc, I started working on two research projects, both of which were staffed with international teams from different campuses and included renowned professors as external collaborators. After 4 months in the job, I took over the management of one of the projects.

Even though the research team in CAR Europe consists of only two people (both starting out as post-docs), my job gives me many opportunities to collaborate with other researchers in the field, both within CAR as well as in academia all over the world. CAR has a relatively good funding basis for research, which allows us to attract high-profile partners that bring a lot of expertise and innovation.

Moreover, my work is inherently international, involves a lot of travel into all parts of the world, and has a high degree of diversity: In a typical week, I talk to one organisation about leadership research, prepare a speech for a

---

[1] Name annonymised.

practitioner audience, work a day or so on academic articles, and spend another two to three days on project related research. In CAR, dissemination of knowledge is seen as very important, so we researchers present our studies at many academic conferences and also partner with our sales team to bring new knowledge to organisations who turn it into practice.

I like this post-doc programme, because it is a wonderful combination of academic research rigor and practical relevance, gives me high flexibility but also accountability, and opportunities to grow into various areas – academic research, training, coaching, training design, or even consulting roles.

Jennifer (graduate in human resource management)

Doctoral strategies for a hybrid career

As described above, hybrid careers offer a huge variety of job opportunities due to their mixture of academic and industrial elements. It will thus be difficult to know in advance precisely in which direction you will go and it will consequently also be difficult to prepare for it: if you are seeking a hybrid career with a stronger focus on academic elements, we suggest you focus on the advice on academic careers. If, on the other hand, you are seeking a hybrid career with a strong focus on the industrial elements, we suggest you more closely follow the advice on industry careers. If you do not know in which direction your career will take you, our advice is to develop a basic knowledge and experience in all aspects relevant to academic and industry. If, at the later stages of your doctorate, you have a better idea about where you are moving, you can then adjust your doctoral strategy accordingly, that is focusing more on satisfying either academic or industrial requirements, as appropriate.

The undecided career

You do not know what you want? Well, you are not alone. It is not uncommon for people to use a doctorate as a 'buffer' period in which to decide how to take their career forward. Ideally you already know what you want to do after your doctorate, so you can tailor the process to your needs, but realistically we know this will not always be the case. Not knowing what you want puts you at a slight disadvantage because it means you will have to prepare for all eventualities. You may not be able to conceive a time when you will want to make academia your choice but a lot can change in the three–five years that it will take for you to complete your doctorate. Academia is a bit like Marmite – you either love it or hate it. (*Note*: For those of you who do not know, Marmite is an edible yeast spread. Try it for yourself and see whether you love it or hate it.)

If you still have not decided what you want to do when your viva is just around the corner or once you graduate, you may like to consider a hybrid career. It gives you some more time to make your decision but we give you that advice with a word of caution – indecisiveness is not a good long-term strategy. If you are in any one area for too long or spread yourself too thin, you are unlikely to remain attractive to employers. So, the sooner you can make decisions, the better for your career.

Doctoral strategies for an undecided career

The best way to work against uncertainty is preparation. This means while your colleagues, who have their sights set on industry focus on gaining practical experiencing and keeping their qualifications up to date and those looking to stay in academia work on research grants and journal papers, you will need to aim for achievement in all those areas. It means working harder during your doctorate but has the advantage of leaving you with more options after graduation by allowing you to build a greater skill set and therefore making you more employable. So, try to build a decent publication portfolio and gain some initial teaching experience (e.g. through tutorials or seminars) but at the same time do not lose sight of industry completely, for example try to get involved in academic consulting projects for companies and work towards your professional qualifications – maybe even do an industry internship.

Clearly, different people have different career preferences based around their knowledge, skills and abilities, as well as aspirations and motivations. Table 9.1 summarizes the preceding discussion.

Table 9.1 Evaluation of different career paths

	Fellowships	Lectureships	Company	Consulting	Government/ Non-profit	Hybrid
Flexibility of working hours	High	Medium	Low	Low	Low	Medium
Autonomy in decision-making	Medium	High	Low	Medium/ high	Low/ medium	Medium/high
Intellectual challenge	High	High	Medium	High	Medium	High
Diversity of work	Medium	Medium	Medium	High	Medium	Medium
Rigour/ethics	High	High	Medium	Medium	Medium	Medium/high
Workload	Medium	Medium	Medium	High	Medium	Medium
Pay	Medium	Medium	Medium	High	Medium	Medium
Job security	Low	High	High	Medium	High	High
Promotion	Low	Medium	High	High	Medium	Medium
Vacation days	High	High	Medium	Medium	High	Medium/high

As mentioned above, these future career choices will have an impact on your doctorate. In other words, knowing what career path you want to take in the future gives you the possibility to shape your doctorate in order to better fulfil the respective requirements. This is what we described in the context of doctoral strategies in this chapter. Table 9.2 below summarizes our discussion about different doctoral strategies in relation to possible career options in order to help you adapt your doctorate to your career plans.

Table 9.2 Overview of career paths and corresponding doctoral strategies

Career	Doctoral strategy
Academic	• Build solid publication record • Gain research expertise (literature, research method and techniques, grant application) • Get experience in teaching and teaching-related activities (includes official teaching qualification, presentation and communication skills) • Participate in consultancy projects, industrial studies and so on
Industrial	• Gain practical experience and industry-specific knowledge • Finish doctorate relatively quickly • Develop presentation, project management, communication and interpersonal skills (includes standard software) • Research and publication experience
Hybrid	• Combination of strategies for academic and industrial career with emphasis on academia • Combination of strategies for academic and industrial career with emphasis on industry
Undecided	• Combination of strategies for academic and industrial career

Active career development

It is never too early to start thinking about what you will do after graduation or to engage in active career development. In this section, we briefly review career seeking, which generally proceeds in four stages: self-assessment, career choice, job search and application. More detailed information is available from the diverse literature on this topic, for example AGCAS, 1998; Bolles, 1999; Parkinson, 2001.

- *Self-assessment* means taking time to think about (a) what you want to do and (b) what you are good at. There are various tools that can support you in this task (e.g. see Israel et al., 2000; Bolles and Bolles, 2008).
- *Career choice* means thinking about the knowledge, skills and abilities necessary for success in a career of your choosing. This could include

building additional skills, for instance with the help of the university career centre.

- *Job search* is not only about looking but also about knowing where to look. Good starting points for your search include *The Times Top 100 Graduate Employers* (Birchall and Allen, 2007) and *Britain's Top Employers 2008* (Clapperton, 2008). While general online job search platforms like www.monster.com host a greater number of job listings, more specific websites like www.jobs.ac.uk (academia only), www.cima.org.uk (for careers in management accounting), www.open.gov.uk (for jobs in government departments) or www.lawsociety.org.uk (for information on education, training and qualifications in law) are also useful. However, not all jobs are publicly advertised and virtual professional platforms have gained increasing importance (e.g. Xing at www.xing.com or LinkedIn at www.linkedin.com). Remember, it is not about who you know, it is about who knows you! The UK government also operates a useful career adviser scheme at www.adviceguide.org.uk.
- *Application*: Once you have found a suitable job, you will need to go through the application process, which includes an application form, cover letter and curriculum vitae (CV) as standard. See AGCAS (1999), Bryon and Modha (2005), Jackson (2005) and Yate (1998) for additional guidance.

Being aware of stereotypes

A final note on the topic before we move on to the next chapter: It is important to take everything we say with a grain of salt – although we have tried to present an unbiased view, we know all too well how easy it is for that bias to sneak back in. Academics love academia and practitioners love industry; that is just how it is. Different people, different views. So, to conclude, as a way of allowing you to understand these prejudices, preconceptions and biases, we present two very different (and polarized) perspectives of careers: The view of a practitioner and the view of an academic (as shown in Table 9.3).

Table 9.3 Stereotypical views of academics and practitioners

	Academic view	Practitioner view
Academia	Academia gives you the freedom to advance scientific knowledge in an interesting and meaningful way. You have the flexibility to work in areas that are important to you and you can gain real satisfaction from helping individuals, organisations, cities and	Academics are funny people. They operate from their ivory tower, producing research without any real world relevance, trying to give advice to the experts in the field (us practitioners). Academics are undoubtedly intelligent, sometimes brilliant people, but it is a

nations. There is no nobler profession than academia. Often it means that work goes unrewarded, except through personal gratification. But I would rather know that I was doing something important than drive a convertible. I love what I do and not many people can say that.

shame that all gets wasted on abstract theoretical papers. There is not enough interaction with industry and often academics lack real experience. Maybe that is why they are in academia – because they cannot make it in industry.

Industry

Practitioners are often too close to the action to see what is really going on. They do not see the trees for the wood and it surprises me every time how little they really perceive. People in industry ignore basic theoretical principles, rules of behaviour, scientific fact. It can be frustrating and infuriating to watch.

Industry is the real world. It is a fast-paced environment that offers many opportunities for advancement and achievement. If you are good and work hard, you will get ahead. You do not always have the time to do everything perfectly or to do what you want; that is because industry is market-driven and that means there is not time to stand still. Standing still means being overtaken – and we cannot afford that.

10

Getting out: the viva and beyond

The viva voce • *Leaving early* • *Life after the doctorate*

In this final chapter we focus on the concluding stages of the doctorate. We discuss the all important viva voce (oral defence) in detail, talk about some of the issues surrounding early withdrawal from a doctoral programme, and describe how interactions and relationships with former colleagues, friends and supervisors may look after you have finished your doctorate and left university.

The viva voce

AAAAaaaaaahhhhhhhhhhhhhhhhh! – Right? The viva, or oral defence, is the dreaded moment at the end of the doctorate that every student worries about. Three to five years of knowledge and hundreds of pages of writing to defend – you have invested a lot and to have everything come down to this single moment is scary. On top of that, the examination is normally a few months after submission, which means that there is a forced delay giving people ample time to find things to worry about.

When you are waiting for your viva in anticipation, it feels like you are about to go through a baptism by fire. Everyone expects their viva to be their worst nightmare – professors trying to make you walk on hot coals by asking very difficult (even impossible) questions and the external examiner not understanding your work at all. The pressure is intense. If you do not do well, you could 'lose' everything you have worked for over the past few years or, and this may feel even worse at the time, have to invest a lot more into it. On the day of our vivas, we remember thinking: 'Please, don't let the past three years have been a waste' . . .

Well, do not worry. If you were not ready for the viva, your supervisor would not have approved your thesis for submission. Getting to this stage means that you have produced a solid piece of work and made an original contribution to knowledge – the core requirement of a doctorate. Now it is up to you, and hopefully it will be 'going through the motions', a formality that confirms what those around you already know – you have achieved enough to be awarded the title 'Doctor', you just have to demonstrate it one last time.

So where to start? First of all, different approaches to oral examinations exist at different institutions, hence we outline some of the models below. We then talk about the all important issue of selecting your examiners. Preparing for the viva, conduct during the viva and post-viva issues are also discussed.

What is a viva and what does it look like?

Viva voce is Latin and literally translated means 'by live voice'. In the context of the doctoral degree, it is an oral examination in which you defend your thesis to an audience of experts as part of the requirement for your degree. This process can take different formats, depending on university guidelines and the preferred style of your examiners. It thus makes sense to be familiar with both of these (more on examiners below). University guidelines on thesis submission and viva are generally available from the postgraduate office and/or research degrees programme. Make sure you get a copy!

At most UK universities, the viva is conducted by two or more examiners (at least one from within and one from outside of your institution) and a chair (who convenes the session, guides the examiners and, if necessary, moderates between them). Your supervisor may or may not be present but, whatever the case may be, they normally do not take an active role in the session and instead act as a supportive observer (e.g. taking notes that will help you to respond to the examiners' change requests).

The whole process starts with you announcing that you intend to submit your thesis. Make sure you plan sufficient time because the examiners get sent a copy of your thesis some time before the viva, at least a month or two in advance, and so will have the opportunity to read your work in detail. The regulations on the official format of your thesis, for example length, literary style, size of margins and so on, vary from university to university. It is in your own best interest to make sure that you are sufficiently familiar with all the necessary rules and requirements early on. You can do this easily by obtaining a copy of the relevant guidelines from your institution.

Unlike in some other European countries, where the viva is public and anyone can watch you defend your work in front of an audience, the viva is generally conducted in private in the UK, behind the closed doors of either an office or an examination room. However, some institutions give you the opportunity to observe a doctoral viva in order to get a better idea of the process (this is generally subject to the defending student's approval, so is not always a possibility – imagine fellow doctoral students asking you to give them the chance to be present during your viva).

It is also important to know that it is common practice for candidates to make a presentation to the examiners, whether this takes the shape of a formal PowerPoint presentation or an informal oral summary of your work. It thus pays to prepare for this ahead of the day. Presentations normally take place at the start of the viva, immediately after introductions have been made. Once the presentation has concluded, the chair opens the session for discussion and questions. These may be around aspects of the presentation but may also focus on elements of the thesis more generally.

There may be formal turn taking, where one examiner asks all his or her questions before the other examiner is given the opportunity to speak but, more often, the examiners take turns to ask questions and complement each other. They frequently go through the dissertation chapter by chapter (and even page by page), highlighting areas of ambiguity and asking clarifying questions as they go along. (As you walk into the examination room, you will often see each examiner with a copy of your dissertation, with various pages marked up with post-it notes – do not let that frighten you, it is just part of the process.)

Hence, we strongly recommend that you are familiar with your work in detail. This does not mean that you have to know exactly what is on which page. However, you should be able to navigate your way around your thesis, being familiar with the order and context of each chapter and section. Roughly committing your table of contents to your memory will help you feel calm under pressure. The last thing you want in a viva is not to know what an examiner is referring to or being unable to support the core of your argument simply because you cannot find the section of your thesis where you alluded to it – it can happen that an examiner asks you to show where in your thesis you argue a particular point or referenced a key piece of literature.

After a few hours of questions and feedback (a viva can vary in length and generally takes between 2–6 hours, with an average of 2.5 hours), the candidate is normally asked to retreat for some time while the examiners make their final decision. Sometimes this decision is already handed to the candidate at the start of the examination, for example 'congratulations, you've passed with minor corrections – now let's discuss them' – but this is the exception rather than the rule, so you should expect to wait to be informed of the decision. This deliberation period tends to be relatively short, lasting around 10–15 minutes (believe it or not – your examiners actually do not want to make you suffer). At this stage the student is called back into the examination room and the verdict is announced. There are three outcome categories of a viva – pass, resubmit, fail – and, as outlined below, these come in various shades:

1 Degree awarded (pass)

   a No corrections
   b Minor corrections
   c Major corrections (without resubmission)

2 Resubmission – major corrections

3 Degree not awarded (fail)

   a Recommend for M.Phil. (or equivalent Master's degree)
   b No degree

Most students who pass the viva get awarded the degree with minor corrections (no corrections are rare because examiners also highlight formatting and structural issues). This is the outcome you should be striving for when having your viva! Usually you will be given up to three months to amend your thesis and write a response to the examiners. However, in some cases the examiners will ask you to rework larger parts of your thesis (e.g. include more recent literature or restructure parts of your thesis etc.). If this is the case, the examiners will allow 3–12 months for corrections and normally want to see the revised version of your thesis before submission but do not see the necessity to conduct another viva.

An official resubmission means that the work requires a substantial amount of rework before being accepted as a doctoral dissertation. This may mean additional data collection or analysis, and can take a significant amount of time (one or two years). In addition, in most instances you will have to go through another viva, as the content of your thesis has changed so dramatically that the degree cannot be awarded on the basis of your initial viva.

A recommendation for M.Phil. means that the examiners do not believe that your work meets the requirements of a doctoral degree, nor do they believe that you can reasonably reshape the work to satisfy the requirements of the degree within a sensible time frame. This is rare and, depending on your performance during the viva, this decision may sometimes be overturned and amended to 'resubmission'. Failing a doctoral viva is extremely rare and normally occurs in those instances where the student rejects all feedback from their supervisor and/or will not accept that they are not ready for submission. At most universities you will have the chance to appeal against the results of the examination if you feel the decision was unwarranted. However, we strongly advise that you only use this as a last resort because it can be an unpleasant procedure!

In the following story William provides you with the description of that special day in the life of a doctorate student.

Doomsday: The day of the viva

I woke up from a nightmare. I dreamt of the day of my viva – I had fainted in the departmental corridor. I got dizzy, I couldn't breathe – I think I had an anxiety attack. My body crumbled away from under me and that's when I woke up. It was 5am, the day of my viva. My viva wasn't until 10am and I had been hoping for a bit more sleep . . . but when you've been building up to a day for such a long time, and so much rests on how that day goes, I guess sleep becomes secondary to your nerves.

I got up and tried to go over some last minute questions, read through some literature summaries (you know, remind myself who that obscure author on page 5 of my thesis was that I just couldn't remember for the life of me), and in general, just put the finishing touches to my examination preparation. Well, I couldn't concentrate no matter how hard I tried. My thoughts kept slipping to that examination room – What would my external be like? Would my internal be okay? How's it going to go? I HOPE I DO OKAY! With thousands of thoughts circulating through my head, I got ready for the long road ahead.

My heart pounding, my palms sweating, I walked into the corridor. A buzz of activity around me. I don't remember much of it – Fellow students wishing me luck, academics congratulating me for reaching this stage, and lots and lots of questions and advice coming from all sides. 'Are you nervous?' 'How do you feel?' 'You'll do well.' 'You can do it.' I was very nervous, even scared. I felt like I couldn't remember anything about my Ph.D. – Which theoretical framework again? My head was dizzy and I felt I had entered my dream from the night before. Please don't let me faint!

I sat down at my old work station, wrote a few last minute emails and waited. About 15 minutes before the agreed appointment, my supervisor walked over to me (he had wined and dined the external the evening before) and told me: 'I think it'll go okay. But he said he wants to give you a hard time in the viva. Part of the process, you know?' My heart skipped a beat. Blimey! – Why did he have to tell me that MINUTES before I enter the room? My name got called. I got up and walked over to the room – A professorial office at the end of the corridor. I was shaking like a leaf. Smiles and nods all around me, as I walked down the corridor. I didn't feel so good. I felt like I was walking down death row, ready to begin my baptism of fire.

I walked into the room and closed the door behind me, and the questions began. I was very uptight initially and my nerves were getting the better of me, but over time I began to relax. The viva was turning into a discussion – a productive academic review of my work. It was actually kind of fun. People had read my work closely, were giving me constructive feedback about how to take it forward and in essence helping me shape it. Yeah! After a few hours, they were ready to release me. They asked me to wait outside the room for the verdict. And, again, the dread set in and I started questioning myself: 'What do they think? Was it okay? Oh, I hope my answer to question X was convincing.'

About fifteen minutes later, I got called back into the room. The door was closed and I sat down. The first person who spoke was my external examiner. He said: 'Congratulations, Dr. . . .' and that's all I heard. There was some more about 'minor corrections' and 'advice' . . . but they'd lost me at that point. Too happy. So excited, so elated. An incredible feeling. Disbelief. I took my examiners' comment sheets and went into the corridor . . . and walked straight into a champagne reception held in my honour!

William (graduate in chemistry)

Selecting and appointing the examiners

One of the most important parts of the defence process is choosing your examiners. Most universities will ask a student's supervisor or the head of department to recommend one or two internal and external examiners to the board. While this means that the student does not officially get to choose who examines them, it does not mean that they cannot offer input into the process.

Indeed, it is common for students, who are now experts in their field of study, to recommend peers from their field to act as examiner and for them to discuss various options with their supervisors. This should be people you know (e.g. through a conference) or people you know of (e.g. through others) – taking a complete stranger on board is a high-risk strategy because it means that you cannot predict how they are going to react on the day of the viva.

Moreover, it is important for you to know who your examiners are before you finish writing your thesis in order to be able to include and refer to their work (believe us, they will expect this from you). When selecting and appointing examiners try to consider the following key issues:

- Ensure approximate equal hierarchical level of internal and external examiners to avoid any political power games during your viva.
- Ensure you know about the examiners, both their professional expertise and their personality type.
  - They should know about your area and be familiar with (and not opposed to) your methods.
  - They should be friendly and open-minded.
- Try to appoint well-known and reputable examiners, as their prestige will reflect on the quality of your thesis (an important issue when applying for jobs in academia; see Chapter 9).
- If possible, choose an examiner in your country. Viva per video conference is possible but associated with additional risk and awkwardness – what if the video link goes down or you cannot judge someone's response because they are not physically present in person?

Preparing for the viva

In order to prepare for your viva, you need to know what the goal of the viva is and what your examiners expect of you. Generally, the viva assesses four areas:

1 your understanding of own research, including being able to justify the theory, methodology and results;
2 the relationship of your own work to other work in the field;
3 the novelty or contribution of your work;
4 the practical and theoretical implications of your work.

This means that you need to be familiar with all aspects of your work. Read through your thesis one last time and see where the potential for ambiguity exists, where questions might arise and what your examiners may challenge. Also run through practice questions and ask your supervisor to conduct a mock viva with you. This will give you some security by taking some of the pressure off your mind. In addition, we consider it very helpful, even vital, for a successful viva that you gain some experience in presenting your work to an academic audience during your doctorate (see pp.96–100 of Chapter 5 on 'Going to conferences'). There are lots of websites that give *free* advice on the types of general question to expect in a viva – these are actually pretty generic across disciplines. Here are some useful websites you can consult:

- www.geocities.com/andrewbroad/cs/cs710/viva.html
- www.phys.unsw.edu.au/~jw/viva.html
- www.missendencentre.co.uk/links

In addition to the four areas of assessment outlined above, you need to keep in mind the aims of examiners, which are to ensure that:

- the standards of quality within the discipline for which the doctorate is awarded are the same across universities;
- the doctoral student demonstrates capability to be an independent researcher;
- the work is the sole work of the doctoral student (fraud and plagiarism are a severe offence against the regulations!)

Conduct during the viva

Think of the viva as a job interview and follow that basic code of conduct. Dress professionally and act professionally. Come prepared and do not be late (even if your examiner is). Take a copy of your dissertation with a post-it note on each chapter, so you can easily move back and forth, a notepad and two pens into the examination room. That way you can refer to any part of your dissertation quickly if the need arises. Having a pen and paper ready enables you to take notes during the viva, which demonstrates to your examiners that you are taking their comments seriously.

Always listen to what your examiners have to say – both their questions and their feedback. Make sure you always let them finish and do not interrupt. Then answer the examiner's questions as calmly and completely as possible. If you do not understand a question, ask the examiner to repeat or clarify it. This will not reflect poorly on you – answering the question incorrectly, on the other hand, could. If you need some time to think about your response, pause for a few minutes and think about it – if you need some time to consider your answer, tell the examiners just that: 'That's an interesting question. I hadn't thought about it like that before. I'll need a few minutes to think about that'. This maturity will impress them – they do not expect you to know *everything* off the top of your head and though it may seem like a period of eternal silence to you, it will only seem like a few moments to your examiners.

The post-viva period

After the initial excitement and euphoria has died down, the post-viva period tends to be marked by inertia. It is often described as an 'anticlimax' by those who have gone through it because after the viva, nothing really changes. This is difficult for students, who often see the viva as the exit point of a doctoral degree, when in fact, some work still needs to be done. Corrections can be tedious, depending on the nature of the work the examiners have asked you to do. By this time, you will know your work inside out and may find it difficult to go back to it. Mentally, you have finished with the project, even if in reality you have not quite yet. We suggest that you have a break – a few well deserved days off – and then throw yourself back into the work. The longer you wait to complete the corrections, the more difficult it will seem. So we suggest you get right back on the horse and make the changes.

Remember, you are officially only awarded the title once your examiners have signed off your corrections and the university's examination board has ratified that decision. Since the examination board has regular scheduled meetings, it may be a few weeks or months before you can officially use the title. By delaying your corrections and your final submission, you are ultimately delaying this process. Most universities will request several bound copies of the thesis, which you will be liable to fund (there are some exceptions to this rule but that largely depends on the goodwill of your supervisor or department and is not standard practice). Corrections can take a few hours, days, weeks or months – depending on the nature of the feedback (see above) and your motivation level. The University of Reading provides some useful tips on how to survive the post-viva period:

www.reading.ac.uk/studyskills/study_resources/study_guides/
vivacorrections.htm

Leaving early

Sometimes you notice only after enrolment in a research degree that it just is not what you expected or wanted to do. The academic life is not for everyone and this means that some people may wish to withdraw partway through their programme. People withdraw from degrees all the time and there is no shame in admitting you want to do something else. Maybe you have come from industry and are not used to the self-directed learning (see Chapter 8) or the politics (see Chapter 7). Maybe you have run out of money (see Chapter 6), you do not get along with your supervisor (see Chapter 4), or you have received a job offer you cannot refuse. As the following quote demonstrates, there are a multitude of reasons why people decide to withdraw from a research programme, all of them legitimate in their own ways:

> 'I decided to quit grad school. Mainly over disagreement with my supervisor and even though I still think I would love doing research in the right environment and can collaborate with people whom I can get along with, I think probably personality-wise I'm more cut out to be in taught Masters'.

According to an extensive research programme instigated by the Council of Graduate Schools (2004), called 'The PhD Completion Programme', only 49–65 per cent of those who enrol in doctoral programmes will complete their degrees. The reasons for premature departure from doctoral degrees (as also cited in Lightfoot and Doerner, 2008) include:

- *Inadequate admission standards*: The minimum entry requirements, which determine who is able to enter graduate school, generally based around qualifications, grades and previous experience, are too low or inappropriate.

  The inherent assumption is that those with higher grades and past industry or research experience are more capable of successful PhD completion than those who do not. However, due to the unique skills required in graduate programmes, specifically toward the end of the degree, the truth of this statement has been challenged in recent years (Lightfoot and Doerner, 2008).

- *Unfavourable student characteristics*: Research suggests that specific individual traits such as gender, race, international student and family status, may be linked to attrition.

  The inherent assumption is that there are strong and weak PhD students, based on their personal characteristics – i.e. male home students with higher socio-economic status will be successful. Research currently cannot support these views (Lightfoot and Doerner, 2008).

- *Unfavourable institutional traits*: Factors like teaching loads and financial aid impact on a student's ability to successfully complete their doctoral degree.

  The inherent assumption is that students who get involved in additional teaching and research activity will defuse the debt burden and enhance their graduate experience. Counterintuitively, students holding teaching assistant roles actually have higher dropout rates due to the strain these tasks place on their intellectual and time resources (Ehrenberg and Mavros, 1995).

Consistent with our experience, the Council of Graduate Schools (2004) suggests that issues like finance (80 per cent; see Chapters 5 and 6), mentorship (60 per cent; see Chapter 4), family support (60 per cent; see Chapter 3), social environment (39 per cent; see Chapter 3), programme quality (39 per cent; see Chapter 2) and professional career guidance (30 per cent; see Chapter 9) are important when considering attrition from graduate school. This research also offers innovative ways to improve graduate programmes. Their key areas of focus include:

- *Selection processes*: Improving selection processes by focusing on a comprehensive skill set including coursework skills, independent research skills and dissertation skills (the last of which is the most elusive; indeed research suggests that attrition rates are highest at this stage of the process – see Groen et al., 2004).

- *Mentors*: Having a close and effective working relationship with one's adviser; creating a fostering relationship that goes beyond advising to actual mentoring.
- *Research environment*: Ensuring that students are working in an environment conducive to learning. This includes not only the formal programme, its quality and its transparency but also the informal social environment and the professional/career guidance offered. Indeed, there is some indication that interactions outside of the formal context are more important for professional identity and degree completion.
- *Field research mode*: The way research is conducted in the given academic field is of crucial importance. This is reflected by high attrition rates in some disciplines, e.g. highest in the humanities and lowest in engineering (Sowell, 2008).
- *Processes and procedures*: University processes and procedures also impact upon the success rate of graduate students. These should be facilitative rather than restrictive.

Regardless of why you decide to leave graduate school, there are some issues and implications you will need to consider:

- What will you do next?
- How will it reflect on your CV or impact your future study or career opportunities?
- How will it impact on you financially (e.g. what will happen to your bursary)?
- What will it mean for your supervisor, department, university?
- How will you tell your family and friends? How will they react to your decision?
- What happens to the research?
- What about your existing teaching commitments?
- Who owns data and authorship rights?

These are big questions but things you should keep in mind if you do decide to go down the route of programme withdrawal. So, before you decide to leave, make sure that this is what you really want and that you are making the decision for the right reasons. Do not let others try to convince you that a research degree is not for you or that you are not capable of meeting the requirements – think about these issues yourself, think long and hard, and take the time to reflect and seek advice.

As far as we are aware, you cannot be penalized if you withdraw from your degree, even if you are receiving a bursary – at least in the UK. We know several people who did just that without problem. It can be difficult politically but legally no one can force you to complete the degree (otherwise, by definition, they would also actually need to be able to guarantee that you pass – and how can that happen?). Nonetheless, we suggest you check your bursary conditions and/or research contract carefully. You may be liable to continue research/teaching for a set period, normally the period you have been paid for or, if you get paid in advance, you may need to pay back some of the funds. However, if you stop the research activity and funding at the same time, it should be relatively issue free.

We would also advise you to consult your student advice office or get confidential advice from one of the postgraduate student bodies. Generally, the university offers a range of financial, career and alternative advice services. Take advantage of them.

Even if there are no serious financial or legal implications of leaving a doctoral programme, you should not take the decision lightly (see Ben's story below). You are likely to encounter some resistance, disappointment and possibly even negative feelings from colleagues, friends, family members and future employers. It is nothing that cannot be overcome but it is important to think about these reactions, as they will impact on how you will feel about your decision. So, remember to be fair about it – if you are funded, you have consumed some university or research council funding that could have been allocated to someone else and, if you were a core part of a research project, you may well end up leaving your supervisor or research team in the lurch. There is bound to be some resentment and disappointment, and you need to be prepared for that. As a general rule of thumb, the earlier you withdraw from a research degree programme, the less harm is done. At the same time it is also important, however, to give your degree a fair chance at success. As discussed in Chapter 2, the move to a doctoral degree is associated with significant change and thus requires some adjustment – do not give up before you start! You may also wish to consider transferring from a full to a part-time programme; this may give you the flexibility you need to continue.

Why I decided to do a doctorate and why I decided to leave

My decision to study for a PhD came as a result of my Master's study. There were various options awaiting me after my graduation, but the prospect of receiving the highest degree that a student can gain from a university seemed too good to miss. I decided to remain at the same university from which I gained my Masters, I had built a good relationship with staff and could freely discuss my research aims, and as a result was offered a place on the PhD programme.

I did not take my offer too lightly, a combination of the RAE rating, the Research Group and staff, funding available and training were all influential factors in my decision. I definitely had the academic knowledge and technical ability to study my chosen subject so accepted the offer.

After successfully completing my first year report and presenting my work at an international conference, my progress at this stage would seem satisfactory to most. However, I felt myself slowly beginning to lose the excitement and joy of learning. As I felt myself researching a subject that was growing towards my supervisor's interest rather than my own, I became unenthusiastic about something I had always been passionate about. Looking back, there were several factors which influenced my decision to withdraw from the PhD programme.

Firstly, although I knew the academic staff very well and their research interests heavily influenced my own research topic, and my contact with them was good in some ways, in other ways it restricted my own research and I lost interest as a result. *Secondly*, even though my department was strong, I was my supervisor's first PhD student. I felt I needed an experienced and supportive supervisor and at times found I was offered very little support compared to other students in the department. Finally, in accepting the PhD offer, I had taken the easiest and first option after my Masters.

As I became less enthusiastic, I started to review what I wanted after a PhD. I had firmly decided that I wanted to obtain industry experience and not spend my future as an academic. Industry was calling for well qualified experts in my area, but very little industry work would use knowledge about my specific research topic. I began to question myself and my decision: 'Why was I studying a topic that would be of little use in the work that I wanted to pursue? Was my PhD really a good decision?' After a considerable period of deliberation, I decided that my PhD was not right for me. Yet I was terrified knowing that I would let my supervisor down and felt I had wasted funding that could have been utilised elsewhere. Similarly, I didn't know how to tell my PhD colleagues, who I'd gone through the good times and the bad times with – after all I had never discussed the idea of quitting.

Once the decision was made, the process was very swift. I arranged a meeting with my supervisors and research director whereby I addressed my concerns. They recommended that I take some leave time to think my decision through; however, as this has been the main issue on my mind for the past year, I already knew which way it would go. The only reason not to quit was to get the title of Doctor and – hey – wouldn't it be nice to be the first Doctor in the family? Despite the pressure I stuck by my guns and left my PhD. I could see obvious disappointment in my supervisor, but my view was that this was down to self interest. My fellow PhD colleagues were very supportive and my biggest regret was that I had let them down.

However, I don't want you to feel bad for me. I didn't and still don't see myself as a quitter. Unlike the many people who I witnessed pursuing a PhD for several years in a subject that they were not enthusiastic about, I saw myself as returning to an ambitious and motivated state where I could pursue my real interests. Indeed, soon after I made the decision to withdraw, I was offered a job working for an IT consultancy. I accepted the position, feeling that I could use the theory I had gained at university and apply the knowledge to real world problems. This is what I really wanted to do, what I had longed for but been unable to do for some time.

So, after a small period of disorientation, I am now back on the path I want to be on. Travelling around the world, helping people with my knowledge, skills and abilities. I am very happy and know that the decision I made to leave the programme was the right decision for me. It felt like a difficult decision at the time but was in many ways also the easiest decision I ever made. And look at me now!

Ben (ex-doctoral student in computer science)

Some useful sources for more information about this topic include: Gemeroth (1991); Hermanowicz (2003); Lovitts (2001); and Tinto (1993).

Life after the doctorate

During the doctorate, you often do not have much of a life and after the doctorate you often do not know what to do with your life. It is a catch 22 situation. Most students do not have a job lined up after their viva, using the months between viva and graduation to finalize plans and submit job applications (see Chapter 9 for more information). In the meantime, the young doctors often temporarily work as researchers in their old departments, finishing research projects and writing papers.

In the sections below, we give some examples of what interactions and relationships with former colleagues, friends and supervisors may look like after you finish your doctorate, and give some tips about how you can learn to let go and move on from your degree.

Interaction with former colleagues and supervisors

All is well that ends well. Even if you did not get along well with your supervisor(s) or some of your former colleagues, you may wish to stay in touch with them for various reasons, for example you start working in your old department, you stay affiliated with your former department, continue writing publications, need references, want to discuss future collaborations and so on. In this section we briefly show how relationships can develop in your postdoctoral life.

The pressure of a doctoral degree means that things often seem worse while you are doing your doctorate than they actually are. Your fellow students are the academic and industry experts of tomorrow and your supervisor and other members of your department are your future peers. So, keep in touch with your colleagues; you never know when you might run into them again or could benefit from their advice. We are a good example of what successful interactions with former colleagues look like – we live in different countries but still managed to write this book together!

Letting go and moving on

Change is difficult and requires a period of adjustment, so it should come as no surprise that leaving a doctorate behind can be hard. Certainly, we graduate students all complain about lives while we are going through the process, but we also tend to love what we do and when the time to say good-bye comes, we may experience some difficulty in letting go. We are not sad about leaving our manic schedules behind or finally earning money, but we are sad about leaving our cohort, our department and our work.

Your doctoral work will have been a big part of your life for several years, and over time you will have become familiar with and learnt to love it – to let all that go and move on to something different and new can be emotionally challenging. It is a bit like the Stockholm syndrome (Bejerot, 1974); we have fallen in love with our captor, the thesis. Do not worry; everyone feels this way and experiences some nostalgia after completion.

You can ease your transition to a 'civilian life' in a number of ways. First of all, remind yourself that exiting is a natural part of the process and just because you are moving on, does not mean that you have to leave everything behind. You can still collaborate with colleagues, draw on ideas from your thesis, write papers and stay in your area of research. Looking forward helps. It is easier to leave the past behind and move on if you have something to move on to, something to look forward to and focus on. Give your energy a new focal point, whether that is the job search, a different research project, a new location or something else. Last but not least, remember that everything will work out just fine. It always does.

We wish you good luck!

References

AGCAS (1998) *Job Seeking Strategies*. Manchester: Association of Graduate Careers Advisory Services Information Booklets, CSU Ltd.

AGCAS (1999) *Going for Interviews*. Manchester: Association of Graduate Careers Advisory Services Information Booklets, CSU Ltd.

Ali, A. and Kohun, F. (2007) Dealing with social isolation to minimize doctoral attrition: a four stage framework, *International Journal of Doctoral Studies*, 2: 33–49.

Ali, L. and Graham, B. (2000) *Moving in Your Career: A Guide for Academics and Postgraduates*. London: Routledge Falmer.

Axelrod-Contrada, J. (2003) *Career Opportunities in Politics, Government and Activism*. New York: Facts on File Inc.

Barley, S.R. (2006) When I write my masterpiece: thoughts on what makes a paper interesting, *Academy of Management Journal*, 49(1): 16–20.

Baxter, L., Hughes, C. and Tight, M. (1998) *Academic Career Handbook*. Maidenhead: Open University Press.

Bejerot, N. (1974) The six day war in Stockholm, *New Scientist*, 61(886): 486–87.

Birchall, M. and Allen, L. (2007) *The Times Top 100 Graduate Employers: The Essential Guide to the Leading Employers Recruiting Graduates During 2007–2008*. London: High Fliers Publication.

Bolles, M.E. and Bolles, R.N. (2008) *Job-hunting Online: A Guide to Using Job Listing, Message Boards, Research Sites, the Under Web, Counselling, Internetworking, Self-assessment Tools, Niche Sites*. Berkeley, CA: Ten Speed Press.

Bolles, R.N. (1999) *What Color is Your Parachute*. Berkeley, CA: Ten Speed Press.

Bryon, M. and Modha, S. (2005) *How to Pass Selection Tests*, 3rd edn. London: Kogan Page.

Clapperton, G. (2008) *Britain's Top Employers 2008: Best Examples of HR Practice*. London: Guardian Newspapers Ltd.

Council of Graduate Schools (2004) *Ph.D. Completion and Attrition: Policy, Numbers, Leadership, and Next Steps*. Washington, DC: Council of Graduate Schools (www.phdcompletion.org/resources).

D'Souza, S. (2007) *Brilliant Networking: What the Best Networkers Know, Say and Do*. London: Prentice Hall.

Davis, G.B. and Parker, C.A. (1997) *Writing the Doctoral Dissertation: A Systematic Approach*, 2nd edn. New York: Barron's Educational Series.

Delamont, S., Atkinson, P. and Parry, O. (2004) *Supervising the Doctorate: A Guide to Success*, 2nd edn. Maidenhead: Open University Press.

Dodge, S. (1990) Culture shock and alienation remain problems for many foreign students on U.S. campuses, *The Chronicle of Higher Education*, 36(25): 33–36.

Ehrenberg, R.G. and Mavros, P.G. (1995) Do doctoral students' financial support patterns affect their time-to-degree and completion probabilities?, *Journal of Human Resources*, 30: 581–609.

Fink, D. (2006) The professional doctorate: its relativity to the Ph.D. and relevance for the knowledge economy, *International Journal of Doctoral Studies*, 1: 35–44.

Fishbach, A. and Ferguson, M.F. (2007) The goal construct in social psychology, in A.W. Kruglanski and T.E. Higgins (eds) *Social Psychology: Handbook of Basic Principles*, pp. 490–515. New York: Guilford.

Fishbach, A. and Labroo, A.A. (2007) Be better or be merry: how mood affests self-control, *Journal of Personality and Social Responsibility*, 93(2): 158–73.

Fisher, R., Ury, W. and Patton, B. (1981) *Getting to Yes: Negotiating Agreement Without Giving in*. Boston, MA: Houghton Mifflin & Co.

Gemeroth, D. (1991) Lonely days and lonely nights: completing the doctoral dissertation, *American Communication Association Bulletin*, 76: 60–89.

Goldberg, L.R. (1981) Language and individual differences: the search for universals in personality lexicons, in L. Wheeler (ed.) *Review of Personality and Social Psychology*, Vol. 2., pp. 141–65 Beverly Hills, CA: Sage Publications.

Grant, W. and Sherrington, P. (2006) *Managing Your Academic Career: Universities into the 21st Century*. Basingstoke: Palgrave Macmillan.

Groen, J., Condie, S., Jakubson, G. and Ehrenberg, R.G. (2004) Preliminary estimates of the impact of the Andrew W. Mellon Foundation's Graduate Education Initiative on Attrition Rates and Times to Degree in Humanities and Related Social Science Doctoral Programs. Unpublished paper.

Halstead, B. (1987) The PhD system, *Bulleting of the British Psychological Society*, 40: 99–100.

Hermanowicz, J.C. (2003) *College Attrition at American Research Universities: Comparative Case Studies*. New York: Algora Publishing.

Hills, P. (1999) *Publish or Perish*, 2nd edn. Dereham: Peter Francis.

Israel, R., Shaffran, C. and Whitten, H. (2000) *Your Mind at Work: Developing Self-knowledge for Business Success*. London: Kogan Page.

Jackson, T. (2005) *The Perfect CV: Today's Ultimate Job Search Tool*. London: Piatkus Books.

Johnstone, A.H. and Percival, F. (1976) Attention breaks in lectures, *Education in Chemistry*, 13: 49–50.

Kitchin, R. and Fuller, D. (2005) *The Academics' Guide to Publishing*. London: Sage Publications.

Lightfoot, R.C. and Doerner, W.G. (2008) Student success and failure in a graduate criminology/criminal justice program, *American Journal of Criminal Justice*, 33(1): 113–29.

Locke, E.A. (1968) Toward a theory of task motivation and incentives, *Organizational Behavior and Performance*, 3: 157–89.

Lovitts, B.E. (2001) *Leaving the Ivory Tower: The Causes and Consequences of Departure from Doctoral Study*. Lanham, MD: Rowman & Littlefield Publishers Inc.

Luthans, F. and Davis, T. (1979) Behavioral self-management: the missing link in managerial effectiveness, *Organizational Dynamics*, Summer, 42–60.

Maslow, A.H. (1943) A theory of human motivation, *Psychological Review*, 50: 370–96.

Maxwell, J.C. (2001) *The 17 Indisputable Laws of Teamwork: Embrace Them and Empower Your Team*. Nashville, TN: Thomas Nelson Publishers.

McCrae, R.R. and Costa, P.T. Jr. (1990) *Personality in Adulthood*. New York: Guilford.

Miller, G.A. (1957) The magical number seven, plus or minus two: some limits on our capacity for processing information, *Psychological Review*, 63: 81–97.

Oberg, K. (1954) *Culture Shock*. Indianapolis, IN: Bobbs-Merrill Series in Social Sciences.

Parkinson, M. (2001) *Graduate Job Hunting Guide*. London: Kogan Page.

Perry, C. and Cavaya, A. (2004) Australian universities' examination criteria for DBA dissertations, *International Journal of Organisational Behaviour*, 7(5): 411–21.

Phillips, E.M. (1980) Education for research: the changing constructs of the postgraduate, *International Journal of Man-machine Studies*, 13(1): 39–48.

Phillips, E.M. and Pugh, D.S. (2000) *How to get a PhD*, 3rd edn. Maidenhead: Open University Press.

Phillips, E.M. and Pugh, D.S (2005) *How to Get a PhD*, 4th edn. Maidenhead: Open University Press.

Punch, K.F. (2000) *Developing Effective Research Proposals*. London: Sage Publications.

Quotec (2007) *Experimental Third Stream Strategic Development Fund Projects: Study B*. Report to HEFCE by Quotec Ltd and SPRU University of Sussex, April 2007.

Ray, S. (2007) Selecting a doctoral dissertation supervisor: analytical hierarchy approach to the multiple criteria problem, *International Journal of Doctoral Studies*, 2: 23–32.

Rugg, G. (2004) *The Unwritten Rules of PhD Research*. Maidenhead: Open University Press.

Schumann, J.H. (1978) The acculturation model for second language acquisition, in R.C. Gingras (ed.) *Second Language Acquisition and Foreign Language Learning*, pp. 27–50. Washington, DC: Center for Applied Linguistics.

Sowell, R. (2008) *Ph.D. Completion and Attrition: Analysis of Baseline Data*, NSF Workshop: A fresh look at Ph.D, Education.

Swales, J.M. and Feak, C.B. (2004) *Graduate Writing for Graduate Students: Essential Tasks and Skills*. Ann Arbor, MI: University of Michigan Press.

Taylor, S. and Beasley, N. (2005) *A Handbook for Doctoral Supervisors*. London: Routledge.

Tinto, V. (1993) *Leaving College: Rethinking the Causes and Cures of Student Attrition*. Chicago, IL: The University of Chicago Press.

Unwin, T. (2007) Reflections on supervising distance-based PhD students (www. gg.rhul.ac.uk/ict4d/distance-based%20PhDs.pdf).

Wetfeet (2006) *Careers in Management Consulting*. San Francisco, CA: Wetfeet Insider Guide, WetFeet Inc.

Wright, A., Murray, J.P. and Geale, P. (2007) A phenomenographic study of what it means to supervise doctoral students, *Academy of Management Learning & Education*, 6(4): 458–74.

Yate, M.J. (1998) *Great Answers to Tough Interview Questions: How to Get the Job You Want*, 4th edn. London: Kogan Page.

Index